STUDIES
IN LINGUISTIC
SEMANTICS

Edited by

Charles J. Fillmore   The Ohio State University

D. Terence Langendoen   The Graduate Center
and Brooklyn College of
The City University of New York

STUDIES IN LINGUISTIC SEMANTICS

Holt, Rinehart and Winston, Inc.

New York Chicago San Francisco
Atlanta Dallas Montreal
Toronto London Sydney

Studies in Linguistic Semantics edited by
Charles J. Fillmore and D. Terence Langendoen

PREFACE

This volume is an outgrowth of a conference informally known as the 1969 Spring Semantics Festival that was held April 14–15, 1969, at the Ohio State University in Columbus, Ohio. Of those who read papers at the conference, all but two, John R. ("Haj") Ross and David M. Perlmutter, are represented here. Ross's paper, which was entitled "The Deep Structure of Relative Clauses," has been replaced by one with the same title by Sandra Annear Thompson; and Perlmutter's, entitled "On Derived Intransitivity," was withheld at the author's request. Except for papers by Postal and Fillmore, all of the papers in this volume are being published for the first time. Postal's paper appears in *Linguistic Inquiry*, Vol. I, No. 1, January 1970; and Fillmore's appears in *Papers in Linguistics*, Vol. I, No. 1, July 1969.

The conference was sponsored by the Department of Linguistics of The Ohio State University, and was organized by Charles J. Fillmore, aided by a dedicated group of Ohio State University graduate students in linguistics. Ample discussion time was provided after the reading of each paper; and although the discussion is not included here, a number of these papers have been revised to incorporate suggestions and criticisms that were made from the floor.

The theme of the conference was chosen to reflect the current concern of generative grammarians to develop an adequate linguistic account of semantics. It should be noted straight off that not all current issues in semantics nor all current theoretical positions are represented in this collection. The major issues that are discussed are the separability of syntax from semantics and the nature of presuppositions; the major position that is represented is that of generative semantics (see particularly the paper by Postal). Only the paper by Langendoen and Savin attempts to develop the deep interpretive semantics position currently held by Jerrold Katz, while surface interpretive semantics as recently expounded by Noam Chomsky, Ray Jackendoff, and others is not represented at all.

The first two papers in this collection, by Partee and Garner, and the last, by Fillmore, attempt to relate current linguistic concerns with semantics to past linguistic concerns or to philosophical concerns, either past or present. Partee in particular provides a useful sketch of the development of concern with semantics by generative grammarians since 1957, and discusses the history and current state of the question: are transformations meaning-preserving? Garner provides an account of the notion of "presupposition" within philosophy, and finds the use of this term by linguists confusing. In particular, it will be observed that the term is being used quite differently in this volume by Langendoen and Savin, the Lakoffs, and Fillmore, and within the same paper, by Keenan. Clearly some sort of conceptual straightening-up is in order. Finally, Fillmore provides a brief account of how philosophers have managed to isolate various kinds of meaning within a sentence, and suggests a framework for representing these distinctions linguistically.

The remaining papers, which are largely reports on research that is still on-going, require no extensive introduction. Their subject matter ranges from the analysis of presupposition to that of relative clauses, to time reference, to the properties of individual lexical items such as the adverb *even*, the verb *remind*, and the conjunctions *and*, *or*, and *but*. They provide excellent clues to the current state of the art of dealing with semantics within generative grammar.

Columbus, Ohio   C.J.F.
New York, New York   D.T.L.
January 1971

CONTENTS

STUDIES
IN LINGUISTIC
SEMANTICS

On the Requirement That Transformations Preserve Meaning

Barbara Hall Partee   University of California, Los Angeles

Introduction

Although the basic notions of semantics are about as little understood by generative linguists now as they were ten years ago, there has been a major shift in the general attitude of linguists toward semantics. Where once the claims made about the "semantic component" virtually ended with the statement that every complete grammar would have to have one, now questions about the relation of semantics to other parts of the grammar are receiving widespread attention and are central to some of the major current controversies. It is difficult to point to anything that might be called a substantive semantic result, but the most important step has been taken: we have stopped playing ostrich about semantics.

Among the important issues in the area of semantics and its relation to the rest of the grammar, the idea that transformations might be meaning-preserving is one that has an interesting history and one whose fate is still far from clear. In Part 1, I will review its history briefly; then in Part 2, I will discuss generally some important factors in disputes about it; and finally in Part 3, I will talk about some of the more interesting phenomena with respect to which the meaning-preservingness of transformations seems to be called into question.

1. Evolution of the Hypothesis 1957–1969

1.1 The Emergence of Deep Structure Semantics 1957–1965

In *Syntactic Structures* Chomsky presented quite emphatically the view that semantic considerations play no role in the linguist's analysis of syntactic structure. He suggested further that although the underlying syntactic structure might well be of considerable relevance to the description of meaning, it was probably not sufficient for it. The following quotation is from the summary chapter:

> The notion of "structural meaning" as opposed to "lexical meaning," however, appears to be quite suspect, and it is questionable that the grammatical devices available in language are used consistently enough so that meaning can be assigned to them directly. (Chomsky, 1957, p. 108)

A major change in this view was brought about through the pioneering efforts in exploring the semantic component of a transformational grammar made by Katz, Fodor, and Postal. In Katz and Fodor's original work (1963), there were two types of semantic "projection rules" envisaged: one type to build up the meaning of kernel sentences from the meanings of their lexical items, a specific semantic rule being correlated with each phrase-

1

structure rule; and rules of another type associated with the transformations, designed to represent how the meaning of a sentence changed as it was transformed. A major theoretical innovation in Katz and Postal (1964) was the suggestion that the second type of rule might be dispensable because it might be the case that transformations never did change in meaning. They stress the empirical nature of the claim in the following words:

> This principle, it should be stressed, is not . . . a statement in linguistic theory, but rather it is a rule of thumb based on the general character of linguistic descriptions. The principle can be stated as follows: given a sentence for which a syntactic derivation is needed; look for simple paraphrases of the sentence which are not paraphrases by virtue of synonymous expressions; on finding them, construct grammatical rules that relate the original sentence and its paraphrases in such a way that each of these sentences has the same set of underlying P-markers. Of course, having constructed such rules, it is still necessary to find independent syntactic justification for them. (Katz and Postal, 1964, p. 157)

The principle presented by Katz and Postal as an empirical hypothesis gained support very quickly, to the point where it was widely accepted as one of the more solidly established generalizations in linguistic theory and used as a criterion for transformational rules. In Chomsky's writings from about 1964 to 1966 this is clearly the case. In *Aspects of the Theory of Syntax,* Chomsky puts it quite succinctly:

> . . . the syntactic component of a grammar must specify, for each sentence, a *deep structure* that determines its semantic interpretation and a *surface structure* that determines its phonetic interpretation. (Chomsky, 1965, p. 16)

Note that as long as the notion of a syntactically defined deep structure is accepted, the claim that semantic interpretation is entirely on deep structure is indeed equivalent to the claim that transformations preserve meaning.

1.2   Early Challenges to Deep Structure Semantics 1965–1967

An early challenge to the claim was made by Kuroda (1965), in the section called "Attachment transformation." There he noted that certain words, notably *even, only,* and *also,* were limited to one occurrence per sentence but that occurrence could be in any of a large number of positions in the sentence. He argued that the one-per-sentence limitation could be reasonably captured only by making such items constituents of the sentence under, for instance, a pre-sentence node, in which case their variety of surface positions would have to be assigned by a transformational rule (which he called an attachment rule).

One part of Kuroda's evidence is now widely rejected, namely the observation that such words are limited to one occurrence per sentence. It seems quite easy to get more than one *only* per sentence, and the difficulty in getting more than one *even* per sentence may just be a performance difficulty connected with the complexity of the semantic interpretation.[1]

(1) a. Only John danced with only one girl all evening.
     b. Most of the fellows either prefer blonds or don't care; only John will date only redheads.

But otherwise the analysis of words like *even* and *only* is still very much at issue, since the apparent generalization that they can have as semantic scope virtually any phrase which is a constituent at the level of surface structure does not seem to be naturally capturable at the level of deep structure.

Chapin (1967) suggests one important reservation that might be made to the claim that transformations preserve meaning, which is a necessary one in distinguishing the lexicalist-transformationalist controversy from the controversy over whether meaning is determined only at the deepest level of structure. Chapin suggests that some lexical transformations must follow some of the ordinary transformations—that, for example, the formation of words with the prefix *self* (*self-starting, self-defrosting,* and so forth) follows the reflexive transformation, and that of words with the suffix *-able* (*breakable, returnable,* and so forth) follows the passive transformation; but the lexical transformations which Chapin sets up to form such words are not meaning-preserving, since even where the basic meaning of a word is consistent with its phrasal source, additional unpredictable bits of meaning are usually associated with the word (compare *payable, admirable, self-reproducing*).

1.3 Current Positions

In the more recent past, Lakoff, McCawley, Postal, and others have accepted the hypothesis that transformations preserve meaning and extended it to the position that all and only sentences which are paraphrases of each other should have the same deep structures. They have shown that consistent adherence to such a principle requires much more abstract deep structures than were previously contemplated. Many of their analyses have independent support from purely syntactic arguments, and it is often not easy to determine how much of the weight of their arguments is borne by the criterion of meaning-preservingness of transformations. Chomsky and Jackendoff, on the other hand, have argued that the more abstract deep structures do not have sufficient independent syntactic motivation, and that a simpler overall grammar will be achieved by keeping a more conservative deep structure and allowing semantic interpretation to take into consideration

[1] Bruce Fraser (1971) has stated that more than one *even* could occur in a sentence. From the semantic interpretation he provides for *even* one would indeed predict difficulty in understanding such sentences.

some aspects of surface structure and perhaps of intermediate structures as well.

It would appear then that within the abstract-deep-structure or generative semantics camp, the principle of meaning-preservingness of transformations is a fundamental condition on most of the grammar, but not necessarily on those transformations which introduce lexical items. This exception would appear to be inconsistent with the strongest version of "generative semantics," which is that the deepest level of structure is prelexical but is the only level relevant to semantic interpretation—in some sense *is* the semantic interpretation. I am not certain whether anyone seriously holds such a view, but it is certainly the view suggested by the term "generative semantics."[2]

2. Basic Issues

2.1 The Notion of Synonymy

The question of meaning-preservingness is a difficult one to discuss in part because of difficulties with the notions of meaning and synonymy. Some philosophers have claimed that no two sentences are synonymous, including even pairs that would unanimously be claimed to be transformationally related. Another extreme is to call any two sentences synonymous if they have the same truth-value. A position which seems closer to what most linguists seem to have in mind is to call two sentences synonymous if they would have the same truth value in all possible worlds. However, this notion is useful only for declarative sentences, and furthermore doesn't seem to get at things like focus and presupposition very easily.

2.2 The Empirical Nature of Hypothesis

The various stands taken on synonymy all have to do with synonymy between *sentences,* and in talk about transformations preserving or changing meaning, the most common examples are transformations which can infor-

---

[2] McCawley in the discussion following this paper asserted that he does indeed hold the strong form of the generative semantics position; in his view, although at least some lexical insertion does indeed follow other transformations, the idiosyncratic details of meaning connected with individual lexical items must be present on the deepest level and constitute conditions on the insertion of the lexical items.

The independence of the lexicalist-transformationalist question from the question of meaning-preservingness can thus ·be illustrated by the following positions:

	Lexicalist/ transformationalist	All transformations meaning-preserving
Chomsky (1968)	Lexicalist	Yes (?)
Chomsky (1969)	Lexicalist	No
Chapin (1967)	Transformationalist	No
McCawley (1969b)	Transformationalist	Yes

mally be thought of as relating sentences to other sentences. But transformations in fact operate not on sentences but on abstract phrase-markers, and it is not obvious that we have any direct semantic intuitions about these abstract structures, in particular any notion of synonymy between them. Failure to distinguish sentences from abstract P-markers is often harmless, as in discussion of very late optional "stylistic" transformations, where the abstract structures involved are very close to surface structures, that is, sentences. But for obligatory transformations the fact that abstract structures and not sentences are involved is significant. For obligatory rules, in fact, the question of meaning-preservingness does not even make sense, for the input to the rule is an abstract structure with which we have no independent acquaintance. This point can be illustrated by considering the affix-switching rule that moves *-ing, -en,* and so forth, into their surface positions: it makes no sense to ask whether the rule preserves meaning or not, because the question presupposes that we have some independent idea of the meaning of sentences whose affixes are not switched.

The question of whether transformations change meaning can therefore be meaningfully asked only of optional transformations. The clearest case is that in which two sentences are derived from the same deep structure, their derivations differing only in the application versus nonapplication of a certain optional rule. If the two sentences are synonymous, and if the same is true of all pairs related by the given rule, the rule is meaning-preserving; otherwise it is not. A slightly more complicated case is that in which pairs of sentences differ in derivation by one optional rule and one or more subsequent obligatory rules; it still seems reasonable in such cases to attribute any change in meaning to the optional rule. An example of this occurs further below: sentences (4)a and b differ by both that rule and the later obligatory *any-no* rule; however, all discussions of such sentences assume that the meaning change is due only to the *some-any* rule.

A case in which it would be much more difficult to assign responsibility for meaning change could arise in the following sort of situation:[3] Suppose a grammar contains the optional rules T_1 and T_2 and an obligatory rule T_3 whose structural conditions are met just when T_1 and T_2 are both applied. Then there might be four sentences with the same deep structures and the following differences in rules applied:

S_0: none of the rules applied
S_1: only T_1 applied
S_2: only T_2 applied
S_3: both T_1 and T_2, and hence also T_3, applied

Then supposing S_0, S_1, and S_2 were all synonymous but S_3 was not synonymous with the others, it would be rather difficult to decide nonarbitrarily

[3] I am indebted to Frank Heny for this observation.

what rule or rules were responsible for the change of meaning. I do not know of any actual cases of this sort, however.

To simplify the remainder of the discussion, we will ignore potential cases of the last-mentioned sort, and assume that the question of meaning-preservingness is meaningful for optional transformations and not for obligatory ones. There is then a corollary of this assumption, a corollary which was illustrated quite clearly in Katz and Postal (1964). Suppose it is observed that a certain optional transformation does change meaning significantly: it will often be possible to add some abstract element to the deep structure which serves as obligatory trigger to that transformational rule, thus exempting that rule from the requirement of meaning-preservingness. Unless such additional deep-structure elements are independently motivated (as they are in all the Katz and Postal examples), they reduce the claim of meaning-preservingness to near vacuity. Insofar as they can be shown necessary on syntactic grounds, they strengthen it. This issue is crucial in subsequent developments in syntax and semantics, although it is sometimes obscured. I will present below first some examples from Katz and Postal illustrating the independent syntactic justification of the introduction of deep-structure elements which make previously optional rules obligatory; then I will discuss a more recent example which seems to lack such justification.

Two of the classic examples discussed by Katz and Postal are the interrogative and negative transformations. In *Syntactic Structures* both were optional rules, so that (2)b had the same deep structure as (2)a, and (3)b the same as (3)a, but the rules were clearly not meaning-preserving under any definition of synonymy.

(2) a. John smokes pot.
    b. Does John smoke pot?
(3) a. John smokes pot.
    b. John doesn't smoke pot.

Katz and Postal cite Klima's arguments, which are purely syntactic and were given prior to the introduction of the meaning-preservingness hypothesis, that interrogative sentences must have an extra morpheme, which might be represented as WH, in their deep structures, and negative sentences must also contain a special morpheme, say NEG, in their deep structures. Then the *b* sentences are no longer optional variants of the *a* sentences but obligatory transforms of the *c* sentences below, so that they are no longer predicted to be synonymous with the *a* sentences.

(2) c. WH   John smokes pot.
(3) c. NEG   John smokes pot.

Katz and Postal did overlook one important violation of their hypothesis in Klima's analysis of negation, namely that for Klima the *some-any* suppletion rule was optional in most environments. For Klima, therefore, an optional transformation related sentences (4)a,b and (4)c,d.

(4) a. I couldn't answer some of the questions.
     b. I couldn't answer any of the questions.
     c. Some of the books were not on the shelf.
     d. None of the books were on the shelf.

The relation of *some* and *any* turns out to be a very interesting problem and has been one of the important factors in a number of recent proposals, including Fillmore's (1967) distinction between $+/-$ specific indefinite articles, George Lakoff's (1970d) proposal of quantifiers as predicates on higher sentences, and Robin Lakoff's (1969) suggestion that there can't be a *some-any* rule. All these proposals start from the position that Klima's *some-any* rule is inadequate insofar as it violates the Katz/Postal hypothesis of meaning-preservingness, thus elevating what started out as an empirical hypothesis to the position of a constraint built into the theory.

Katz and Postal took great pains to point out the need for independent syntactic justification for analyses, being fully aware that as soon as meaning-preservingness itself is taken as a criterion for transformational rules, it loses almost all empirical content (except for the empirical question of whether it is possible to write a grammar conforming to that principle; but the answer to that is almost certainly affirmative, given the present power of transformational grammar—see Peters and Ritchie's (1969) refutation of the empiricalness of the universal base hypothesis). An example which seems to me to illustrate this weakening of empirical content is the causative analysis of transitive/intransitive verbs like *break*.

In Partee (1965) it is argued that transitive *break* is not a causative of intransitive *break* in English, on the grounds that transitive *break* not only fails to be fully synonymous with *cause to break*, but differs from it in co-occurrence properties. Thus (5)a and (5)b are not alike in meaning, and (6)a and (6)b are not alike in well-formedness; the latter fact gives a syntactic argument against the causative analysis, the former showing that such an analysis does not even have strong semantic support.

(5) a. John broke the window.
     b. John caused the window to break.
(6) a. A change in temperature caused the window to break.
     b. *A change in temperature broke the window.

In Lakoff (1965), where a causative analysis is defended, it is claimed that the above argument is irrelevant, because his causative analysis involves not the lexical item *cause* but a dummy verb CAUSE which presumably differs semantically from *cause* in just whatever ways will account for the meaning difference between (5)a and (5)b, and differs from it in co-occurrence restrictions in just the right ways to account for the impossibility of sentences like (6)b. Since this dummy verb has no lexical realization, the causative transformation must be obligatory and is therefore exempted from the criterion of meaning-preservingness. But since no independent reasons are given for this dummy trigger element being analyzed as a verb, let alone for its being related in any principled way to the verb *cause,* the empirical claim that seems to be made by the statement that English has a causative transformation is greatly weakened, and in particular the analysis offers no support to the Katz/Postal hypothesis.

In short, I am suggesting that the hypothesis that all transformations preserve meaning, so long as it remains an empirical hypothesis, is interesting, debatable, and important. But although it is a plausible hypothesis with a considerable amount of evidence in its favor, it seems to me a mistake to prematurely shut the door on its investigation by accepting it as a criterion for transformations.

2.3 Alternative Hypotheses

The position that transformational rules *don't* preserve meaning is of much less inherent interest than the contrary position, since it amounts simply to the position that a certain strong hypothesis is false. It may of course turn out to be the correct position, but it doesn't seem like anything one could rationally *want* to champion—it is analogous to the position that synchronic rules don't reflect historical development, or that not all languages use the same stock of phonological features, and so forth, the sum of all such positions being that "languages can differ from each other without limit and in unpredictable ways" (Joos, 1957, p. 76). Of course, just being strong doesn't make a hypothesis right; in fact it increases its chances of being wrong—but it does make it interesting, in the sense that it increases our stock of generalizations about the structure of language if it is right.

So for the position that transformational rules can change meaning to be comparable in interest to the position that they can't, it would have to be coupled with some alternative claims of comparable strength, such as the following:

(*a*) Most transformational rules preserve meaning; those of such-and-such a form, however, do not, and their effect on meaning is predictable in such-and-such a way from their form. (This is a very rough generalization of Kuroda's position as described above.)

(*b*) All meaning is determinable at the surface-structure level. (This position is certainly strong enough to be of interest, but is unfortunately extremely easy to falsify.)

(*c*) All meaning connected with the basic grammatical relations between major lexical categories is determined at the deep-structure level, but that connected with reference and with logical relations such as quantification and negation is determined at the surface level. (This bears some resemblance to the Chomsky/Jackendoff position, but for pronominalization, at least, they need to let rules of semantic interpretation apply cyclically, which weakens the position considerably.)

(d) All those parts of meaning that have to do with truth-value (in all possible worlds) are determined at the deep structure level and preserved by transformational rules; what can change in the course of a transformational derivation are just those subtler aspects of "meaning" which are suggested by terms such as "topicalization," "focus/presupposition," or other equally ill-understood notions. (This is the position I tend toward but it is not a well-defined one because of the vagueness of the distinction between the different sorts of meaning.)

2.4 Possible Counterevidence

The last general matter that I want to bring up in this section is the question of counterevidence to the hypothesis that transformations preserve meaning. Just as no empirical support is gained for it by those analyses for which the assumption of its truth lay behind a major part of the evidence, no valid empirical counterargument can be made simply by showing that there exists for a given phenomenon one possible analysis violating the hypothesis. Counterevidence must rather take the form of showing that the best available analysis based on syntactic evidence alone is one which violates the hypothesis. One cannot expect there to be a final word in such arguments, of course, since presumably no analysis will ever be immune from overthrow by a better one.

3. Relevant Phenomena

3.1 Quantifiers

A good bit of the current interest in quantifiers stems from the fact that there are a number of transformations which, as traditionally formulated, preserve meaning except when quantifiers are involved. This is particularly true of those transformations which delete or pronominalize an NP when it is identical to some other NP in the sentence: when identity of NP's is taken to include quantifiers as part of the NP, a change of meaning generally results. The pairs of examples in (7), (8), and (9) illustrate such a change with reflexivization, equi-NP deletion, and relativization, respectively.

(7) a. Every man voted for himself.
     b. Every man voted for every man.
(8) a. Every contestant expected to come in first.
     b. Every contestant expected every contestant to come in first.
(9) a. Every Democrat who voted for a Republican was sorry.
     b. Every Democrat [every Democrat voted for a Republican] was sorry.

Since there are so many transformations which change meaning only when quantifiers are present, it is natural that suspicion should fall on the analysis of quantifiers. So far the choices seem to be among syntactically simple analyses for which the rules of semantic interpretation have to be applied throughout the transformational cycle in rather complex ways, and analyses with semantically more plausible deep structures but some rather unnatural-looking syntactic rules (insofar as the syntactic rules have been made explicit). If an analysis which is elegant in both respects should be found, it ought to have considerable effect on the outcome of the general theoretical dispute.

3.1.1 *Each*-hopping: a surfacist argument and the rebuttal.

In Chomsky (1969) a number of interesting phenomena are discussed. Most of them purport to illustrate the need to have some semantic interpretation rules be sensitive to surface structure, but to me it seems questionable whether any of them actually do so. I will single out for discussion one which seems particularly vulnerable, in that there are purely syntactic counterarguments which lead one to a solution which supports the meaning-preservingness hypothesis. The phenomenon in question is *each*-hopping, typically illustrated by sentence pairs like (10)a and b.

(10) a. Each of the men is involved in this.
      b. The men are each involved in this.

Chomsky's argument, attributed to Dougherty (1968, 1969),[4] is that since it is possible to make a syntactically simple statement of *each*-hopping without concern for any constituents to the right of the Aux, the rule will have to be allowed to derive (11)b from (11)a, with subsequent adjustments to the semantic interpretation.

(11) a. Each of the men hates his brothers.
      b. The men each hate his brothers.

---

[4] Since I have not seen Dougherty (1968, 1969), it is possible that my objections apply only to Chomsky's representation of his arguments.

But such a derivation is questionable on syntactic grounds alone, since purely syntactic arguments can be found for changing *his* to *their* when applying *each*-hopping to a sentence like (11)a. Consider first some facts about conjunction. The distributional facts illustrated in (12) support the intermediate stages shown in (13), which have been independently proposed by a number of people.[5]

(12) a. John hates himself and Bill hates himself.
   b. *John hates themselves and Bill hates themselves.
   c. John and Bill hate themselves.
   d. *John and Bill hate himself.
(13) a. John and Bill hate $himself_1$ and $himself_2$ respectively.
   b. $himself_1$ and $himself_2$ respectively $\Rightarrow$ themselves

That is, we can take all conjunction-reduction as derivative from *respectively-* conjunction, with the generalization that formally identical conjuncts may be collapsed (each collapse accompanied by deletion of *respectively*), the collapsed nouns keeping their number intact if they are coreferential, but becoming plural otherwise. Thus (14)a has two reduced forms, the difference depending on whether the two occurrences of *book* are coreferential or not.

(14) a. John read a book and Bill read a book.
   b. John and Bill read a book and a book respectively.
   c. $\begin{cases} \text{a } book_1 \text{ and a } book_1 \Rightarrow \text{a book} \\ \text{a } book_1 \text{ and a } book_2 \Rightarrow \text{books} \end{cases}$
   d. John and Bill read $\begin{cases} \text{a book} \\ \text{books} \end{cases}$

The same process can be seen to apply twice in a case like the following:

(15) a. $John_1$ hates his_1 $brother_3$ and $Bill_2$ hates his_2 $brother_4$.
   b. John and Bill hate his_1 $brother_3$ and his_2 $brother_4$ respectively.
   c. John and Bill hate his_1 and his_2 $brother_3$ and $brother_4$ respectively.
   d. John and Bill hate their brothers.

That *each*-hopping has a good bit in common with conjunction-reduction appears from examination of sentences containing *each* and a reflexive pronoun. The distribution shown below is parallel to that in (12).

[5] See the reference to Postal (personal communication) in McCawley (1968, p. 166); also Schacter in the conjunction section of Stockwell *et al.* (1969).

(16) a. Each of the men shaves himself.
      b. *Each of the men shaves themselves.[6]
      c. The men each shave themselves.
      d. *The men each shave himself.

Exactly the same kind of distribution appears for sentences like (11)a and b
if we add *own*; this case was noted by Chomsky, who proposed handling it
by a surface filtering rule.

(17) a. Each of the men hates his own brothers.
      b. *Each of the men hates their own brothers.
      c. The men each hate their own brothers.
      d. *The men each hate his own brothers.

Chomsky explicitly suggests deriving (17)d from (17)a and then filtering out
(17)d; he does not point out that (17)c would then have to be derived from
(17)b and (17)b also filtered out; nor does he point out that the same kind
of problems would arise for (16). Although I don't know how to state the
pluralization rule so as to make it apply "in the same way" to conjunction-
reduction and *each*-hopping, it seems to be that this is clearly what's going
on. Otherwise it must be counted as a coincidence that the derivation which
would preserve meaning (namely from the *a* to the *c* cases) in both conjunction-reduction, (12), and *each*-hopping, (16) and (17), is also the derivation
that eliminates all the ungrammatical sentences without appeal to filtering
devices. Thus it seems to me that the example Chomsky offers in support of
the need for surface structure interpretation plus filtering devices in fact
provides an argument against them.

3.1.2 Conjunction-reduction: a problem for everyone.
Another case
where a rule as traditionally stated is meaning-preserving most of the time
but not so when quantifiers are involved is the case of conjunction-reduction,
noted in Partee (1970) and discussed further in G. Lakoff (1968b). The rules
for conjunction-reduction as proposed by Chomsky (1957) and subsequently
refined by a number of writers would allow the derivation of (18)b from
(18)a, but the two sentences are clearly not synonymous.[7]

---

[6] A commonly accepted form is *each of the men shave themselves* where the verb as well
as the reflexive pronoun is pluralized. The existence of such a dialect, together with the
absence (as far as I know) of any dialect which accepts (16)b, simply lends support to the
claim that pronouns as well as verbs can change number transformationally.

[7] For those speakers who can understand "few students" as referring to a *specific* few in
both sentences, the resulting readings will be synonymous; however, for all speakers "few
students" can be taken as nonspecific, and the two sentences are nonsynonymous on the
resulting readings.

(18)   a.   Few students are popular and few students are likely to succeed.
      b.   Few students are both popular and likely to succeed.

A priori there is no way to choose between a complication of the syntactic
rules for conjunction-reduction and a complication of the semantic rules
of interpretation; the choice must depend on how one can make the greatest
generalizations with the least amount of extra apparatus, taking both syntax
and semantics into account.

    One suggestion made by Lakoff (1968b) has considerable initial attrac-
tiveness but runs into some serious problems. The analysis of quantifiers suggested in G. Lakoff (1965) would lead to deriving (18)b from something like
the synonymous (18)c,

(18)   c.   Students who are both popular and likely to succeed are few.

but nothing suggested in that analysis would block the derivation of (18)b
from (18)a, so that there would be two derivations of the unambiguous[8]
(18)b. What Lakoff (1968b) suggested was that the derivation from (18)a to
(18)b could be blocked by a quite general and plausible condition, namely
that conjunction-reduction should not take place on nonreferential NP's:
this would correctly allow reduction of cases like (18)a and b with subjects
like *those three students, John,* and so forth, and with *few students* for
those speakers who can interpret it as referring to a specific few. It would
block the cases which make the problem, namely those with indefinite quantified subjects. However, it would also block reduction of nonreferential
NP's in cases where such reduction does not lead to any change in meaning,
and therefore it seems to be too strong a restriction. For example, the phrase
"few questions" in (19)a and b does not appear to differ in any significant
regard with respect to referentiality from the phrase "few students" in (18)a
and b, and yet the application of conjunction-reduction to (19)a to yield
(19)b is perfectly meaning-preserving.

(19)   a.   Mary will answer few questions and Susan will answer few
        questions and Joan will answer few questions.
      b.   Mary, Susan, and Joan will answer few questions.

There appear to be many complicating factors. One significant factor seems
to be the relative order of the quantifier and the conjoined phrase, or perhaps the subject position of the quantifier, since the passives of (19)a and b
are not synonymous.

---

[8] There would presumably be four derivations if (18)b can be understood two ways, as
either specific or nonspecific; in either case, that is, there are too many derivations.

(19) c. Few questions will be answered by Mary and few questions will be answered by Susan and few questions will be answered by Joan.

d. Few questions will be answered by Mary, Susan, and Joan.

It seems that (19)d is ambiguous for many speakers (apparently more so than (19)b, so that on one reading it is indeed synonymous with (19)c, but on the other reading it is not. Another complication is the apparent alternation of *and* and *or*. Thus (19)e below is much closer in meaning to (19)g than to (19)f.

(19) e. Many airplanes stop at Dallas and many airplanes stop at Chicago.

f. Many airplanes stop at Dallas and Chicago.

g. Many airplanes stop at Dallas or Chicago.

The first and third sentences are not fully synonymous, however, since (19)g asserts only that the total number of airplanes stopping at the cities is many, and that not necessarily many airplanes stop at each, as is asserted in (19)e. Although (19)g does not appear to involve phrasal conjunction, it has no obvious sentential source with either an *and* or an *or*.

Still another complicating factor is the behavior of words like *both*, *each*, and *apiece* with conjunction and quantification. Despite considerable attention, these words are still very poorly understood, and they are obviously of crucial importance in relating conjoined full sentences to sentences with phrasal conjuncts. Thus it is still not at all obvious whether the eventual solution to the problem of (18)a and b will involve reanalyzing the syntax in such a way that all the rules are meaning-preserving or alternatively allowing the semantic component to take into account certain aspects of derived structure or of the derivations themselves.

3.1.3 Q-magic: a generative-semantics argument and a rebuttal.

Another interesting problem with meaning-preservation in the area of conjunction and quantifiers arises with the Lakoff/Carden rule of quantifier-lowering ("Q-magic"; see G. Lakoff (1968b), Carden (1967)). Lakoff (1968b) suggests that sentence (20)a shows that quantifier lowering cannot apply into conjoined structures, that is, obeys the Ross (1967) coordinate structure constraint, because (20)a cannot have as one of its readings anything like (20)b.

(20) a. Abdul believes that few men and many women like baba ganouze.

b. There are few men such that Abdul believes that they and many women like baba ganouze.

But if there is indeed such a rule as quantifier-lowering, the relation between it and conjunction is more complicated than Lakoff noticed, and in a way which seems very peculiar indeed within the framework that Lakoff proposes.

Recall first of all the ambiguities noted by G. Lakoff (1965) for sentences such as (21)a.

(21) a. 100 soldiers shot two students.
      b. A group of 100 soldiers shot a total of two students.
      c. 100 soldiers each shot two students.
      d. Two students were each shot by 100 soldiers.

Virtually all speakers can interpret (21)a as either (21)b or (21)c; some can also interpret it as (21)d while others have that reading only for the passive of (21)a. What is significant here is not how many readings one obtains, but the fact that exactly the *same* number of readings (for any given speaker) will be obtained for (22)a, namely (22)b, (22)c, and perhaps (22)d. One does not, however, get any "mixed" readings, such as (22)e below.

(22) a. On that safari, five hunters shot three lions and two tigers.
      b. On that safari, a group of five hunters shot three lions and two tigers.
      c. On that safari, five hunters each shot three lions and two tigers.
      d. On that safari, three lions and two tigers were each shot by five hunters.
      e. On that safari, a group of five hunters shot three lions and five hunters each shot two tigers.

What makes this set of data interesting is that starting with a sentential conjunction like (23),

(23) On that safari, five hunters shot three lions and five hunters shot two tigers.

one has, assuming coreferentiality of the hunters, either $2 \times 2 = 4$ or $3 \times 3 = 9$ readings for the unreduced sentence; but when (23) is reduced to (22)a one has

  i.   not, as blind conjunction-reduction would predict, four or nine readings,
 ii.   not, as Lakoff would predict, only one reading (namely (22)b, since the quantifiers supposedly could not be lowered from higher sentences),
iii.   but rather either two or three readings, corresponding exactly to the two or three readings for an unconjoined sentence like (21)a.

This would appear to be prima facie evidence in favor of treating conjunction-reduction as one formal operation, letting semantic interpretation depend in part on the output, since the generalization indicated by iii above is that in conjoined NP's containing quantifiers, the quantifiers must have the same scope. The transformationalist position must have two different rules for conjunction-reduction, one for specific and one for non-specific NP's. Otherwise, if conjunction-reduction is to be treated as a single rule followed by quantifier-lowering, as Lakoff appeared to regard it, then quantifier-lowering must be allowed to violate the coordinate structure constraint just in case it violates it equally for all conjuncts.

The facts when stated informally do not after all seem terribly peculiar; they are obviously related to the fact noted by Chomsky (1966) that (24)a is only two ways ambiguous, like (24)b, not four ways ambiguous as one might have expected.

(24)   a.   John likes Mary better than Susan, and so does Bill.
       b.   John likes Mary better than Susan.

But these facts are nevertheless not explained within any of the current frameworks, and until an explanation is found it can only be a question of plausibility of what sort of framework is most likely to harbor a satisfactory explanation. It is the fact that the reduction of ambiguity accompanies the transformational processes of conjunction-reduction, (23) to (22)a, and verb-phrase ellipsis, (24)a, that suggests that semantic interpretation must take into account either the processes involved or the outputs thereof.[9]

3.2   Subject and Object: the Problematical Relation of Surface Structure to Semantic Interpretation

The last four sets of examples I want to discuss all concern the semantic significance of subject and object position, particularly of what appears to be derived subject and object position.

3.2.1   *Easy*.   Firstly, classical syntactic arguments[10] have favored assigning a single deep structure to the sentences of (26), and hence presumably to those of (27).

[9] Lakoff's most recent suggestions (G. Lakoff 1969a,b) seem to present a new alternative, namely that aspects of the semantic interpretation—dependent only on or perhaps equated with deep structure—may be carried along in some manner through a derivation and may determine constraints on the operation of syntactic rules. Lakoff claimed in the discussion following this paper that his suggestion makes the question of meaning-preservingness quite vacuous and offers a framework in which examples like (22) might indeed be able to be handled. However, unless it can be shown that there are some empirical claims connected with the introduction of such a powerful new device (and particularly some possibility of falsification), it would appear to be a matter of making the meaning-preservingness question vacuous by begging it.

[10] See Chomsky (1964), Partee (1968).

(26)   a.   It is easy to please John.
       b.   John is easy to please.
(27)   a.   It is particularly easy to get this baby into these overalls.
       b.   This baby is particularly easy to get into these overalls.
       c.   These overalls are particularly easy to get this baby into.

It is clear from co-occurrence restrictions that the surface subjects *John,*
this baby, and *these overalls* must each occur in deep structure in the clause
which ends up as an infinitive phrase, but it is not out of the question that
they *also* occur as deep structure subjects of *easy,* after the manner of (28):

(28)   This baby is ADJP[particularly easy S[NP gets this baby into these
       overalls]]

If a structure something like (28) could be justified on independent (that is,
nonsemantic) grounds[11] as underlying (27)b, and analogous deep structures
for (26)b and (27)c, then there would not necessarily be a violation of the
meaning-preservingness condition in deriving those sentences. But there is
certainly a violation by the classical analysis, since the raising of a constituent
sentence NP into matrix subject position has always been treated as an
optional transformation.

Note, incidentally, that even if (28) could be syntactically justified as the
deep structure for (27)b, there would remain a significant unexplained cor-
relation. Sentence (27)a with heavy stress on *these overalls* seems synonymous
with (27)c. It would seem that adding stress and raising to subject are two
ways of accomplishing the same result, namely the bringing into focus (speaking vaguely) of one of the NP's. Without some way of relating (28) to the
corresponding stressed version of (27)a, then, (28) is only half a solution to
the problem for representing the differences between (27)a, b, c.[12]

3.2.2   *Appears.*   The second set of examples exhibits a similar pattern
with even less semantic difference but still not quite total synonymy.

(28)   a.   It appears that John is shooting at Bill.
       b.   John appears to be shooting at Bill.
       c.   Bill appears to be being shot at by John.

Whereas the difference among the sentences of (27) seems to involve attribu-
tion of different properties to the derived subjects, the difference here seems

---

[11] Tentative but unpublished suggestions along these lines have been made by R. P. V.
Kiparsky and David Perlmutter.

[12] Probably of relevance here is the discussion of clefting and stress in Postal (1968).

to be a difference in point of view of the speaker—in *a* he is taking in the whole situation, in *b* and *c* focussing on John and Bill respectively. Following the direction taken by Postal (1971) for the verb "remind," we might look for a relation between the sentences of (29) and those of (30) below:

(30) a. I see that John is shooting at Bill.
      b. I see John shooting at Bill.
      c. I see Bill being shot at by John.

However, the analysis of *see* and its complements is much less clear than the analysis of *appear* has generally been believed to be, so it is of no immediate help for (29) to suggest relating *appear* to *see*. But it is no doubt at least relevant that the verb *appear* is a psychological verb, so that the differences in (29) may be related to different perceptions leading to essentially the same assertion.

3.2.3   Certain.   For contrast, consider the third set of examples with the nonpsychological sense of *certain*.

(31) a. Nobody is (absolutely) certain to pass the test.
      b. It is (absolutely) certain that nobody will pass the test.
      c. It is not (absolutely) certain that anybody will pass the test.

The problem here is that (31)a, which is sharply nonsynonymous with both (31)b and (31)c, would seem to be derivable from both of them on the classical analysis of *certain*.[13] *Certain* must allow subject-raising because of sentences like (32).

(32)   There is certain to be an argument over that.

And yet to allow subject-raising to apply to either (31)b or (31)c would lead to a change in meaning of a much more fundamental sort than that in either (27) or (29). (31)a can be paraphrased by (33).

(33)   There is nobody of whom it is (absolutely) certain that he will pass the test.

(Thus under a common kind of grading system, (31)b and (31)c are both false, while (31)a is true.) A logician would have no difficulty in representing the differences in the sentences of (31) in terms of differing "scopes" of three elements: negation, an existential quantifier, and a modal operator "certain"; and a linguist might be tempted to simply translate these scope differences into spatial configurations, with trees roughly as in (34).

---

13 See Rosenbaum (1967) and Partee (1968).

(34)

a.

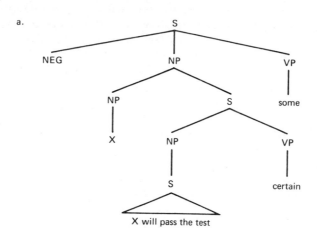

b.

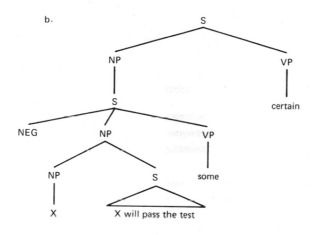

c.

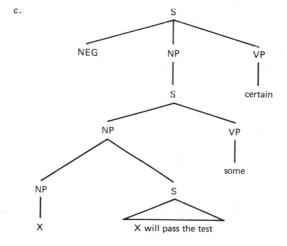

But the problem clearly does not end with the postulation of such deep structures, since it still remains to show how the syntactic rules would map such structures onto the right surface structures. A naive linguist might suppose, for instance, that a deep structure like (34)a would turn into something more like (35) or (36) below than (31)a, and it is incumbent upon the hypothetical proposers of (34)a to show in a non-*ad hoc* way why it can turn into (31)a.

(35)   Those who it is certain will pass the test are none.
(36)   There is no one who it is certain will pass the test.

If one were to maintain the classical syntactic analysis, allowing (31)a to be derived from (31)b or perhaps (31)c (or perhaps both), there would be both the particular problem of characterizing the semantic effect of subject-raising in such cases and the more general problem of stating constraints on how transformational rules (or more global properties of derivation) in general can affect semantic interpretation. The corresponding problem for the analysis suggested in (34) is to find constraints on the transformational rules (or on derivations) so that the rules never apply in cases where their application would change meaning. At the moment there seem to be no obvious solutions in either direction.

Examples (27), (29), and (31) all involve matrix subjects derived in some sense from embedded sentences. What is clear is that appearing in matrix subject position is of semantic relevance, and what is in dispute is how that fact is to be captured. A second-order problem which faces any analysis is to explain why the three quite different semantic effects observed all are associated with the single phenomenon of raising to subject, and why, for instance, contrastive stress has a similar effect only in (27)a.

3.2.4   *Loading the truck with hay.*   The last set of examples concerns the direct object position in simplex sentences. Partee (1965) and Fillmore (1968) consider pairs of sentences like (37)a and b:

(37)   a. We loaded the truck with hay.
        b. We loaded hay onto the truck.

Both authors argue that the distributional similarities between the *a* and *b* type sentences are striking enough that they must be transformationally related. The verbs which show this kind of relation, sometimes with different prepositions, include *spray (wall, paint), spatter, spread (bread, honey), sprinkle, smear, plant (garden, corn), splash, wrap (Johnny, towel).* But as Fillmore notes (p. 48, footnote 49), there is often a slight semantic difference between the paired sentences. For instance, (37)a suggests that the truck was filled, but (37)b does not. Similar differences appear in (38) and (39).

(38) a. David planted his garden with corn.
      b. David planted corn in his garden.
(39) a. Wrap the baby with/in a soft towel.
      b. Wrap a soft towel around the baby.

Sentence (38)a, but not (38)b, indicates that the garden had only corn planted in it; sentence (39)a more than (39)b suggests that the baby should be entirely wrapped up.

The fact that the *a* sentences use *with* with most of these verbs may not be pure accident. Although the *with*-phrases in (37)a, (38)a, and (39)a do not seem to be instrumental adverbs, they are not far removed. If one's object is to get the truck loaded, get the garden planted, or get the baby wrapped up, one can use hay, corn, or a towel to accomplish the task. Such paraphrases with *use* are typical behavior for instrumental adverbs (see G. Lakoff, 1968a). The main argument against calling these *with*-phrases simply instrumental adverbs is that they co-occur with other *with*-phrases which are much more clearly instrumental.

(40) a. We loaded the truck with hay with pitchforks.
      b. David planted his garden with corn with a hoe.

In any case, the similarity to instrumental adverbs might suggest a direction to look for an explanation of the difference between the *a* and *b* sentences of (37)–(39).

4. Conclusions

The suggestion that transformations might be meaning-preserving has led to the investigation of a number of intriguing problems. The great majority of transformations can easily be stated so as to be meaning-preserving for the great majority of sentences; this fact alone strongly supports such a requirement on the theory, and undoubtedly constitutes the major argument of most of the defenders of such a requirement. However, the radical differences among alternative proposals for handling the recalcitrant minority of cases make it clear that the burden of semantic interpretation cannot simply be placed on the shoulders of the syntactic deep structure (no matter how deep) without some accompanying contortions and readjustments of the latter. In short, I would suggest that the hypothesis of meaning-preservingness of transformations has so far eluded both demonstration and refutation; that it is clearly worth pursuing as far as possible; and that further work on the sorts of apparent counterexamples discussed above may well be the key to a deeper understanding of the relation between semantics and syntax.

"PRESUPPOSITION" IN PHILOSOPHY AND LINGUISTICS*

Richard Garner   The Ohio State University

* This work was supported in part by The Ohio State University through its Grant-in-Aid Program.

The theme that has been suggested for this collection of papers is "presuppositions of utterances to the extent that they can be linked with what the linguist sees as linguistic structure." I wish to approach this topic by starting with a discussion of two of the crucial terms employed in it: *presupposition* and *utterance*. I propose to conduct my examination of the former word by pointing out differences among the ways three philosophers have used it and then by contrasting these with some views of linguists about presupposition. In the end I shall suggest that there is not one concept of presupposition, differing but slightly from one person who employs it to another, but several radically different concepts, all of which have been related to the word *presupposition*. The dangers of this are, I trust, sufficiently obvious to require no comment.

Utterances

The word *utterance* has both an "act-object" and a "type-token" ambiguity, as well as being neutral among words, phrases, and sentences. Someone talking about "utterances" may be speaking of any of the following:

(1) a specific occurrence of a particular word (phrase, sentence), or what I shall call a word (phrase, sentence) object token

(2) the individual act of producing a particular word (phrase, sentence), or what I shall call a word (phrase, sentence) act token

(3) a word (phrase, sentence) treated as a repeatable type, or what I shall call a word (phrase, sentence) object type

(4) any act of uttering an instance of a given word (phrase, sentence), or what I shall call a word (phrase, sentence) act type[1]

---

[1] Strawson draws our attention to the act-object ambiguity in connection with the word *statement* in Strawson (1950b). Both distinctions are elaborated in Cartwright (1962), Garner (1968a) and (1968b). We may fill in the details by taking as our examples the word *troglodyte*, the phrase *the sullen troglodyte,* and the sentence *The sullen troglodyte is annoyed,* and by observing that one professing an interest in an "utterance" might be concerned with:

    (a) a specific word object token—some particular occurrence of the word *troglodyte*
    (b) a specific phrase object token—some particular occurrence of the phrase *the sullen troglodyte*
    (c) a specific sentence object token—some particular occurrence of the sentence *The sullen troglodyte is annoyed*
    (d) a specific word act token—some individual act of producing the word *troglodyte*
    (e) a specific phrase act token—some individual act of producing the phrase *the sullen troglodyte*
    (f) a specific sentence act token—some individual act of producing the sentence *The sullen troglodyte is annoyed*
    (g) a word object type—the word *troglodyte* considered as a repeatable type
    (h) a phrase object type—the phrase *the sullen troglodyte* considered as a repeatable type [Footnote continues on the following page.]

It is also possible that one making claims about "utterances" might be advancing general statements about

    (5)   every word (phrase, sentence)

or about

    (6)   every act of uttering a word (phrase, sentence)

We may identify this as a concern with word, phrase, or sentence objects or acts in general.[2] When we turn our attention to complete sentences, and the acts of uttering them, it may be our intention to say things about

$$(7) \quad \text{every} \left\{ \begin{array}{l} \text{declarative} \\ \text{imperative} \\ \text{interrogative} \end{array} \right\} \text{sentence object token}$$

or about

$$(8) \quad \text{every} \left\{ \begin{array}{l} \text{declarative} \\ \text{imperative} \\ \text{interrogative} \end{array} \right\} \text{sentence act token}$$

The word *utterance* gains its entry here if we speak of utterances which *are* declarative (imperative, interrogative) sentences, or of utterances which are *utterances of* declarative (imperative, interrogative) sentences. In the former case the concern is with utterances as objects and in the latter with utterances as acts.

    Unfortunately the word *utterance* may be called upon to refer to any of the items distinguished above, but, what is worse, that word has been used in other ways as well. I can best explain how this has come about by making use of the notion of an "illocutionary act," introduced in Austin (1962). Let us suppose that Jones (whom we shall call our "locutionary source") utters the sentence *I will come to the orgy* to Smith (whom we shall

---

    (i)   a sentence object type—the sentence *The sullen troglodyte is annoyed* considered as a repeatable type

    (j)   a word act type—any act of uttering the word *troglodyte*—this too is repeatable and (like phrase and sentence act types) may be performed by any number of people or by one person on several occasions

    (k)   a phrase act type—any act of uttering the phrase *the sullen troglodyte*

    (l)   a sentence act type—any act of uttering the sentence *The sullen troglodyte is annoyed*

[2] One could also, of course, try to deal with classes of word acts or objects, which classes could be delimited by any of the many possible principles of grouping.

call our "locutionary target").[3] Under certain circumstances (which might be called the "circumstances of the locutionary act" (CLA)) it will be correct to say that Jones made a promise to Smith; but if the CLA are different we should instead say that he gave Smith a warning, made a statement to him, or expressed his intentions to him. Now at this level too we are likely to encounter the notion of an utterance; only here the word *utterance* is used to talk about illocutionary acts or objects (types or tokens).

At the extreme of greatest generality one may speak of (what is presupposed by)

    (9)   every illocutionary act

or

    (10)   every illocutionary object

and less generally of (what is presupposed by)

$$
(11)\quad \text{every illocutionary act of} \left\{ \begin{array}{l} \text{giving an order} \\ \text{making a promise} \\ \text{making a statement} \end{array} \right\}
$$

or

$$
(12)\quad \text{every illocutionary object which is a(n)} \left\{ \begin{array}{l} \text{order} \\ \text{promise} \\ \text{statement} \end{array} \right\}
$$

At this level no "content" has been brought in, for we are not interested in promises to do this or that, promises made by Jones, or promises made to Smith, but promises (or orders or statements) in general.[4]

---

[3] I shall use the abbreviations *LS* and *LT*. These terms were first introduced in Garner (1969) and have since been adopted and supplemented in Fillmore (1969b).

[4] If we place considerations of the LS and the LT in the background for a moment but begin to specify the content of the promise, we can concentrate on (a) promises to attend an orgy (any orgy at all) and (b) promises to attend a specific orgy. Now here we may find ourselves concerned with discussing such topics as what is presupposed by

    (a) every illocutionary act of making a promise to attend an orgy (any orgy at all)
or
    (b) every illocutionary act of making a promise to attend a specific orgy

as well as with what is presupposed by the illocutionary objects related to those acts. And when we bring in our LS and LT, we may find ourselves asking about what is presupposed by

    (a1) every illocutionary act of Jones of making a promise to attend an orgy (any orgy at all) [Footnote continues on the following page.]

Even when we do specify some content as well as the LS and the LT (as illustrated in footnote 4) we have not reached the maximum degree of specificity, for we have been speaking of *types* which are, by definition, repeatable. So we must add to our list the following items which also fall under the heading of "utterances":

(13) a specific illocutionary act of making a promise to attend a specific orgy, made by Jones and given, on some definite occasion, to Smith

(14) a specific illocutionary object which is a promise to attend a specific orgy, made by Jones and given, on some definite occasion, to Smith.

In the case of (13) we are concerned with an illocutionary act token, and in the case of (14) with an illocutionary object token.

The potentially confusing thing is that a discussion of "utterances" or of "presuppositions of utterances" can turn out to be a discussion of any of the items distinguished above, or of their presuppositions; and while it is doubtless true that there are relations among them, and that everything that is presupposed by the more general items of a given sort is also presupposed by the less general items of the same sort, there are important differences that can be blurred if we allow the word *utterance* to range indiscriminately over all of them. Thus, the very first thing to make clear, when we say that we are concerned with presuppositions of utterances, is what we are talking about when we use that very dangerous word *utterance*.

Presupposition

Leaving the word *utterance* for the moment, let us turn to the word *presupposition*. As I understand the situation there are two very important questions to be raised at the outset. First, it must be asked what sort of thing or things one who is talking about presuppositions of utterances wishes the variables *x* and *y* to range over in the formula "*x* presupposes *y*"

(b1) every illocutionary act of Jones of making a promise to attend a specific orgy

or by the corresponding illocutionary objects. In addition to this, we might also find ourselves worried about the presuppositions of

(a2) every illocutionary act of making a promise to Smith to attend an orgy (any orgy at all)

(b2) every illocutionary act of making a promise to Smith to attend a specific orgy

or by the corresponding objects. And, of course, we may be concerned with the presuppositions of those acts or objects when we have specified more fully the content (for example, the date and place of the orgy) as well as the LS and the LT. Naturally, similar distinctions could be made were we to speak of statements, bets, warnings, and so forth, rather than (or in addition to) promises.

(I shall call this *the presupposition formula*). One who specifies the range of *x* will help us to understand how he is using the word *utterance,* but in addition to this it is quite likely that as the values of both variables change, the concept of presupposition will also change; and so a specification of the range of the variables will also help clarify the particular use of the word *presupposition* involved. But further, we cannot hope to understand the way someone is using the word *presupposition* unless we are able to discover what is thought to result when a presupposition fails, and so the second question we should ask is this: What is the alleged consequence (penalty) of a presupposition failure? As the answers to our two questions vary (and we should not suppose that they vary independently) it is likely that the concept of presupposition being employed will undergo (sometimes subtle and sometimes marked) alterations.[5]

Now I want to bring out some facts about the notion of a presupposition (and also that of an utterance) by examining what three philosophers have had to say about presupposition. The notion was not, as many seem to believe, introduced by Strawson. Frege, in "On Sense and Reference" (1892), appealed to it when he pointed out that "if anything is asserted[6] there is always an obvious presupposition that the simple or compound proper names used have a reference" (p. 69). (Frege treated all singular referring expressions as proper names so that definite descriptions, as well as ordinary proper names like Gottlob and Wolfgang, were called proper names.)

Let us say that if Jones and Smith utter assertively the sentence *Kepler died in misery,* then (if certain other conditions are satisfied) they have both performed illocutionary act tokens of the same type and produced illocutionary object tokens of the same type. But if Laubner utters assertively the sentence *Kepler did not die in misery,* he will have performed an illocu-

---

[5] One potential source of trouble is the fact that most people who write about presuppositions talk (at least sometimes) about what *a speaker* presupposes. This is a potential source of trouble because one concerned with the presuppositions of any of the kinds of things we have distinguished may express this concern by speaking of what is presupposed by the speaker when he utters a word, phrase, or sentence, or when he makes a statement or a bet, asks a question, or gives an order. Or, using "the speaker" in another sense, we may ask what "the speaker" (that is, *any* speaker) presupposes when he utters any interrogative sentence or performs any illocutionary act. I have chosen to make my distinctions among the various kinds of acts and objects a speaker may perform or produce, but we could always rephrase what I have said by talking explicitly about what, as a performer of an act of a certain kind, or as a producer of an object of a certain kind, a speaker does (or would) presuppose. Rescher (1961) speaks of propositional, property, and inferential presupposition and explicitly asks the second question I have distinguished of each. He argues that the latter two are definable in terms of the first and understands the first as taking the form "to assert that *p* presupposes *q*," thus introducing, as above, the notion of what a speaker asserting a proposition presupposes.

[6] Frege uses the words *assert* and *assertion* rather than *state* and *statement,* but his usage of these words is close enough to my usage of *statement* that no harm will come, I believe, from speaking always of statements when talking about Frege's views.

tionary act token of a different type, and the illocutionary object token he has produced is a token of a different type from that of which the tokens produced by Jones and Smith are instances.[7]

When a presupposition fails Frege would, I think, be inclined to say that no statement was made. In Austin's terminology we could say that the *purported* act "did not come off," and in my terminology we could say either that no statement act token was performed or that no statement object token was produced. We must, therefore, understand Frege's remark that if anything is asserted there is always a presupposition that the proper names used have a reference as amounting to the view that a necessary condition of anyone's being able to use a sentence to make a statement is that the proper name serving as the grammatical subject of the sentence does have a reference.

It would be a mistake to interpret Frege as committed to the general formula that a statement made by using a sentence containing a proper name presupposes that the name used designates something, for if the name fails to designate (as it would if it were *the present king of France*) there *is* no statement to do the presupposing. Here we might resort to talk about what *a speaker* presupposes (see footnote 5) and say that a speaker, purporting to make a statement, presupposes certain facts. If those facts do obtain there is no real harm in talking about what is presupposed by the statement act type of which his successful token is an instance, or by the statement object type, a token of which he produced, or even by the tokens themselves. The interpretation of Frege I am adopting here is similar to that found in Black (1958), who says that Frege holds that "when the presupposition is not the case, we have no assertion, but only the utterance of a form of words . . ." (p. 51). Apparently Nerlich (1965) understands Frege differently—see p. 40, footnote 6.

Frege has nothing to say about the presuppositions of other kinds of illocutionary acts or objects, or even of general (as opposed to singular) statements, but (if we remember what was said in the previous paragraph) we will not go too far wrong if we understand him as having said that the *x* in the presupposition formula may be understood as referring to all illocutionary act or object types of a given kind (singular statements), any illocutionary act or object type of that kind, or any illocutionary act or object token which is a token of one of those types. I repeat that we can say this as long as we realize that to say that a given statement presupposes a fact is to say that unless that fact obtains no such statement can be made. Finally,

---

[7] When a specific singular statement object type is in question we may, if we can identify the proper name used, state the presupposition more explicitly. Rather than saying that there is a presupposition that the proper name used designates something, we can say, as Frege does about his own example, "that the name *Kepler* designates something is just as much a presupposition for the assertion *Kepler died in misery* as for the contrary assertion" (p. 69). It is interesting to compare this claim with some of Fillmore's comments about a "negation test" for presuppositions. (See Fillmore, 1969a, p. 62 and 1969b.)

we might notice that y in the presupposition formula ranges over "facts" (whatever they are supposed to be).[8]

The second treatment of presupposition by a philosopher that I wish to discuss (and by far the most influential one) is Strawson's. Strawson (and most other philosophers in the same tradition) insists that we enforce the distinction between a sentence and a statement, and says that "it is about statements only that the question of truth and falsity can arise; and about these that it can sometimes fail to arise" (1952, p. 175). This distinction is also discussed in Strawson (1950a), (1950b), Austin (1950), (1962), Cartwright (1962), (1968), and many other publications.

In (1952) Strawson defines the presupposition relation by saying that a statement S presupposes a statement S' if, and only if, the truth of S' is a precondition of the truth or falsity of S (p. 175). In other words, to say that a statement object type S presupposes another statement object type S' is to say that the truth of S' is a necessary condition for the truth or falsity of S. There is good reason to say, as I have just done, that when Strawson speaks of "statements" which presuppose he is talking about statement *objects* rather than statement acts. Obviously in Strawson's view the sort of thing which does the presupposing (as well as the sort of thing which is presupposed) must be susceptible of truth and falsehood, and in his debate with Austin about truth (1950b) he argues that it is correct to apply *true* and *false* to statements only if they are understood as objects and not as acts, or, as he puts it, as "what I say" rather than "my saying it" (pp. 33–35).

Strawson speaks not only of the presuppositions of singular statement object types, such as those made by utterances of sentences like *The present king of France is bald,* but also of what is presupposed by quantified statements of any of the four standard forms:

All S is P.
No S is P.
Some S is P.
Some S is not P.[9]

His prime example involves the statement made by the sentence: *All John's children are asleep.* As in the king of France case, he says that the truth

---

[8] In Frege (1956) it is claimed that a fact is a true thought. If we understand this as amounting to the view that it is possible to identify facts and true statements we will find that there is almost no difference between Frege and Strawson about the values of the variable y in the presupposition formula.

[9] Another difference between Frege and Strawson might be seen in their treatment of y. For Strawson y ranges over statement object types whereas for Frege it seems to range over facts. Black (1958) says that according to Frege "a presupposition of the assertion, *The king of France is wise,* is that one and only one man reigns over France, that is, something that either is, or is not, the case. For Strawson, however, if we are to follow his formal definition, the presupposition is always a *statement,* that is, something that may itself be true or false, genuine or spurious" (pp. 52–53). But, as pointed out in footnote 8, the difference here may be illusory.

of the statement that John has children is presupposed by the statement
that they are asleep. If John has no children then the statement that they
are asleep is neither true nor false (1952, pp. 173 ff). I think that both Frege
and Strawson would allow that statement object types or tokens may replace
the variable x in the presupposition formula (if we keep in mind the qualification made at the end of the section on Frege), but, unlike Frege, who
remains silent on this point, Strawson seems prepared to generalize his
remarks to include quantified statements of the four standard forms as well
as singular statements containing (Fregean) proper names.

The qualification referred to in the last paragraph involved the recognition that, for Frege, when a presupposition fails no statement is made.
Strawson's view, as I have presented it, is quite different. For Strawson if
a statement S presupposes another statement S', the falsity of S' leads to
the result that the statement S lacks a truth value and does not result in
the speaker failing to make a statement at all. I can find no evidence in
Strawson's writings that he was ever tempted to adopt the alternate (Fregean)
conception of presupposition,[10] though Nerlich (1965) argues that he "oscil-
lates" between the following two incompatible positions:

    i. When a meaningful sentence is uttered by a speaker of the language on a
       certain occasion, then a necessary condition for the statement thus made to
       have a truth value is that the (main) referring expression in the sentence
       has, on that occasion, a reference.

and

    ii. When a meaningful sentence is uttered by a speaker of the language on a
       certain occasion, then a necessary condition of the speaker's thereby making
       a statement is that the (main) referring expression in the sentence has, on
       that occasion, a reference. (p. 34)

I find Nerlich's evidence for the occurrence of i in Strawson's writings
quite inconclusive, though there are reasons to believe that more recently
Strawson has come to adopt ii.[11] Perhaps the strongest reason for abandon-

[10] Compare the remark from p. 175 of Strawson (1952) quoted earlier. A perusal of Strawson (1950a) may satisfy the reader that Strawson is very careful there to leave this matter
unresolved. Whenever a simple remark would make clear which alternative he would
adopt, he avoids the issue by saying that a presupposition failure results in a failure to
make a true or false statement; but this could be because the speaker failed to make a
statement at all, or because the one he did make lacks a truth value. Part of getting clear
about what Strawson means by *statement* depends on finding the answer to this question.
[11] During his visit to The Ohio State University in the academic year 1966–1967, Strawson
seemed disposed to ii rather than i. He spoke of "propositions" rather than of statements
and claimed that when there is no king of France the sentence *The present king of France
is bald* does not express a proposition. Still Strawson's interpretation as well as the question
of what, aside from Strawson's own views, the best account of presupposition is, is a
matter of continuing debate. Hancock (1960) argues that the very fact that on i we are

ing i in favor of ii is that ii allows a natural generalization to speech acts of other kinds and their objects, since it seems desirable to speak of the presuppositions of promises, commands, questions, bets, warnings, and so on as well a those of statements. More accurately, of course, we would speak of what someone who purports to perform such an act (and thereby to produce such an object) presupposes (see footnote 5).[12]

The third treatment of presupposition by a philosopher that I wish to discuss is presented by Wilfrid Sellars (1954) in the context of a discussion of Strawson's view.[13] After criticizing what he takes to be Strawson's notion of presupposition Sellars offers his own analysis. He says that if a person utters assertively the sentence *Harry has stopped beating his grandmother,* he has *asserted* both that Harry once beat his grandmother and that he no longer

---

forced to say that a statement need not have a truth value counts against i. This, however, seems to be rather a matter of legislation. He also suggests that, according to Strawson, statement *acts* count as values of *x* in the presupposition formula, but it is far from clear that Strawson is *required* to say this and perfectly obvious, given his explicit definition of presupposition in (1952) and his claims about the proper subjects of predications of truth and falsity in (1950b), that he is committed to deny it. Linsky (1967) distinguishes between statements and propositions and argues that the latter must (by definition) be either true or false. He then suggests that Russell could have defended himself against Strawson's criticisms by arguing that the *proposition* that the present king of France is wise does entail the *proposition* that there is one and only one individual now occupying that position (p. 91). Both Linsky and Nerlich argue that Strawson fails to make a clear distinction between entailment and presupposition. According to Nerlich the view labeled i breaks down over just this point. His argument is thoroughly but inconclusively, discussed in Montague (1969). If it is impossible to distinguish between entailment and presupposition on i that seems another reason for moving in the direction of ii. But ii is also criticized by Nerlich.

12 This places Strawson's view much more in line with Austin (1962). Geach (1950) does talk about the presuppositions of questions, but when discussing the classic example *The present king of France is bald,* he vacillates between treating sentences and statements as the values of *x* in the presupposition formula. He also says that when there is no king of France the "use of *the King of France* as a logical subject is out of place," (p. 34) and the assertion of *The present king of France is bald* (I have changed the example slightly) is "not false but simply out of place." It is unclear whether he had in mind something like i, ii, or something more in line with the view of Sellars, next to be discussed.

13 Strawson (1954) is a reply to this article and contains minor modifications of position i. On the mistaken belief that "Strawson nowhere gives an explicit analysis of *x presupposes y*" (p. 212), Sellars attempts to explain what Strawson "might have meant" by considering a number of possibilities, including:

   (a) To say that *x* presupposes *y* is to say that it is incorrect for a speaker to make an utterance *x* unless he believes that *y* is the case.

and

   (b) To say that *x* presupposes *y* is to say that it is incorrect for a speaker to make an utterance *x* unless he believes, and believes truly, that *y* is the case.

Both of these alternatives are criticized by Sellars, but there is little reason to believe that Strawson would have subscribed to either of them, and attention to his explicit definition (1952, p. 175) makes it plain that neither (a) nor (b) captures his notion of presupposition. The only thing to be said in defense of Sellars is that it is not perfectly clear from Strawson (1950a) that Strawson did not have something like (a) or (b) in mind. See pp. 34 and 36, for example.

does so: and his assertion is false if either of these facts fails to obtain.[14] But further, there is a sense in which it is *incorrect* for this person to utter this sentence assertively unless he *believes* that Harry once beat his grandmother and *believes* also that his LT shares this belief. Finally, it is also *incorrect* for his LT to say "That's false" unless he (the LT) *believes* that Harry once beat his grandmother "and thus has as his reason for saying *That's false* the belief that Harry continues his wicked ways" (p. 206).

Turning from "complex" statements to singular ones (see footnote 14), Sellars seems to adopt a modified Russellean view to the effect that someone who makes an assertion by uttering the sentence *This table over here is large* also "asserts" (in part) that there is one and only one table *over here* (p. 207). But he adds that this fact is also *presupposed* by an utterance of that sentence.

> An utterance of "The table over here is large" does indeed presuppose that there is one and only one table "over here." To say that the utterance presupposes this is to say that it is correct to make the utterance . . . only if one believes there is to be one and only one table "over here" and that this belief is shared by the listener. Furthermore, to say "That's false" when told that the table is large equally *presupposes* that the uniqueness condition is satisfied: where this in turn means that it is correct to say "That's false" only if one believes the uniqueness condition to be satisfied and that the original speaker shares this belief. But even though the original utterance and the reply presuppose that the uniqueness condition is satisfied, the utterance is nevertheless *false* if the uniqueness condition is not satisfied, *even though it is not correct to say that it is false unless one believes that the condition is satisfied.* (pp. 207–208)

The crucial move occurs when Sellars attempts to explicate what it means to say that an utterance presupposes the existence and uniqueness of the table. His explication differs from Strawson's view (that is, from i) in at least two crucial respects: first in the values for y and second in the conception of the results of a presupposition failure. What is presupposed here is, according to Sellars, distinct from what is asserted, in that what is "asserted" is that there is one and only one table *over here,* whereas what is "presupposed" is that the LS believes that this is so and that the LT shares this belief.[15] For Strawson if the presupposed statement is false we are left with a statement that is neither true nor false, but for Sellars if the (dif-

---

[14] Sellars also seems to believe that these facts are presupposed as well as asserted, but see the next two footnotes. Here we may speak of "complex" statements rather than of ("simple") singular or quantified statements. I shall not have much to say about statements of this sort, though I believe that any treatment given the other kinds I shall discuss could also be given "complex" ones.

[15] Sellars' way of speaking here does not make this clear. He says that an utterance of *The table over here is large* presupposes *and* asserts that there is one and only one table *over here,* and it is not until it is clearly seen what he means when he says that such an utterance presupposes this that it becomes obvious that he holds that what is presupposed differs from what is asserted.

ferent) presuppositions fail we can say only that, in some sense, the LS has spoken "incorrectly."[16] In his reply to Sellars Strawson freely admits that it would be "incorrect" for someone to make an assertion unless he believed that the presupposed existence statement was true (p. 217), but he makes it clear that this "pragmatic" feature of discourse has nothing to do with *his* notion of presupposition.[17]

Notice that whereas for Strawson (at least on the position identified as i) it is statement objects which presuppose, on Sellars' view what must presuppose is something to which the terms *correct* and *incorrect* can apply: and that seems to be illocutionary act types or tokens. This interpretation is also supported by the reflection that when, in the above passage, Sellars glosses his claim that the correct usage of such statements presupposes, he certainly seems to be saying that this means that the *act* of making such a statement

[16] Perhaps we should say that since an essential part of Strawson's explication of pre-supposition involves a specification of what results from a presupposition failure, it is a mistake for Sellars to allow that "presuppositions" similar to those pointed out by Strawson hold, but then to deny that a presupposition failure has the consequences mentioned by Strawson in his definition of the notion. Perhaps Sellars should have taken the trouble to find out how Strawson actually used the word *presupposition,* for then he could have tried to show that there are no presuppositions in this sense because the statements Strawson identifies as presuppositions do not, when false, result in statements without a truth-value. He could then have gone on to talk about the conditions under which it is "correct" or "incorrect" for speakers to say certain things, and the assumptions they make about the world and about the beliefs of their audiences when they speak in certain ways. This topic has certainly been treated in the literature, only usually under the heading of what a speaker *implies.* See Grice (mimeo). It is very tempting to say, with Black (1958), that "confusion between presupposing (in Strawson's sense) and implying led Pro-fessor Sellars to misunderstand the doctrine under discussion" (p. 57, footnote 16).

[17] In his replay to Sellars, Strawson suggests that Sellars actually has two conflicting ac-counts of presupposition, one, which Strawson calls account A, covering the presupposi-tions of singular (and "complex") statements, and one, called account B, covering the presuppositions of affirmative universally quantified statements. This does not seem quite fair because Sellars' notion as to what is presupposed is, in both cases, the same—the difference involves what is thought to be asserted by one who makes such statements. But Strawson is almost certainly right when he suggests that "there is surely no reason what-ever, except a determination to adhere at all costs to the orthodox modern analysis, for simultaneously adopting account A in the case of statements containing definite descrip-tions and account B in the case of universal statements" (p. 219). Strawson also points out that account A is given not only for singular referring statements, but also for par-ticular (as opposed to universal) quantified statements. Thus a statement such as *Some A is B* will, on Sellars' view, have the presupposed statement (that the subject class is not empty) as a part of its assertion content. According to Sellars, then, one who says that *some* of his shirts are at the laundry will also have said (and/or implied) that he has shirts (and will also have presupposed, but not said, that the LT believes that he has); while one who says that *all* of his shirts are at the laundry will only have said (and/or implied) that it is not the case that he has shirts which are not at the laundry, and not that he has any shirts (but he too will have presupposed that he has shirts and that the LT believes that he has). Strawson remarks, concerning this: "Who, if he had never seen a bound variable, would have supposed that the difference between saying that all his shirts were at the laundry and that some of them were, involved *this* difference?" (p. 220) More recently Sellars (1968) has reaffirmed his earlier position, without reference to any of Strawson's objections (pp. 122–125.)

is correct only under certain conditions. If the presuppositions (in Sellars' sense) fail, the *act* of making the statement must still be said to have been successfully performed, but it is, in some way, "incorrect." Further, the object produced (the statement made) still has a truth value. Thus for Sellars the values of *x* should probably be understood to be illocutionary act types or tokens. (The generalization to other kinds of illocutionary acts would not be a difficult matter however.)

We are now in a position to exhibit some of the differences among the differing conceptions of presupposition we have so far encountered, and I think that what I have said can best be summarized and drawn together in the following chart:

	Values of *x* in the presupposition formula	Values of *y* in the presupposition formula	Result of a presupposition failure
Frege	A speaker purporting to make a singular statement or, more loosely, All illocutionary act or object types of a given kind (singular statements), any illocutionary act or object type of that kind, or any token of one of those types	The fact that the names used have a reference	No act is performed or no object is produced
Strawson I	Singular statement object types or tokens and quantified statement object types or tokens	Existence statements pertaining to what is mentioned by the subject terms of the sentences employed (or, more strictly, the truth of such statements)	The statement produced lacks a truth value
Strawson II	Singular statement object types or tokens as well as singular statement act types or tokens: quantified statement object types or tokens as well as quantified statement act types or tokens; and probably other kinds of illocutionary act and object types and tokens (for example, promises, bets, warnings, and so forth)	Existence statements pertaining to what is mentioned by the subject terms of the sentences employed (or, more strictly, the truth of such statements)	No act is performed or no object is produced
Sellars	Singular, "complex," and quantified statement act types or tokens	Facts about the beliefs of the LS in the existence and uniqueness of what is mentioned by the subject terms of the sentences employed, and facts about the beliefs of the LS about the beliefs of the LT about the existence and uniqueness of what is mentioned by the subject terms of the sentences employed (something further would have to be said to enable this to cover "complex" statements)	One who makes such a statement speaks incorrectly

The Linguists

One very important difference between philosophers' talk about presupposition and that of the linguists lies in the matter of what it is that is said to do the presupposing. Each of the three philosophers we have considered has been concerned to draw attention to the "presuppositions" of some class of illocutionary object types or act types, some specific illocutionary object type or act type, or some specific illocutionary object token or act token.[18] Those linguists who talk about presupposition, however, are usually found to be treating presuppositions of a class of *sentence* types (for example, all interrogative sentences), a specific *sentence* object type (for example, the sentence *Have you stopped beating your wife?*), or some token of a *sentence* object type. Most recently linguists have attempted to deal with what they call the presuppositions of words, or, as it is sometimes said, of "predicate words" and nouns used predicatively. See Fillmore (1968b, pp. 84 and 87). Such concerns can, of course, still be described as concerns about "presuppositions of utterances," due to the overwhelming looseness of *utterance* discussed above.

Katz and Postal (1964) discuss "the presuppositions of questions," but by this they clearly do not intend to be referring to either illocutionary acts or objects, but rather to interrogative sentences. They suggest that "the constituent structure of the underlying P-marker of all questions" can be diagrammed in the following way (p. 115):

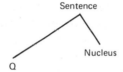

and that the presuppositions of any question are

> all the sentences whose reading at the "Sentence" node is the same as the reading of the constituent Nucleus in the underlying P-marker of the question (except for the syntactic marker Nucleus and for the *wh*-bracketing) and all the sentences that are entailed by sentences that are presuppositions in this sense. (p. 116)

Without attempting to raise objections to their view it is possible to extract from this passage the fact that Katz and Postal assume (at least when

---

[18] In one place (1950a) Strawson speaks about the word *the,* saying that "to use the word *the* in this way is then to imply . . . that the existential conditions described by Russell are fulfilled" (p. 36). But this is obviously different from saying anything about the presuppositions of a word object type. More recently Searle (1959) and (1969) has had something to say about "presuppositions of concepts" (1969, pp. 145–146), and in both places explains what he means by saying that "an expression [this is the (1969) formulation— in (1959) he uses the word *term*] *a* presupposes an expression *b* if and only if in order for *a* to be true or false of an object *x*, *b* must be true of *x*" (1969, p. 126). So far philosophers have made little of this, and it remains true that most of the talk about presupposition by philosophers is of the sort I have been discussing. Further, if Rescher (1961) is correct "concept presupposition" is definable in terms of "statement (or proposition) presupposition." (See footnote 5.)

interrogative sentences are involved) that the variables x and y in the presupposition formula take sentences as their values. What presupposes is an interrogative sentence and what is presupposed is a set (presumably infinite) of declarative sentences.[19]

It is more difficult to discover what Katz and Postal believe to result from a presupposition failure. They say that "the notion of a 'presupposition of a question' concerns a condition that the asker of the question assumes will be accepted by anyone who trys to answer it" (p. 116). Now this sounds vaguely similar to Sellars' view that one of the things a speaker making a statement presupposes is that the LT has a certain belief. And it certainly differs from either of Strawson's notions of what is presupposed, for he would say that while the speaker may or may not assume that his hearer has a certain belief, or that he would accept this or that condition, what is *presupposed* is the truth of some existence statement, not the truth of some statement about the beliefs of the LS or the LT concerning the existence of what is mentioned by the subject term of the sentence.

Now on Sellars' view, when a presupposition fails the only discernible result is that the speaker has done something "incorrect," but Katz and Postal do not seem to have *any* suggestions as to what results from a presupposition failure, and given that, unlike Sellars, they seem to believe that both variables in the presupposition formula range over sentences, it is far from clear what they could say in answer to this question. They are not, for example, in a position to talk about statements which lack a truth value, or even of illocutionary acts which misfire. Perhaps the best hypothesis would be that, in their view, a speaker who utters a sentence presupposes that other *sentences* would be accepted by the LT, and if they would not be accepted there will be some "hitch" in the communication situation—

---

[19] This is roughly the interpretation of the view of Katz and Postal found in Fillmore (1966), who, commenting on Katz and Postal's view, says:

> A second type of relation *between sentences,* described by Katz and Postal, is that between a question and its presuppositions. This is revealed most directly by relating interrogative words to indefinite words, in such a way that the presupposition of a question is in fact a part of the underlying structure of the question. Thus the question WHERE DID HE GO? presupposes (and has as a part of its underlying structure) the *sentence* HE WENT SOMEWHERE: and the question WHO DID THAT? presupposes that SOMEONE DID SOMETHING. (pp. 222–223, italics mine)

In passing, I must remark that there is something very odd about the construction *that SOMEONE DID SOMETHING* when what follows *that* is a complete sentence. This seems to be a confusion of direct and indirect discourse. More importantly, however, I think that it is going somewhat beyond the actual position of Katz and Postal to suggest, as Fillmore seems to do here, that *every* presupposition of a question is a part of the underlying structure of the interrogative sentence used to ask it. I do not think that anything Katz and Postal say justifies an interpretation which would commit them to this position. If that is their view, they will be committed to the consequence that the underlying structure of an interrogative sentence can never be given, since it will contain an infinite number of presupposed sentences (on the assumption that any given sentence has an infinite number of entailments and that the presuppositions of a sentence include all the sentences it entails).

but this is just a guess.[20] At any rate it is clear that since their view as to the values of the variables x and y in the presupposition formula, as well as their view as to the consequences of a presupposition failure, differ from the views of Frege and Strawson, it is reasonable to suggest that, like Sellars, they are using *presupposition* in a way radically different from either Frege or Strawson. If this is so, I submit that it would be advisable for anyone sympathetic with the Katz-Postal treatment of what they call *presupposition* to scrap the word, so that readers will not be led to suppose that the remarks of Katz and Postal are either compatible with, or opposed to, those of Frege and Strawson. I would also recommend this course of action to anyone wishing to elaborate on the remarks of Sellars. (See in this connection footnote 16.)[21]

The most complete and informative treatment of *presupposition* I have encountered in the writings of linguists is Fillmore (1969b), where the presuppositions of a sentence are said to be "those conditions which must be satisfied before the sentence can be used [to make an assertion, ask a question, give a command, express a feeling, etc.]." The sentence *Please open the door,* he says, "can be used as a command only if the LT is in a position to know what door has been mentioned and only if that door is not, at TLA [the time of the locutionary act] open." The presuppositions of this *sentence* are broken down into three categories:

(i)   There are certain presuppositions having to do with the fact that the LT must understand English, be believed by the LS to be awake, not be totally paralyzed, etc., which have to do with "questions of 'good faith' in speech communication. . . ."

[20] Another possibility is that a presupposition failure results in some sort of defect in the sentence which is said to presuppose. I can find no reason for supposing that this is what Katz and Postal have in mind however. Later treatments of "presupposition" by linguists seem to suggest that there is some way that a failure of a presupposition is connected with ungrammaticalness, but none of the suggestions I have seen or heard have been worked out sufficiently to require or allow comment.

[21] It is not so easy to contrast the treatment of presupposition found in Fillmore (1969a, Section 9) with that of the philosophers we have considered. According to Fillmore what "an expression" (a term almost as ambiguous as *utterance*) presupposes is treated as an aspect of its meaning (p. 52). Fillmore claims that the sentence *A borrowed B from C at T* asserts that A had B after T, but presupposes that C had B before T. Here what seems to be presupposed (the value of y) is a fact, and in spite of the fact that sentences are said to do the presupposing (to be values of x) there is an obvious concern with sentences as they are being used to make statements. It seems clear that in this article Fillmore is drawing closer to Frege and Strawson, but in talking about the results of a presupposition failure he says things which make it very difficult to reach a clear understanding of his position. He says, for example, that if A did not have B at least for a while after T (part of what is *asserted*) the sentence in question "would be simply inappropriate" (p. 52). But then, he remarks, of another sentence, that "if any of the conditions *presupposed* by the sentence fails to hold, however, the sentence is merely not relevant," as opposed to being false (p. 53). I find it impossible to understand the difference between saying that a sentence is *inappropriate* and that it is not *relevant,* especially when the first ill results from a failure of an asserted fact and the second from a failure of a presupposed fact.

(ii) There are presuppositions about the existence and specificity of the door, and these relate to the "use of the definite article."

(iii) There are presuppositions about the closed state of the door which must be treated as properties of the verb *open*.

I would be inclined to agree here that the items mentioned in (i) are involved with the success or failure of purported speech acts, and it might do to say that they are conditions which are necessary for the performance of any illocutionary act of a type which calls for action from the LT. In terms of the distinctions made at the beginning of this paper, we might say that these are "presuppositions of utterances" in the sense of *utterance* singled out in (ii). Such conditions have been treated by Austin (1962) as "happiness conditions" for the successful performance of illocutionary acts and by Searle (1969) as "normal input and output conditions" (p. 57).

On the whole it is probably better not to speak of the presuppositions of *sentences*. The same sentence (that is, two tokens of the same sentence object type) can be used, on different occasions to perform different kinds of illocutionary acts. For example, the sentence *I will go to the orgy* may be used in differing circumstances to make a statement, a prediction, or a promise, to give a warning or to express a resolution. Further, even a single sentence act token may count as the performance of several different illocutionary acts—for an example see Searle (1969, pp. 70–71). In the light of these facts it is difficult to see what might be gained by treating happiness conditions as presuppositions of *sentence* act or object types. If we follow Fillmore (1969b), we will bring in the notion of an illocutionary act anyway, in order to explain what it is that "does not come off" when a presupposition fails, so it cannot be for the sake of economy that presuppositions are attached to sentences (economy that could be gained only if *no* mention of illocutionary acts or objects occurred).

Consider a speech situation in which the LS utters assertively the sentence:

(15) The present king of France is bald.

to a single LT. A list of the happiness conditions for the successful performance of *any* locutionary act (or the successful production of *any* illocutionary object) might include:

(a) The LT understands English.

(b) The LS is conscious of what he is doing.

(c) The LT hears the sentence spoken (or, if it is written, sees it).

(d) The LS is not performing in a play, reciting poetry, or giving an example of a grammatical sentence, etc.

Whatever the general happiness conditions for the performance of any illocutionary act are (and the above are given only for the purpose of illustration), they can be stated together and should be related to a particular *sentence* act or object only by the general maxim that no one who utters any sentence can be said to have performed an illocutionary act of any sort unless they are satisfied.

Now (15) was uttered, we may assume, in an attempt to make a statement; and we may wonder whether there are any special happiness conditions related to the act of making statements. It is possible that one such condition is:

(e)   The LS has some basis for believing that the statement he is trying to make is true.[22]

On the other hand, a list of necessary conditions for the successful act of making a statement would probably *not* include:

(f)   There is some point in the LS uttering the sentence he did.
(g)   The LS has some interest in imparting a belief to the LT.
(h)   The LS has some interest in having the LT believe that he (the LS) has a certain belief.

These three conditions (and others like them) have sometimes been treated as things that the speaker "implies," but almost never as necessary conditions for successful illocutionary acts. Speaker implication has been discussed primarily in Grice (1961 and mimeo).[23]

(15) is a fairly simple sentence which is (grammatically at least) of the subject-predicate form with a definite description serving as the subject term.

---

[22] This, of course, is very questionable. What I have in mind here, however, is the notion that if the speaker does not have some grounds for saying what he does then it might be better to talk about estimates, conjectures, or guesses, rather than statements. Lies introduce another problem, but even there it seems that the speaker must at least represent himself as having some grounds for saying what he does. Austin (1962) suggests that "often there are things you cannot state—have no right to state—are not in a position to state. You *cannot* now state how many people there are in the next room; if you say *There are fifty people in the next room,* I can only regard you as guessing or conjecturing" (p. 137). See also Searle (1969, p. 64).

[23] I believe that Fillmore (1969a) trips over a point related to this when he suggests that the sentence *Bill doesn't even know that if he weren't in jail, he'd be assassinated within 24 hours* presupposes

(a)   that if he weren't in jail, Bill would be assassinated within 24 hours

and

(b)   that Bill is now in jail. (p. 53)

Applying the "negation test" (see footnote 7) we can see that here Fillmore is committed to the view that any sentence of the form "S knows that p" or "S doesn't know that p" presupposes the factuality of p. It can be granted that if p is not the case there is a sense in which the sentence "is not relevant" but, if we accept the result of a presupposition failure suggested by Fillmore (1969b) it would seem that we would have to say that unless p were the case nobody could either assert or deny (successfully) that p was known by anyone. This is, at the very least, highly problematic.

Now let us consider what should be said if one utters this sentence when either

(i) There is no king of France.

or

(j) There is more than one king of France.

Here we come to the factors Fillmore identifies under (ii) as related to the "use of the definite article." But there is clearly more to be said here. (1) It is not merely the use of definite article that is important here, but the referring use of any singular referring expression to identify an individual. Frege's example, *Whoever discovered the elliptical form of the planetary orbits died in misery,* must also be included, as well as sentences with ordinary proper names in subject position. (2) There are uses of the definite article in contexts where something like (j) is the case—that is, the uniqueness condition is not really satisfied—yet the circumstances of the utterance are sufficient to guarantee that a successful and complete reference, and hence a successful act of stating, has been performed (see Strawson, 1950a, Section III and Searle, 1969, Chapter IV). (3) When we place the definite description elsewhere in the sentence the conditions that govern "the use of the definite article" no longer seem to apply. Each of the following sentences, I believe, may be used to make a statement even when there is no French monarch:

> Soon Claude will become the king of France.
> I had lunch with the present king of France.
> Abdul believes that De Gaulle is the present king of France.
> But he is wrong because De Gaulle is not the present king of France.[24]

The third sort of "presupposition" Fillmore discusses is treated as a property of words, but again the matter is more complicated than his treatment suggests. The LS who attempts to order someone to open a door has gone wrong *in some way* if the door in question is open at TLA. But it is not clear whether we should say that no order was given, that the order was pointless, or that the order just cannot be obeyed. There is an interesting discussion of this problem in Alston (1964, pp. 40 ff.). What is clear, how-

[24] Strawson (1954) discusses such sentences and qualifies his doctrine of presupposition by admitting that "*in certain cases and circumstances* it might be quite natural and correct to assign a truth-value to a statement of one of these kinds (to say that it is false or even that it is true), even though the condition referred to is not satisfied" (p. 225). He says, for example, that when someone states that Jones went to lunch with the king of France he is "talking about" Jones and what he says is false even if there is no king of France (p. 226). See also Searle (1969, pp. 157–162).

ever, is that if we understand ourselves to be talking about "a property of the verb *open*," much more must be said than is suggested by Fillmore's lexical entries for *blame, accuse,* and *criticize* (1969b); for when we say to someone *If the door is not already open, go and open it,* or ask whether or not anyone has opened the door, there is no presupposition that the door is closed. One is almost tempted to suggest that what is required, if we are to speak of presuppositions of words in this way, is a statement of "context-sensitive" presupposition rules. That would, however, take us back to illocutionary acts again.

Let us return now to what Fillmore says about the presuppositions of the noun *bachelor* when used as a predicate. He suggests that "only the property of *having never been married* is part of the meaning proper" of that word, and adds that "uses of this word (as predicate) *presuppose* that the entities being described are human, male and adult." The sentence *That person is not a bachelor*

> is only used as a claim that the person is or has been married, never as a claim that the person is a female or a child. That is, it is simply not appropriate to use this sentence, or its non-negative counterpart, when speaking of anyone who is not a human, male adult.

But now let us suppose that someone utters this sentence referring by *that person* to a female. We may grant that there is something "odd" and "inappropriate" about his utterance, but should we really say that he failed to make a true statement, that his purported illocutionary act did not come off? I think not. Rather, we are likely to say that his statement, though true, was very misleading. See the remarks about "the assertion fallacy" in Searle (1969, pp. 141–146) for a discussion of some related points.

When selectional rules were more popular than they now are it was thought that a grammar would not generate sentences with such violations. A selectional violation was considered to be a syntactical error. Now Fillmore (and others) want to replace the notion of selection with something they call "presupposition" so that the problem with *My toothbrush admires sincerity* is not syntactical but involves a presupposition failure. But, as we have seen, there are general conditions for all speech acts and special conditions for assertions which, if not satisfied, lead to a failure of the illocutionary act. Among these the special conditions about the necessity for a successful reference—if I don't have a toothbrush I have failed to make a statement—are the sorts of things Strawson and Frege (and in some respects Sellars) had in mind when they talked about presuppositions. Next there are "implications"—if I assert *p* then I imply that I believe it—but here if the implied statement is false the original statement is not disqualified.

Assuming now that all of the above types of conditions are satisfied, just what is the problem with *My toothbrush admires sincerity*? I confess a temptation to say that the speaker has made a false statement and leave it at that on the grounds that the statement that it is false that my toothbrush admires sincerity seems to be true.

Another example of the way lexical items are supposed to have presuppositions involves the word *blame*. If Clark Kent reports that Jones blamed Smith for the accident then, according to Fillmore (1968b), Clark *asserted* that Jones judged that Smith is responsible but *presupposed* that Jones judged that the accident was "bad." Now if Jones had merely ascribed responsibility for the accident to Smith, either withholding judgment or judging that an accident now and then is a good thing, Clark would have made a mistake. But I think that his mistake would have resulted in a false statement, not an illocutionary misfire. Jones did not blame Smith, he merely said that Smith was responsible. Both this case and the toothbrush case suggest that what happens when a "presupposition" (considered as a property of a lexical item) fails is quite different from what happens with other failures which have also been given the same name, and this is evidence that there is a new concept at work here, and not just an extension of an old one.

I believe that linguists from Katz and Postal to Fillmore go wrong when they speak of the presuppositions of sentences or of their parts.[25] A speaker who presupposes does not do so as a performer of a sentence act token, but in the performance of an illocutionary act (or the purported performance of one). When it is granted that this is so, it becomes important to see that just as there are more ways of killing a cat than drowning it in butter, so there are ever so many different sorts of things that might go wrong when we attempt to perform illocutionary acts. It is no more help to lump all of these together under the general heading of presupposition than it is to rely on weasel words like *odd, inappropriate,* and *irrelevant.* When we really begin to set out what does go wrong in different sorts of cases, a watered down notion of presupposition failure adequate to cover them all can only cover up differences it must be the job of any adequate treatment of language to expose and explain.

---

[25] I have not discussed the distinction between the presuppositions of a "concept" and the presuppositions of a "word," but there is an obvious parallel here with the distinction between a sentence and a statement (in any of the many senses of that word).

TWO KINDS
OF PRESUPPOSITION
IN NATURAL LANGUAGE

Edward L. Keenan   The University of Pennsylvania

I shall propose, in this paper, a general and informal definition of the notion of presupposition in natural language, and then consider two ways the general idea can be more clearly and rigorously defined.

1. The Informal Idea

In general I want to consider that the presuppositions of a sentence are those conditions that the world must meet in order for the sentence to make literal sense. Thus if some such condition is not met, for some sentence S, then either S makes no sense at all or else it is understood in some nonliteral way, for example as a joke or metaphor.

2. The Logical Notion of Presupposition

We can define one notion of presupposition solely in terms of the basic semantic concepts used in mathematical logic: truth and logical consequence. In standard mathematical logic, truth is conceived of (informally) as a relation between a sentence, considered as a syntactic object, and the world (model, interpretation). Thus the notion of world is defined by the logic (in the metalanguage of course) and then, for each sentence type in the logical language, the conditions that a world must meet for the sentence to be true in it are specified. For "simple" sentences this is done somewhat arbitrarily, and for the complex ones it is done as a function of the truth conditions of simpler ones.

Given the definition of truth, logical consequence is defined as follows: a sentence S is said to be a logical consequence of a set of sentences S* just in case S is true in every world (that is, under all the conditions) in which all the sentences of S* are true. In such a case we also say that S follows logically from S*, and that S* logically implies S.

It should be clear, and will not be substantiated here, that what consequences we can draw from a sentence (or set of sentences) depends on the meaning of that sentence. Hence if we are to characterize the basic meaning relations between sentences of English in our grammar, we must define the notion of consequence in the base. Henceforth I assume this has been done.[1]

We now define logical presupposition as follows: A sentence S logically presupposes a sentence S' just in case S logically implies S' and the negation of S, ~S, also logically implies S'. In other words, the truth of S' is a necessary condition on the truth or falsity of S. Thus if S' is not true then S can

---

[1] In Keenan (1969), I provide a mathematical logic in which consequence is defined for factive predicates, many of the definite names mentioned in Section 2, and cleft sentences.

be neither true nor false (and must in the formal logic be assigned a third or "nonsense" value).

Below, on the left, I give many examples of sentences which logically presuppose the sentence to their right. That is, the left hand sentence, as well as its negation, logically implies the sentence on its right. I include in parentheses the negated verb as it would occur in the negated version of the left hand sentence. In no case does the sentence on the right exhaust the presuppositions of the sentence on its left. Further, to verify, informally, that the right hand sentence does indeed follow from the one on its left the reader should try to imagine the world any way at all such that the sentence on the left is true and then see if the one on the right is also true. If not, then I am mistaken and the implication does not hold.

Notice that the sentences on the left are syntactically and semantically quite diverse. They have in common only that they all preserve some consequences under negation. But they do this for different reasons and in different ways.

Sentence	Presupposition of Sentence
(1) "Factive" Predicates (see Kiparsky and Kiparsky, 1968)	
That Fred left surprised (didn't surprise) Mary.	Fred left.
It is (isn't) remarkable that Fred left.	Fred left.
Mary resented (didn't resent) that Fred left.	Fred left.
Fred's driving annoys (doesn't annoy) Mary.	Fred drives.
Chad's declaration of war on Russia shocked (didn't shock) most Americans.	Chad declared war on Russia.
(2) "Definite" Names	
John called (didn't call).	John exists.
John married (didn't marry) Fred's sister.	Fred had a sister.
John wrecked (didn't wreck) this truck.	There exists a truck.
Mary loves (doesn't love) the puppy she found.	Mary found a puppy.
Chicago is (isn't) where Fred met Sally.	Fred met Sally.
How the thief escaped will always be (will not always be) a mystery.	The thief escaped.
John saw (didn't see) who mugged Sally.	Someone mugged Sally.

Sentence	Presupposition of Sentence
John believed (didn't believe) what the doctor said.	The doctor said something.
John is (isn't) the one who caught the thief.	Someone caught the thief.

(3) "Cleft" Sentences

It was (wasn't) John who caught the thief.	Someone caught the thief.
It was (wasn't) in August that John quit.	John quit.
It was (wasn't) to escape the draft that John went to Canada.	John went to Canada.
It was (wasn't) because he was tired that John left.	John left.

(4) Selectional Restrictions

That arithmetic is incomplete surprised (didn't surprise) Magrid.	Magrid is animate, intelligent.

(5) Temporal Subordinate Clauses

John left (didn't leave) $\left\{ \begin{array}{l} \text{when} \\ \text{before} \\ \text{after} \end{array} \right\}$ Mary called.   Mary called.

(6) Nonrestrictive Relatives

The Tiv, who respected Bohannon, are (are not) a generous people.	The Tiv respected Bohannon.

(7) Certain Aspectuals

Fred $\left\{ \begin{array}{l} \text{quit (didn't quit)} \\ \text{continued (didn't continue)} \\ \text{resumed (didn't resume)} \end{array} \right\}$ speaking.   Fred was speaking.

(8) Iteratives

Fred called (didn't call) again.	Fred called at least once.
Fred ate (didn't eat) another turnip.	Fred ate at least one turnip.

Fred $\left\{ \begin{array}{l} \text{went back (didn't go back)} \\ \text{returned (didn't return)} \end{array} \right\}$ to Boston.   Fred has been in Boston.

(9) Presuppositional Quantifiers

(Not) only Fred shot himself.	Fred shot himself.
(Not) everyone but Fred left.	Fred didn't leave.

3. Four Comments on Logical Presupposition

1. We can extend logical semantics to account for the presuppositions of questions by defining their presuppositions to be the sentences which are logical consequences of every one of their answers. (But a logical characterization of the question-answer relation is far from trivial.) Thus we could expect to show that (10)a–(10)c below presuppose the sentences to their right:

(10)	a.	Did it surprise Mary that Fred left?	Fred left.
	b.	Where did they bury the survivors?	They buried the survivors.
	c.	Should you pray with your eyes open, or closed?	You should pray.

2. In general "definite" names are syntactic constructions which function semantically as names in such a way that the existence of an object named is presupposed by the sentence in which the definite name occurs. Thus definite names tack our sentences onto reality, even, it seems to me, when the names occur embedded under nonfactive predicates. Thus, in my opinion, (11)a and (11)b below presuppose the sentence to their right but (11)c does not:

(11)	a.	It is probable that Mary lost the watch Fred gave her.	Fred gave Mary a watch.
	b.	John imagined that Mary lost the watch Fred gave her.	Fred gave Mary a watch.
	c.	John imagined that Fred gave Mary a watch and that she lost it.	Fred gave Mary a watch.

3. The logical notion of presupposition is defined solely in terms of abstract sentences and the world. Whether anyone actually utters or believes some sentence has nothing to do with whether the sentence makes a particular logical presupposition. *The greatest prime number is odd* presupposes that there exists a greatest prime whether anyone says or believes the sentence or not, in the same way that *Two is a prime number* logically implies that there exists a prime regardless of whether anyone asserts or believes the sentence.

4. The logical notion of presupposition correctly accounts for the oddity of the sentences (12)a–(12)c below by showing them to be logical

consequences of their own presuppositions. That is, they presuppose them-selves. Thus, if they are meaningful at all they must be true.

(12)   a.   John loves the girl he loves.
       b.   The man who won won.
       c.   The cop who clubbed John is the cop who clubbed John.

4.   The Pragmatic Notion of Presupposition

We consider now a notion of presupposition defined on the relation be-tween the utterance of a sentence and the context in which it is uttered.

By an utterance of a sentence I refer to an actual act of speaking—a space-time event. By the context of an utterance I refer to those individuals, participants, involved in the speech act, as well as the physical and cultural setting of the speech act. More specifically, the context of an utterance will be defined to consist of, at least, the speaker, the addressee(s) if any, the audience, if any, the physical environment of the utterance (including other people and objects present to the participants), and the "cultural" environ-ment of the utterance (for example, the speech act is part of a ritual, com-mercial transaction, songfest, and so forth). I do not pretend of course that these context categories are exhaustive or even exclusive.

Now many sentences require that certain culturally defined conditions or contexts be satisfied in order for an utterance of that sentence to be understood (in its literal, intended meaning). Thus these conditions are naturally called presuppositions of the sentence; if they are not satisfied then the utterance is either not understandable or else is understood in some nonliteral way—insult or jest for example. These conditions include among many others: (a) status and kind of relations among the participants; (b) age, sex, and generation relations among the participants; (c) status, kin, age, sex, and generation relations between participants and individuals men-tioned in the sentence; (d) presence or absence of certain objects in the physical setting of the utterance; and (e) relative location of participants and items mentioned in the sentence itself.

Once these particular relations have been elucidated we might hope for a general definition of *appropriateness* of an utterance in a context. Then we could state the general definition of pragmatic presupposition as follows: An utterance of a sentence pragmatically presupposes that its context is appropriate.

For the moment however we have no such general definition and must be content to give examples of pragmatic presuppositions, each of which will serve as a test case of the general definition. A few examples follow.

Sex and Relative Age of Speaker/Hearer

Mary Haas (1944) has discussed a Louisiana Indian language, Koasati, in which *lakawatakkos* (I am not lifting it) presupposes that the speaker is a man, and contrasts with *lakawatakko* which presupposes that the speaker is a woman. She cites other languages, for example Thai, which also have a male and female *I*.

Haas further cites Biloxi, an extinct Siouxan language, in which presuppositions are made on the sex and relative age of both the speaker and the addressee. Thus:

Utterance presupposes	the speaker is	the addressee is
ki-kanko (carry it)	male	adult male
ki-tki′ (carry it)	male or female	adult female
ki-tati′ (carry it)	female	adult male
ki (carry it)	male or female	child

Physical Setting of the Utterance

In the Malagasy sentence (13) below the deictic particle *any* forces the presupposition that the speaker is not in Tamatave. On the other hand (14) presupposes that the speaker is in Tamatave.

(13)   Avy   any Tomasina izy
         Comes-from there Tamatave he
         He comes from Tamatave
(14)   Avy   aty Tomasina izy
         Comes-from here Tamatave he
         He comes from Tamatave

Similarly (15) below presupposes that the house in question is visible to the speaker and contrasts with (16) in which it is presupposed that the house is not visible to the speaker.

(15)   Ety   ny tranony
         Here the house his
         His house is here
(16) · Aty   ny tranony
         There the house his
         His house is there

Personal and Status Relations among Participants

That address and reference terms codify status relations is well known. I only mention the French *Tu es dégoûtant,* in which it is presupposed that the addressee is an animal, child, socially inferior to the speaker, or personally intimate with the speaker.

5. Conclusion

The two notions of presupposition I have specified are not intended to exhaust the semantic properties of natural language that can be appropriately called presuppositional. Notice in particular that neither of the notions I propose are defined on the beliefs of a speaker or of someone mentioned in the sentence. Logical presupposition is defined ultimately on the relation between base structures and the world. Pragmatic presupposition is defined on the relation between utterances and their contexts.

To see that these two notions of presupposition are belief independent we consider two kinds of cases in which the speaker does not believe the presuppositions of what he has said. First, a speaker need not believe the presuppositions of what he is saying if he is speaking with intent to deceive, or speaking in jest, or if he simply does not understand very well what he is saying, even if he believes it. That is, one can believe what one is saying without realizing that what one has said has certain presuppositions.

Second, there are many instances in which one accepts something "for sake of argument" precisely to show that it is false. *Reductio ad absurdum* proofs in logic codify this type of reasoning as follows: Assume some proposition P, reason your way to a contradiction, and then conclude that P is false. Now the sentences we use to derive the contradiction may naturally presuppose P, for they are sentences which depend on the world being the way P says it is. But notice that the entire proof in no sense implies (much less presupposes) P, for it is a proof of not-P. The assumption of P during the proof was simply a strategy to get us to the desired conclusion. Thus we have a clear case where certain sentences in a discourse have a certain semantic property (implying or even presupposing P) but where the entire discourse does not have that semantic property. Thus it is natural for someone giving a *reductio* proof to utter sentences whose presuppositions he does not believe.

Furthermore *reductio* reasoning occurs frequently in natural languages, although many of the steps in the argument are often left inexplicit. By way of example, consider the following argument (which will dispose of an interesting counterexample to my claim that cleft sentences are presuppositional as in (3) above²): *You say that someone in this room loves Mary. Well, maybe so. But it certainly isn't Fred.* (that is, It certainly isn't Fred who loves Mary). *And clearly it isn't John. And* . . . We continue in this way until we have enumerated all the people in the room, and then conclude: *Therefore no one in this room loves Mary.* Thus it is reasonable to say that *It is John who loves Mary* presupposes that *Someone loves Mary* even though a speaker of the above discourse would not believe the presupposition. Thus there are a variety of ways a sentence can be uttered without it being true or even believed.

² This putative counterexample was originally pointed out to me by Thomas Bever and Harris Savin.

THE
PROJECTION PROBLEM
FOR PRESUPPOSITIONS*

D. Terence Langendoen   Graduate Center and Brooklyn College of the City University
of New York
Harris B. Savin   The University of Pennsylvania

* This work was supported in part by The Advanced Research Projects Agency, U.S. Department of Defense, under Grant No. DAHC15 68 G-5 to The Rockefeller University.

We are concerned in this paper with the question of how the presupposition and assertion of a complex sentence are related to the presuppositions and assertions of the clauses it contains. This is a question which arises quite naturally within the original Katz and Fodor (1963) conception of semantics within linguistic theory, but one which, to our knowledge, has not previously been asked. By "presupposition" we mean, following Frege (1892), the expression of the conditions which must be satisfied (be true) for the sentence as a whole to be a statement, question, command, and so forth. By taking the notion in this Fregean sense, the projection problem for presuppositions turns out to have a strikingly simple solution, a fact which strongly suggests that this notion has linguistic reality.

To see how the projection rule for presuppositions works, consider first the sentences:

S1. John accused Mary of beating her husband.
S2. John stopped doing it.

The sentence S1 makes roughly the assertion A1 and has the presupposition P1; sentence S2 makes roughly the assertion A2 and has the presupposition P2:[1]

A1. John claimed that Mary beat her husband.
P1. John judged that it was bad for Mary to beat her husband.
A2. After time t, John didn't do it.
P2. Before time t, John did it.

Now consider the complex sentence, formed by embedding S1 as the object complement of the verb *stop*:

S3. John stopped accusing Mary of beating her husband.

We want to know how the presupposition and assertion of S3 are related to the presupposition and assertion associated with the main verb *stop* and with the subordinate verb *accuse*. For convenience, let A″ and P″ be the assertion and presupposition respectively of the subordinate clause of S3:

A″ = A1. John claimed that Mary beat her husband.
P″ = P1. John judged that it was bad for Mary to beat her husband.

[1] These sentences have other presuppositions as well, for example those concerning the existence and uniqueness of the entity denoted by *John*, but these can be ignored for our purposes.

Notice first of all that S3 presupposes P″, but that it neither presupposes nor asserts A″. Now consider the assertion and presupposition of the main clause of S3, which we call A′ and P′ respectively:

A′. After time t, John didn't X.
P′. Before time t, John did Y.

where X and Y are things to be found in the subordinate clause of S3. The question is: what things? The obvious possibilities for both X and Y are A″ and P″. Substituting A″ for X, we get:

A′ (A″). After time t, John didn't claim that Mary beat her husband.

Substituting P″ for X, we get:

A′ (P″). After time t, John didn't judge that it was bad for Mary to beat her husband.

Substituting A″ for Y, we get:

P′ (A″). Before time t, John claimed that Mary beat her husband.

Substituting P″ for Y, we get:

P′ (P″). Before time t, John judged that it was bad for Mary to beat her husband.

Clearly, S3 does assert A′ (A″), and presupposes P′ (A″). Clearly also, A′ (P″) is no part of the meaning of S3; indeed, it is probably false even if S3 is true. We contend further that P′ (P″) is no part of the meaning of S3 either, although it is not obvious from the present example because it is implied by P″, which we have already seen is presupposed by S3. To see why P′ (P″) cannot be part of the meaning of a complex sentence like S3, consider the sentence:

S4. John accused Mary of criticizing him for riding his bicycle to work.

The presupposition P″ of the subordinate clause of S4 is:

P″. Mary judged that John rode his bicycle to work.

and the presupposition P′ of the main clause of S4 is:

P′.   John judged that Y was bad.

But, when P″ is substituted for Y in P′, we get:

P′ (P″).   John judged that it was bad that Mary judged that John rode his bicycle to work.

In this case, P′ (P″) is not implied by P″, and indeed could well be false even if S4 is true. Other examples show even more dramatically that neither A′ (P″) nor P′ (P″) are part of the meaning of a complex sentence of the form S′ (S″). Consider:

S5.   John regretted that he pretended to have bad breath.
S6.   John pretended to regret that he had bad breath.

If we construct A′ (P″) for example S5, we find that it is:

A′ (P″).   John wished that he had bad breath.

But clearly S5 makes no such assertion. If we construct P′ (P″) for example S6, we find that it is:

P′ (P″).   John didn't have bad breath.

However, P″ by itself is:

P″.   John had bad breath.

But P″ and P′ (P″) cannot both be presuppositions of S6, since if they were, the sentence would have a contradictory presupposition and hence it could never be used to make a statement. Since P″ is clearly presupposed by S6, we conclude that P′ (P″) cannot be.

The projection principle for presuppositions, therefore, is as follows: presuppositions of a subordinate clause do not amalgamate either with presuppositions or assertions of higher clauses; rather they stand as presuppositions of the complex sentence in which they occur. If either an assertion or a presupposition contains a variable which stands for a subordinate clause (say, an object complement), then it follows that that variable is replaced only by the assertion of the subordinate clause.

We find also that the only constituents of a clause that contribute to its presupposition are the main verbal (verb or adjective) and the nominals which stand in grammatical relation to it as subject or object. Adverbs (including negation) affect the assertion only, never the presupposition. If adverbs originate as verbals in higher clauses, then the projection rule as stated above explains this fact. If not all adverbials originate in higher clauses, we still need no new machinery to prevent adverbs from affecting presuppositions. The only variables that appear in the semantic representation of presuppositions in the lexicon will be variables standing for nominals and verbals. All the facts will then be described correctly, although there will be no explanation for the invariable absence of abverbials from presuppositions.

It is instructive to restate the projection rule for presuppositions in terms of the Fregean definition of presupposition. The principle that the presupposition of subordinate clauses stand as part of the presupposition of the complex sentence containing them means that a necessary condition for a sentence to be a statement is that each of the subordinate clauses in it must be a statement. This state of affairs has a gratifying air of plausibility about it, even though we have so far been unable to find an argument to show that the world would be an unhappier place otherwise. Given that the presuppositions of clauses do, in fact, stand as presuppositions of the whole sentence, we can, however, explain after a fashion the fact that they do not also amalgamate freely with adverbials, higher clauses, and the like. If a presupposition of a clause amalgamated freely in addition to standing as a presupposition of the whole sentence, then it would be difficult to avoid anomalies and contradictions of the sort discussed in connection with example S6.

We would now like to address ourselves to two of the comments that were raised in the discussion following the presentation of the foregoing material. First, it was claimed that in a conditional sentence such as:

S7. If I hadn't left Bloomington, I would have regretted it.

the presupposition of the object complement of *regret,* which ordinarily would be in this case:

P7. I haven't left Bloomington.

is suspended, and that therefore a mechanism for suspending presuppositions in conditional sentences is required.

But this characterization of the facts is not correct. A conditional sentence has the property that its presupposition is presupposed in a (possibly imaginary) world in which its antecedent is true. This accounts for the anomaly of a sentence such as:

S8. If I hadn't left Bloomington, I would have regretted having left Bloomington.

Therefore there is no reason to suspend P7 as a presupposition of S7, and no mechanism for suspending presuppositions is required.

Second, it was suggested that instead of having a projective mechanism for obtaining the presuppositions of complex sentences, the presuppositions should be represented independently in the mind of the speaker, and that they constrain in the appropriate way the lexical insertion of such verbals as *accuse, criticize, pretend, regret,* and so forth. The proposal is, at present, vague, but insofar as we understand it, it fails to meet its presumed objective—to handle the facts discussed above within the framework of generative semantics. Each presupposition cannot be represented in the minds of speakers as an unanalyzable element, because there are an infinite number of them. If, on the other hand, the presuppositions are given the same sort of semantic representation in the mind of the speaker that they would get if they were assertions instead of presuppositions, there would then be only a finite number of elements in the vocabulary that is used to state lexical insertion rules, but the insertion rules themselves would become so inordinately complex as to make the proposal completely unattractive as an alternative to interpretive semantics. As the following examples illustrate, the lexical insertion rules would no longer replace one subtree with a single lexical item; rather, they would take two trees that stand in a very complex relation to one another, match them up, and then effect lexical insertion into one of them. Consider the sentences:

S9.   John acted as if he didn't wish to have bad breath.
S10. John acted as if he regretted that he had bad breath.
S11. John pretended not to wish to have bad breath.
S12. (=S6) John pretended to regret that he had bad breath.

The assertions of S9–S12 are the same, namely:

A′ (A″). (=S9) John acted as if he didn't wish to have bad breath.

Each of these sentences would therefore receive, under this approach, the same semantic interpretation. In case the speaker had no relevant presuppositions in mind, the expressions *act as if* and *not wish* would have to be lexically inserted, yielding S9. In case the speaker had the presupposition:

P″. John had bad breath.

then *act as if* and *regret* would have to be inserted, yielding S10. In case he had the presupposition:

P′ (A″). John wished to have bad breath.

then *pretend* and *not wish* would have to be inserted, yielding S11. Finally, if he had the presupposition:

> P″ and P′ (A″). John had bad breath and John wished to have bad breath.

then *pretend* and *regret* would have to be inserted, yielding S12. The reader is invited to work out the details of the lexical insertion rules necessary for each of these examples.

THE ROLE
OF DEDUCTION
IN GRAMMAR*

George Lakoff   The University of Michigan

* This work was supported in part by Grant GN-1934 from the National Science Foundation to Harvard University. The author thanks Georgia Green and Robin Lakoff for pointing out to him the regularities of *too* and *but* on which this paper is based.

In G. Lakoff (1970d) I showed that for many sentences it makes no sense to ask whether or not they are grammatical in any absolute sense, but only to ask whether they are grammatical relative to certain presuppositions. For example, in reciprocal contrastive stress constructions:

(1) Jóhn insulted Máry and then shé insulted hím.

(2) *Jóhn praised Máry and then shé insulted hím.

(3) Jóhn called Máry a virgin and then shé insulted hím.

The pronouns on the right can be stressed in (3) only if it is presupposed that to call someone a virgin is to insult that person. (2) is judged ungrammatical since by the definition of *praise,* praising someone cannot be an insult, at least not in our culture.

Let us now ask what are the regular conditions under which reciprocal contrastive stress occurs. The simplest case occurs in (1), where no special presupposition is required. If one has two conjoined sentences of the form:

(4) $[_{S_1} \cdots [_{NP}a] \cdots [_{NP}b] \cdots _{S_1}]$ and $[_{S_2} \cdots [_{NP}b] \cdots [_{NP}a] \cdots _{S_2}]$

where S_1 is identical to S_2 in meaning, except that wherever S_1 mentions a, S_2 mentions b, and vice versa, then a and b get stressed. For convenience we will refer to S_1 and S_2 as $f(a,b)$ and $f(b,a)$ respectively, where f stands for a phrase-marker minus the elements a and b. Thus the simple rule is that in sentences of the form:

(5) $f(a,b)$ and $f(b,a)$

stress a and b.[1]

Now consider the more complicated cases like (3) where a sentence with reciprocal contrastive stress can only be grammatical relative to a certain presupposition. Take (3). Let 'x called y a virgin' be $g(x,y)$ and 'x insulted y' be $f(x,y)$. (3) is of the form:

(6) $g(a,b)$ and $f(b,a)$
     where: $a = John$
            $b = Mary$

[1] Actually, the condition is more general than this. The rule applies not only in conjunctions, but whenever disjoint clauses of this form occur in a sentence. For example:

The fact that John insulted Mary indicated that shé would soon insult him.
Note that the time adverb *soon* must be considered semantically external to its clause if one is to state the identity condition uniformly.

As we noted, (3) is grammatical only relative to the presupposition that calling someone a virgin is an insult. That is,

(7) $(x)(y) (g(x,y) \supset f(x,y))$

Thus (6) can receive reciprocal contrastive stress on *a* and *b* only if (7) is presupposed. But this is no accident or idiosyncratic peculiarity of this example. As we have seen, the general rule applies to structures of the form (5), and we would like to reduce all cases to cases of this form. It just so happens that given (7) as a presupposition, we can *deduce* from (6) a structure of the form (5).

(8)   a. $g(a,b)$ and $f(b,a)$ (the sentence of (6))
       b. $g(a,b)$ (by simplification of a)
       c. $(x)(y) (g(x,y) \supset f(x,y))$ (presupposed as in (7))
       d. $g(a,b) \supset f(a,b)$ (instantiation)
       e. $f(a,b)$ (modus ponens, from steps b and d)
       f. $f(b,a)$ (by simplification of a)
       g. $f(a,b)$ and $f(b,a)$ (conjunction)

The general principle here seems to be that a structure of the form (6) may receive reciprocal contrastive stress only if the sentence makes one or more presuppositions such that from (6) and those presuppositions, a structure of the form (5) can be deduced.

Let us now consider another example. Georgia Green (1968, 1969) has discussed with great insight the occurrence of *too* and *either,* and the basic facts discussed below are due to her observations. There are two basic cases where *too* occurs.

(9)   a.   John is honest and Bill is honest too.
        b.   John is a Republican and John is honest too.
(10)   a. $f(a)$ and $f(b)$
            where: $a = John$
                   $b = Bill$
        b. $g(a)$ and $f(a)$
            where: $g = is\ a\ Republican$
                   $f = is\ honest$

In (10)a the *f*'s are the same; in (10)b the *a*'s are the same. Thus, given a sentence of either the form (9)a or (9)b with no special presuppositions, we can get a *too* inserted. These are the simple cases.

Now consider a complex case.

(11)   The mayor is a Republican and the used-car dealer is honest too.

(11) has two readings which can be differentiated by stress as in (11)a and (11)b.

(11) a. The mãyor is a Repŭblican and the used-câr dealer is hŏnest
          tóo.
      b. The mãyor is a Repúblican and the used-câr dealer is hŏnest
          tóo.

In (11)a *honest* is unstressed and refers anaphorically back to *is a Republican*. *The mayor* and *the used-car dealer* are both stressed and so the latter cannot have anaphoric reference to the former; thus, they are not presupposed to be the same individual. In (11)b, however, *the mayor* and *the used-car dealer* are unstressed and so the latter does have anaphoric reference to the former; thus, they are presupposed to be coreferential.

(11)a and (11)b both require presuppositions to be considered grammatical—and they are different presuppositions. (11)a requires the presupposition that Republicans are honest. (11)b requires the presupposition that *the mayor* and *the used-car dealer* are the same person. These are given in (12)a and (12)b respectively.

(12) a. $(x) (g(x) \supset f(x))$ (all Republicans are honest)
      b. $a = b$ (the mayor is the used-car dealer)

(11) has the form of (13):

(13) $g(a)$ and $f(b)$ *too.*
      where: g = *is a Republican*
             f = *is honest*

Again, it is no accident that a sentence of the form (13) happens to be grammatical only given presuppositions of the form (12)a and (12)b. The reason is that from just these presuppositions we can deduce structures of the form of (10)a and (10)b—the simple cases where *too* can be inserted.

(14) a. $g(a)$ and $f(b)$ (sentence as in (13))
      b. $(x) (g(x) \supset f(x))$ (presupposition of (12)a)
      c. $g(a) \supset f(a)$ (instantiation)
      d. $g(a)$ (simplification of a)
      e. $f(a)$ (modus ponens from d and c)
      f. $f(b)$ (simplification of a)
      g. $f(a)$ and $f(b)$ (conjunction)

(14)g is of the form of (10)a and corresponds to the reading of (11)a, where *honest* is unstressed and is understood as being anaphoric. What *honest* is anaphoric to turns out not to be in the first half of the sentence of (11)a, but rather in what can be *deduced* from that first half given the presupposition of (12)a. Thus anaphora seems to depend on deductions.

Let us now consider the reading of (13) where (12)b is presupposed.

(15) a. g(a) and f(b)   (sentence as in (13))
      b. a = b   (presupposition of (12)b)
      c. g(a)   (simplification of a)
      d. g(b)   (substitute identicals for identicals)
      e. f(b)   (simplification of a)
      f. g(b) and f(b)   (conjunction)

(15)f is of the form of (10)b. Thus, with *too,* the generalization seems to be that a sentence can take *too* if one of the forms (10)a or (10)b can be deduced from the sentence and from the presupposition relative to which it is grammatical. The simplest case is where the presuppositions are null as in (9)a and (9)b.

Let us now consider the even more complicated use of *but*. What follows is based on the insightful observations of Robin Lakoff (1971), who has begun to make sense of the regularities involved in the use of *but*. I will consider only one of the senses of *but,* that which involves a statement contrary to one's expectations. Consider, for example,

(16)   It is June, but it is snowing.

(16) asserts that it is June and it is snowing, and it presupposes that one would not expect it to be snowing in June. That is, (16) has the form:

(17)   Assertion: S_1 and S_2
       Presupposition: $Exp(S_1 \supset \sim S_2)$[2]
       where: $S_1 = $ *it is June*
              $S_2 = $ *it is snowing*

This, I think, is the basic form of this sense of *but*; it differs from *too* and reciprocal contrastive stress in that even in its most basic form, it requires

---

[2] Richard Thomason has pointed out to me that 'expectation' isn't exactly the right concept for expressing the meaning of *but,* although it is close in most cases. He suggests instead that the appropriate concept would be something closer to 'a belief on the part of the speaker that, according to some general rule, S_1 should entail $\sim S_2$'. In those cases where the speaker has no special information which would lead him to believe that the rule should not hold, it would be rational for him to expect S_1 to entail $\sim S_2$. I accept Thomason's observation, and I would not be surprised if the appropriate concept were to be even more complex. In the absence of a more thorough understanding of these matters, I will use the notation "Exp" to stand for whatever the appropriate concept should be, whether expectation, belief as to general rules, differential probabilities, and so forth. Since the differences among these alternatives is not relevant to the main issue under consideration, I will continue to speak in terms of expectations, for the sake of simplicity of exposition.

a presupposition. Thus, the basic rule is that *but* replaces *and* in an assertion like that of (17) when the corresponding presupposition is as given there.

There are, however, more complicated examples of *but* in this sense. Consider (18).

(18) John is a Republican, but he is honest (too).

(18) is grammatical relative to the general presupposition that one would expect Republicans not to be honest. Thus, (18) has the form:

(18) Assertion: $f(a)$ and $g(a)$
      Presupposition: $(x) \, \text{Exp}(f(x) \supset \, \sim g(x))$
      where: $f = $ *is a Republican*
             $g = $ *is honest*
             $a = $ *John*
             $f(a) = S_1$
             $g(a) = S_2$

(18) does not have the form of (17); however, there is a trivial deduction from the presupposition of (18) to a structure that will correspond to (17).

(19) a. $(x) \, \text{Exp}(f(x) \supset \, \sim g(x))$ (presupposition of (18))
      b. $\text{Exp}(f(a) \supset \, \sim g(a))$ (instantiation)

Recalling that $f(a) = S_1$ and $g(a) = S_2$, we see that (19)b has the form Exp $(S_1 \supset \, \sim S_2)$. Thus, the general principle for the occurrence of *but* is that when S_1 *and* S_2 is asserted and there are one or more presuppositions from which $\text{Exp}(S_1 \supset \, \sim S_2)$ can be deduced, then *but* can replace *and* and the sentence will be grammatical only relative to those presuppositions.

Now consider a slightly more complex example.

(20) John's father belongs to the Republican party, but John belongs to the Republican party too.

(20) is grammatical relative to a number of presuppositions; one of the most interesting for our discussion is 'one would expect a son not to belong to the same party has his father'. We can represent (20) with this presupposition as (21).

(21) Assertion: $B(F(a),r)$ and $B(a,r)$
      Presupposition: $(x)(y) \, \text{Exp}(B(F(x),y) \supset \, \sim (B(x,y)))$
      where: $B(x,y) = $ x *belongs to the* y *party*
             $F(x) = $ x's *father*
             $r = $ *Republican*
             $a = $ *John*

(21) also does not have the form of (17), but again there is a simple deduction that will yield the appropriate form.

(22) a. (x)(y) Exp(B(F(x),y) $\supset$ $\sim$ (B(x,y)))   (presupposition of (21))
      b. (x) Exp(B(F(x),r) $\supset$ $\sim$ (B(x,r)))   (by instantiation of
                                                              r for y)

      c. Exp(B(F(a),r) $\supset$ $\sim$ (B(a,r)))   (by instantiation of
                                                          a for x)

Letting B(F(a),r) = S_1 and (B(a,r) = S_2, we see that (22)c reads Exp(S_1 $\supset$ $\sim$ S_2). Thus, (20) is grammatical relative to the presupposition of (21), since Exp(S_1 $\supset$ $\sim$ S_2) can be deduced from that presupposition. Much more complicated examples than these occur in normal discourse, and they often involve many presuppositions and a long chain of deduction. Take a typical example.

(23) Nixon was elected, but the blacks won't revolt.

(23) involves the assertion of (24), and is grammatical relative to a set of presuppositions like that given in (24).

(24) Assertion: Nixon was elected, and the blacks won't revolt.
                        S_1 and S_2
      Presuppositions:
        1. Nixon is a Republican.
        2. If a Republican is elected, then social welfare programs will
            be cut.
        3. If social welfare programs are cut, the poor will suffer.
        4. Blacks are poor.
        5. Blacks are discriminated against.
        6. Blacks form a substantial part of the population.
        7. One would expect that poor, suffering people who are dis-
            criminated against and who form a substantial proportion of
            the population would revolt.

I will not go through the deduction here, but it should be obvious that Exp(S_1 $\supset$ $\sim$ S_2) can be deduced from these presuppositions. Thus, (23) will be grammatical relative to these presuppositions. Since these presuppositions do not conflict with our knowledge of the world, (23) is a perfectly normal sentence. Of course, there are innumerable other sets of presuppositions relative to which (23) would be grammatical—all of those from which Exp(S_1 $\supset$ $\sim$ S_2) can be deduced.

It should be clear that the general principles governing the occurrence of *too, but,* and reciprocal contrastive stress can be stated only in terms of presuppositions and deductions based on those presuppositions. This means that certain sentences will be grammatical only relative to certain presuppositions and deductions, that is, to certain thoughts and thought processes and the situations to which they correspond. This seems to me wholly natural.

The consequences of these observations are important for both linguistics and natural logic. Logic, as it is normally studied, involves a formal system containing axioms and rules of inference which are not constrained with respect to either form or content by empirical linguistic considerations. But these observations show that natural logic must be so constrained, at least with respect to the form of expressions. Recall that we have been using the notation f(a,b) to stand for an S containing noun phrases *a* and *b*. That is, we have been describing semantic representations of sentences and lines of deductions in the same notations, and for a good reason—the general principles determining the distribution of *but, too,* and reciprocal contrastive stress require that *identity* relations hold between syntactic structures and lines of deductions in natural logic. The sorts of representations needed for natural logic must be of the same form as those needed for linguistics. This should hardly be surprising, but it's nice to have a demonstration of it.

The consequences for linguistics are not too surprising either, namely, that gramaticality must be defined relative to assumptions about situational contexts and to thought processes, assuming that natural logic deductions are a first approximation to a formal representation of thought processes. In formal terms this means that a syntactic derivation must not only include a sequence of phrase-markers $P_1, \ldots, P_n$ and a semantic representation, $SR = (P_1,$ presuppositions, topic, focus, . . .), but it must also include a member of the class of deductions from those presuppositions. In this sense, the study of linguistics and the study of natural logic are inextricably bound up together.

One more point: The general question of whether a given expression in a system with the expressive power of first-order logic with identity can be deduced from some arbitrarily given set of axioms is known to be undecidable, and it is generally believed that the same is true of all logics incorporating at least this much expressive power. Though an adequate natural logic is nowhere near completion, it does seem clear that any adequate natural logic will have to have at least the expressive power of first-order predicate calculus. As we saw, the question of whether a sentence with *but* is grammatical relative to a given set of presuppositions depends on the question of whether $Exp(S_1 \supset \sim S_2)$ can be deduced from these presuppositions. If this is undecidable in natural logic, as would be a good bet, the question of whether a given sentence containing *but* is grammatical relative to a given set of presuppositions would be undecidable in natural logic. In general, the notion of grammaticality relative to some set of presuppositions would then be an undecidable property of sentences. This should give some second thoughts to investigators working in the field of discourse analysis, since it means that given a sentence and given some formal description of a context and given a completely adequate grammar of the language in question, there would still be no general solution to the question of whether that sentence was appropriate to that context. But this should not be surprising.

If the arguments in this paper are correct, we can conclude the following:

1. The general principles governing when certain sentences are grammatical relative to certain presuppositions can only be stated in terms of deductions from those presuppositions.

2. An anaphoric expression may have as its antecedent an expression which is not in the sentence itself, nor in the presuppositions of the sentence, but in some line of a deduction based on those of presuppositions. (See the discussion of (11)a.)

3. In order to determine whether a sentence containing the contrary-to-expectations sense of *but* will be grammatical relative to a set of presuppositions, it is necessary that a line of deduction be *identical* to some S in a linguistic representation of the sentence. Consequently, logical form must match up with linguistic form, at least for natural logic.

4. The question as to whether an arbitrary sentence is well formed relative to an arbitrary set of presuppositions seems to be in general undecidable.

ON
REPORTED
SPEECH

Arnold M. Zwicky   The Ohio State University

In this brief communication I address myself to the relationship between sentences and reports of sentences, primarily reports using the verb *say*, but also some employing *tell* and *let someone know*. In my exposition I shall distinguish the (original) "speaker," who gives a "speech," and the person who describes the content of this speech—the "reporter," who supplies a "report." Consider, for example, speech (1), where the speaker is Harry, and the reports of (1) in (2):

(1) My only brother, Frank, who is a genius at chess, will be staying with me for a week.

(2) a. Harry said that his brother is going to stay at his place for seven days.
   b. Harry said that someone will visit him for a while.
   c. Harry said that his brother is very good at some game.
   d. Harry said that his only brother is named Frank.

Those who are competent in English have the ability to judge sentences with main verb *say* as satisfactory or unsatisfactory reports of a given speech. The same ability is manifested when those who are competent in English make judgments about the acceptability of examples like those in (3):

(3) a. Harry said, "My only brother, who is a genius at chess, will be staying with me for a week," but he didn't say that anyone would visit him.
   b. Harry said, "My only brother, who is a genius at chess, will be staying with me for a week"—that is, he said that someone would visit him.

The sentences in (2) are satisfactory reports of speech (1), but the sentences in (4) are not:

(4) a. Harry said that there will be no space for me to stay at his house.
   b. Harry said that he was thinking of someone named Frank.
   c. Harry said that he has only one brother.

To distinguish satisfactory reports, like those in (2), from unsatisfactory reports, like those in (4), it seems necessary to distinguish various aspects of sentences (see the discussion in Fillmore 1969b).

First, the "meaning" of a sentence, what is asserted, requested, demanded, and so forth.

Second, the "presuppositions" of the sentence, the conditions on the correct use of the sentence.[1]

[1] I realize that this characterization of the notion of presupposition is unsatisfactory in a number of respects, and that it is in fact doubtful that there is any usefulness in the term *presupposition* construed very broadly. Some of the papers accompanying this one make these points quite clearly. But for present purposes it is sufficient to distinguish presuppositions, in some rather loose sense, from certain other aspects of sentences.

Third, the "messages" that might be conveyed by the sentence—what the speaker might mean by the sentence, or what the hearer might take the sentence to mean. Such messages are at times totally unrelated to the meaning of the sentence (as when (5) is to be understood as code for (6)), even precisely contradictory to the meaning (as when (7) is spoken with sarcastic intent).

(5)   Uncle dreadfully ill, dying fast.
(6)   Meet me in London tomorrow at noon.
(7)   What a beautiful dress!

Fourth, "inferences" to be drawn from the meaning of the sentence, or from the messages that might be conveyed by it, or from both. For instance, from (8) one can conclude that Fermat's Last Theorem is false, although no one would want to claim that 'Fermat's Last Theorem is false' is the "meaning" of (8).

(8)   There is a number such that 3,267, when raised to that power and added to 6,987 also raised to that power, gives 9,812 raised to that power.

Similarly, on hearing (9) one can reasonably suppose that some sort of assistance is in order.

(9)   I think I'm going to faint.

But (9) is nevertheless a declaration, not a request. Inferences may be strict, as in the case of (8), or only likely, as in the case of (9). Other types of inferences are drawn not from the content of utterances but from their form (roughly, not from what was said but from the way in which it was said), as when choice of vocabulary and aspects of phonology are used to classify speakers as to their geographical origin, age, status, and so forth.

In drawing a distinction between meanings, presuppositions, messages, and inferences, I do not claim to be very clear about the characteristic features of these aspects of utterances, in particular about the differences between presuppositions, messages, and inferences, although there does seem to be a fair number of clear cases of each.

Consider now (4)a and (4)b, both unsatisfactory reports of (1). (4)a conveys, not the meanings of (1), but rather a possible inference from (1), or a message that might be conveyed by (1). (4)b conveys, not the meaning of (1), but rather a presupposition of (1), roughly that the speaker has in mind someone with the proper name being used. From these examples, and many more of similar type, we can conclude that a satisfactory report conveys the meanings of a speech, and not its presuppositions or its possible messages or possible inferences from it. This is a property of the verb *say*, not of verbs of report in general. Compare *let someone know*, which can convey any of the previously mentioned aspects of a speech; thus (10) is a satisfactory report of (1) which conveys a possible message of (1).

(10)   Harry let me know that there would be no space for me to stay at his house.

And (11), which conveys one of the presuppositions of (1), is also a satisfactory report of (1).

(11)   Harry let me know that he has a brother.

In my speech *tell* is ambiguous as between a sense like that of *say* and a sense like that of *let someone know*, so that (12) is a satisfactory report of (1), but only in the 'let someone know' sense of *tell*.

(12)   Harry told me that there would be no space for me to stay at his house.

It is a satisfactory report of (13), spoken by Harry, but only in the 'say' sense of *tell*.

(13)   There will be no space for you to stay with me.

Now I return to the verb *say*, which I have thus far argued to report the meanings of speeches but not various other aspects of them. More precisely, *say* reports only the assertions in speeches. Speech (1) does not "assert" the existence of Harry's brother, nor does it "assert" that Harry has no brothers besides the one mentioned (hence (4)c is an unsatisfactory report of (1)). On the other hand, (1) does assert that this brother of Harry's is a genius at chess, and that he will be staying with Harry for a week, and that his name is Frank. Similarly, (14), spoken by Harry, asserts that a friend of Harry's is good at chess and that he will be staying with Harry for a week.[2]

(14)   A friend of mine who is good at chess will be staying with me for a week.

[2] Restrictive relative clauses within definite NP's are not assertive, and restrictive relative clauses within indefinite NP's are frequently not assertive. It seems quite clear to me, however, that (14) has at least one reading involving two assertions, although I have at the moment no characterization of the class of assertive relative clauses.

In consequence, (15) is a satisfactory report of (14):

> (15)   Harry said that the guy who will be staying with him is good at chess.

Note next that a report need not, of course, convey all of the assertions in a speech, nor need it convey all of the content in any particular assertion.[3] These observations are exemplified by the reports in (2) above. Thus, (2)a omits the assertion that Harry's brother's name is Frank, and the assertion that Frank is a genius at chess, and also the information that Frank is Harry's *only* brother.

> (2)   a.   Harry said that his brother is going to stay at his place for seven days.

(2)b omits the same things, and in addition provides no description of Harry's visitor, no indication of the length of the visit, and no specification that the visitor will actually be staying at Harry's house.

> (2)   b.   Harry said that someone will visit him for a while.

Finally, recall the familiar observation (as in McCawley, 1968e) that identifications in reported speech may be reports of the speaker's identifications or may be independent identifications supplied by the reporter. Thus, (16) is a satisfactory report of (1), given the reporter's judgment that Harry's brother Frank is a famous Fascist.

> (16)   Harry said that a famous Fascist will visit him.

Similarly, the reporter may substitute synonyms for terms of the original speech, as in the following satisfactory report of (1):

> (2)   a.   Harry said that his brother is going to stay at his place for seven days.

where *for seven days* replaces the *for a week* of the original speech (1), and where *stay at his place* replaces the *stay with me* of (1).

A rough approximation to a statement of the relationship between speeches and reports is then:

---

[3] In these respects the notion of report under discussion here differs from a characterization of a satisfactory job of (newspaper) reporting. A newspaper report is expected to be complete with respect to "significant" items of information, in some special sense of *significant*.

(17) A report is a subset of the set of assertions of the speech, with possible replacements of identifications or lexical items in the speech by identifications or lexical items supplied by the reporter.

If anything like (17) is the correct statement, we can draw several conclusions about the representations of sentences at the level at which the relationship between speeches and reports is to be expressed. First, that declarative sentences at this level are sets of representations of assertions. Second, that some of these assertions are overt existentials (recall the fact that a sentence like (18) is a satisfactory report of Harry's speech (19)).

(18) Harry said that someone was coming.
(19) John is coming.

Third, that identifications are represented independently of the remaining content of the assertions. Fourth, that the choice of particular lexical items either has not yet been made at this level, or is (somehow) represented independently of the remaining content of the assertions. Fifth, that the presuppositions of the assertions are represented independently of the meanings of the assertions.

The
Deep Structure
of Relative Clauses

Sandra Annear Thompson   University of California, Los Angeles

A number of general studies in transformational grammar (including Chomsky (1965), Rosenbaum and Jacobs (1968), G. Lakoff (1966), Langendoen (1969), Ross (1967b)) have assumed that the appropriate underlying representation for a relative clause sentence involves a sentence embedded into a noun phrase. I would like to question this assumption, and to suggest that in fact the appropriate underlying representation for a relative clause sentence is a conjunction.

The argument will be developed in several stages. First, I will suggest some facts which indicate that conjunctions must underlie relative clause sentences. Next, I will show the general process of relative clause formation and some of the implications of my analysis. Finally, I will indicate in what respects the derivation of sentences containing nonrestrictive relative clauses is similar to that of sentences with restrictive relative clauses.

1. Indications That a Conjunction Source for Relative Clause Sentences Is Correct

a. To my knowledge, no arguments defending an embedding analysis against a conjunction analysis for relative clause sentences have ever been presented either in the literature or informally.

b. There is virtually no agreement among those who assume that relative clauses are underlying embedded as to what configuration of nodes is appropriate to represent the relationship between the two sentences. Stockwell *et al.* (1969) presents a summary of the various approaches which have been taken and the arguments given to support each.

c. There is a significant but generally overlooked set of structural distinctions between relative clause sentences and those complex sentences which are clearly realizations of structures containing embedded sentences, namely those containing sentential subjects or objects, such as:

(1) That Frieda likes to cook is obvious to me.
(2) I think that Frieda likes to cook.

For sentences like (1) and (2), an embedding analysis is well motivated since the contained sentence is required as an obligatory argument of the verb; it plays a role with respect to the verb which Fillmore (1968) has called the *objective* role and without which the verb cannot stand. Furthermore, the verb governs both the occurrence of clause and the type of clause which can occur. These conditions do not hold for relative clause sentences. A relative clause is always structurally superfluous; it plays no role whatever with respect to the main verb and no morphemes in the language are marked as requiring it. A relative clause sentence is equivalent to two independent predications on the same argument. These differences are captured by an analysis in which sentential subjects and objects are instances of underlying embedding, and relative clauses are only superficially embedded. If relative clause sentences are not underlyingly embedded structures this could account in part for the general disagreement, pointed out in **b** above, as to the underlying representation of the position of the embedded sentence.

2.   The Derivation of Relative Clause Sentences

A.   Assumptions

In order to present the schematic outline for forming relative clause sentences, two assumptions must be made explicit.

   a.   The difference between parts of sentences such as the following:

   (3)   I know *a* student who plays the harmonica.
   (4)   I know *the* student who plays the harmonica.

will be assumed to be introduced at some level of derivation other than the one at which "content morphemes" and the relations among them are specified. I leave open the question of just where such a distinction must be made; for the present discussion, it suffices to point out that (3) and (4) must have identical representations insofar as the meanings of the nouns and verbs and the relations among them are concerned. I shall further assume that the choice of the definite determiner will in general correlate with certain presuppositions which the speaker makes about the extent of his listener's knowledge.

   b.   As pointed out by Bach (1968), numerals and quantifiers must be introduced outside the clause in which they ultimately appear. That this must be so is illustrated by the fact that the sentences of (5) are not matched by the respective pairs in (6):

   (5)   a.   I have three students who are flunking.
         b.   I know few people who smoke cigars.
         c.   I saw no students who had short hair.
   (6)   a. $\begin{cases} \text{I have three students.} \\ \text{Three students are flunking.} \end{cases}$
         b. $\begin{cases} \text{I know few people.} \\ \text{Few people smoke cigars.} \end{cases}$
         c. $\begin{cases} \text{I saw no students.} \\ \text{No students had short hair.} \end{cases}$

B.   Derivation

Returning now to the proposal for deriving relative clause sentences from conjunctions, I suggest that underlying (7) is a structure like (8):

(7) I met the girl who speaks Basque.
(8) (I met girl) (girl speaks Basque).

The choice of the clause to become the relative clause correlates with certain suppositions on the part of the speaker about what the hearer knows, and accordingly with the choice of the determiner. Consider (8) again. If the speaker presupposes that the hearer knows neither about his meeting a girl nor about a girl's speaking Basque, then both of the following conjunction realizations of (8) are acceptable:

(9) I met a girl and she speaks Basque.
(10) There's a girl who speaks Basque and I met her.

as well as both of the following relative clause sentences with indefinite head nouns:

(11) I met a girl who speaks Basque.
(12) A girl I met speaks Basque.

If, on the other hand, the speaker presupposes that there is a girl such that it is known by the hearer that he met her, the relative clause sentence corresponding to this presupposition will have the conjunct containing *met* as the relative clause, and the head noun will be definite:

(13) The girl I met speaks Basque.

Similarly, if the speaker presupposes that his hearer knows about the girl who speaks Basque, the corresponding relative clause sentence will have the conjunct *speaks Basque* as the relative clause, and again the head noun will be definite:

(14) I met the girl who speaks Basque.

C. Implications

a. The distinction then, between the "matrix" and "constituent" sentences in a relative clause structure can be seen to be related to nothing in the structural portion of the representation of such sentences. The meaning difference between sentences (13) and (14), in other words, is not a function of the fact that the matrix and the constituent sentences have been interchanged; if it were, then we should expect the same meaning difference to characterize the pair (11)–(12). But (11) and (12) do not have different meanings in any usual sense of the word *meaning*. Instead, the semantic difference between (13) and (14) is a function of the presuppositions which the speaker has about the extent of his hearer's knowledge.

b. Similarly, the "restrictiveness" of a relative clause is also shown not to be a property best described in terms of an embedding underlying representation. Relative clauses with indefinite nouns do not "restrict" these nouns in the way that relative clauses with definite nouns seem to, and yet underlying embedding structures do not reveal a basis for this difference. Again, I think that the apparent "restricting" nature of relative clauses with definite head nouns is a function of the presuppositions discussed above.

c. Postal (1967) has shown that a certain ambiguity can be explained only if relative clauses are assumed to be derived from conjunctions. The sentence he gives is:

(15)   Charley assumed that the book which was burned was not burned.

On one reading, Charley assumed that a certain book had not been burned when in fact it had been. On the other reading, Charley assumed a contradiction. On the hypotheses that relative clause sentences are underlyingly embedding structures, there is no way to represent the ambiguity. This is because corresponding to (15), only one embedding structure can be constructed, namely:

(16)

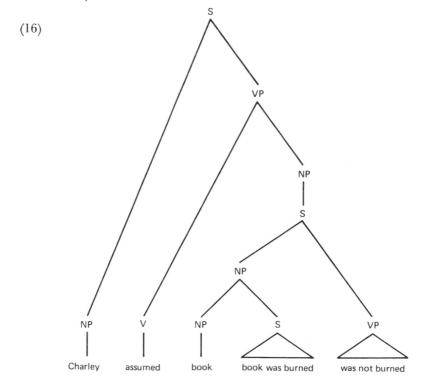

But there are two conjunction sources for (15). Underlying the first reading, in which Charley is merely mistaken, is the representation:

(17) (Charley assumed (book not burned)) (book burned).

Notice, that, as we would expect, (17) also underlies:

(18) The book which Charley assumed was not burned was burned.

which results from the first conjunct's becoming the relative clause, as well as the conjunction:

(19) Charley assumed that the book was not burned but it was burned.

Underlying the second reading, in which Charley assumes a contradiction, is:

(20) Charley assumed ((book burned) (book not burned)).

As with (19), (20) underlies two sentences besides (16). By selecting the second of the two conjuncts of (20) as the relative clause, we can derive:

(21) Charley assumed that the book which was not burned was burned.

which is an exact paraphrase of the second reading of (15). The conjunction derivable from (20) is, of course:

(22) Charley assumed that the book was burned and that it was not burned.

At this point, it should be made clear that there is one class of relative clause sentences which do not seem to be related to conjunctions in the manner just described. A sentence such as:

(23) Men who smoke pipes look distinguished.

which contains a relative clause with a generic head noun, obviously does not have a conjunction such as:

(24) (Men smoke pipes) (men look distinguished).

as its source. It is generally assumed that such a sentence is instead derived from the representation underlying an *if-then* sentence like:

(25) If a man smokes a pipe, he will look distinguished.

The extremely interesting semantic and syntactic issues raised by this assumption are unfortunately left unexplored here.

3.   Nonrestrictive Relative Clauses

The similarities between nonrestrictive clause (=NR) sentences and conjunctions have been remarked upon by a number of linguists (see, for example, Thompson (1968), Drubig (1968), G. Lakoff (1966), Postal (1967), Ross (1967a)). I will not review these similarities, but I will assume that NR sentences must be derived from conjunctions. Again, as far as I know, no arguments have been advanced in favor of an embedded analysis for NR sentences; in those studies which present underlying embedding representations for NR's, the question of there being alternative analysis is not even raised.

At the outset, two types of NR sentences must be distinguished; I will refer to them as Type I and Type II NR sentences. Type I NR sentences are exemplified by:

(26)   Jerry, who used to play football, now has a sedentary job.
(27)   I had a date with the librarian, who read to me all evening.

Type II NR sentences are exemplified by:

(28)   She took the children to the zoo, which was very helpful.
(29)   Joe debated in high school, which Chuck did too.

In Type I NR sentences, the relative pronoun replaces a referring noun phrase; in Type II, it replaces an entity, the nature of which will be clarified later in this section. For the moment, we will consider only Type I.

A.   Type I NR's

Ross's proposal (1967b, p. 174) that all Type I NR's be derived from second conjuncts seems to be correct. That is, at some intermediate level before anaphoric pronominalization has applied, given a conjunction each of whose clauses contains an occurrence of a coreferential noun, the second conjunct can be moved to a position immediately following the noun in the first conjunct. Pronominalization can then apply, moving either backwards or forwards,[1] so that from the conjunction

---

[1] Ronald Langacker pointed out this fact to me.

(30) George noticed that Margie refused the candy, and George didn't take any candy.

any of the following can be derived:

(31) George, who didn't take any either, noticed that Margie refused the candy.
(32) George, who noticed that Margie refused the candy, didn't take any either.
(33) George, who didn't take any candy, noticed that Margie refused it too.
(34) George, who noticed that Margie refused it too, didn't take any candy.

One apparent counterexample to the claim that NR's are derived from second conjuncts is the following sentence:

(35) Is even Clarence, who is wearing mauve socks, a swinger?

As Ross (1967) points out, its conjunction counterpart does not exist:

(36) *Is even Clarence a swinger, and he is wearing mauve socks?

It seems to me that Ross's solution to this problem is not as radical as he indicates. As a source for (36) he proposes the structure underlying:

(37) Is even Clarence a swinger? Clarence is wearing mauve socks.

Instead of following Ross in his conclusion that all NR's must be derived from sequences of sentences, I claim instead that the connector is deleted between a question and a declarative.

Imperatives are similar to questions in this respect. The source of:

(38) Tell your father, who is outside, that supper is ready.

apparently cannot be:

(39) *Tell your father that supper is ready, and he is outside.

But if there is a rule deleting *and* between imperatives and declaratives, the problem disappears. Notice that it would not help to posit a conjunction source in which the declarative sentence came before the question or imperative; questions and imperatives simply cannot be connected to declaratives by *and,* either before them or after them.

(40)   *Clarence is wearing mauve socks, and is even he a swinger?

(41)   *Your father is outside, and tell him that supper is ready.

Finally, a restriction must be placed on the NR rule to the effect that questions and imperatives themselves cannot become NR's.

At this point two objections might be raised; I would like to consider these in slightly greater detail. First, it has often been suggested that an NR represents an assertion by the speaker, a comment injected into the sentence whose truth is being vouched for by the speaker independently of the content of the rest of the sentence. An example of the type of sentence which makes such an analysis seem likely is

(42)   The mayor, who is an old windbag, designated himself to give the speech.

An implication of this analysis is that NR sentences should be represented in such a way as to reflect that the NR is an independent assertion made by the speaker, perhaps by positing a separate superordinate declarative performative for it. However, it is not correct to assign the responsibility for the truth of every NR to the speaker of the sentence in which it occurs. Bach (1968, p. 95) points out that a sentence like

(43)   I dreamt that Rebecca, who is a friend of mine from college, was on the phone.

which might be thought to contain an NR asserted by the speaker, can be made ambiguous by changing *is* to *was*. The case is even clearer in a sentence in which the subject is different from the speaker. It seems to me that the following sentences are ambiguous as to whether the subject or the speaker is vouching for the truth of the NR:

(44)   Harold says that his girlfriend, who is a little bit crazy, wants to go to Hanoi.

(45)   The claims agent said that the paint job, which should have been done long ago, would cost $150.

In fact, each of the above sentences can be disambiguated by adding a clause which forces the interpretation in which it is the subject, rather than the speaker, who asserts the NR.

(46)   Harold says that his girlfriend, who is a little bit crazy, wants to go to Hanoi, but I think she's too rational to try it.

(47)   The claims agent said that the paint job, which should have been

done long ago, would cost $150, but he doesn't know that now is when it should be done.

The other possible objection to my thesis is that if both nonrestrictive and restrictive relative clause sentences are derived from conjunctions, then sentences of both types, which may have very different meanings, can be derived from identical sources. Arguments against having identical sources for the two types of sentences carry weight only for sentences with numerals in them, which I will discuss shortly. In other cases, it seems that once again, the differences between restrictive and nonrestrictive relative clause sentences are not of the sort that ought to be represented structurally; instead they are differences representing a speaker's decision about how to present to the hearer information present in the underlying representation. For example, consider the two sentences:

(48)   The boy, who works at the library, is majoring in philosophy.
(49)   The boy who works at the library is majoring in philosophy.

The representation underlying both of these is:

(50)   (Boy works in library) (boy is majoring in philosophy).

For (48) the speaker has decided that the boy is already known to the hearer; the speaker is adding two pieces of information about the boy. For (49) the speaker assumes that the hearer knows about the boy who works at the library; *the* can be used with this NP, and the information which the speaker assumes to be new appears as the main predicate. I can see no way in which such a difference as that which exists between restrictives and nonrestrictives could be represented in a consistent way for all such sentences in terms of some underlying structural distinction.

Restrictive and nonrestrictive relative clause sentences with numeral associated with the head nouns do have different representations. Consider the sentences:

(51)   Three boys who had beards were at the party.
(52)   Three boys, who had beards, were at the party.

The assertions are quite different: (51) means not that three boys were at the party, but that there were three boys all of whom both attended the party and had beards. But (52) *does* mean that there were three boys at the party. Understanding very little about the representation of numerals, I can do no more now than to suggest that underlying (51), the numeral is associated with neither of the conjuncts, while underlying (52) it appears in both. This is confirmed by the fact that corresponding to (51) there is no two-clause conjunction, but corresponding to (52) we find:

(53)   Three boys were at the party, and they had beards.

B. Type II NR's

Type II NR's are also derived from second conjuncts only. The examples given above of Type II NR's were

(28) She took the children to the zoo, which was very helpful.
(29) Joe debated in high school, which Chuck did too.

I suggest that these are immediately derived from the sentences.

(54) She took the children to the zoo, and that was very helpful.
(55) Joe debated in high school, and that Chuck did too.

Before outlining the process by which Type II NR's are formed, let us consider a derivation in reverse, with (28) as an example. Its immediate source is (54). The *that* of (54) is a pro-form for certain repeated portions of a sentence; directly underlying (54) would be

(56) She took the children to the zoo, and her taking the children to the zoo was very helpful.

Disregarding the tense of the first conjunct, we can see that the *that* in (54) has replaced the repeated portion of the second conjunct of (56). Let us take a derivation in reverse with another example:

(57) They said she could play the marimba, which she can.

The sentence containing *that* which immediately underlies (57) is

(58) They said she could play the marimba, and that she can.

Directly underlying (58) is the full form with the repeated portion preposed:

(59) They said she could play the marimba, and play the marimba she can.

The immediate source for (59) is

(60) They said she could play the marimba, and she can play the marimba.

In detail, the derivation of a Type II NR sentence proceeds as follows: Given a near-surface-level conjunction in which part of the surface VP of the first conjunct matches part of the VP of the second conjunct, (a) the repeated portion may be preposed;[2] (b) the preposed portion may be replaced by *that*;[3] and (c) the connector may drop, with concomitant change of *that* to *which*.

Notice that, as outlined by Chomsky (1957), when there is no auxiliary element to carry emphasis or negation, a *do* must be added, as in the following examples:

(61) She promised to dance for us, and she did dance for us.
    a. She promised to dance for us, and dance for us she did.
    b. She promised to dance for us, and that she did.
    c. She promised to dance for us, which she did.
(62) She dances well, and I don't dance well.
    a. She dances well, and dance well I don't.
    b. She dances well, and that I don't.
    c. She dances well, which I don't.

The following examples show the operation of an optional rule of "parenthesis":

(63) That Cornelius was pleased was to be expected, and he certainly seemed to be pleased.
    a. That Cornelius was pleased, and he certainly seemed to be pleased, was to be expected.
    b. That Cornelius was pleased, and pleased he certainly seemed to be, was to be expected.
    c. That Cornelius was pleased, and that he certainly seemed to be, was to be expected.
    d. That Cornelius was pleased, which he certainly seemed to be, was to be expected.

A special set of examples is the following, in which a *do* appears:

(64) She taught me to bake a cake, and I couldn't bake a cake before.
    a. She taught me to bake a cake, and bake a cake I couldn't do before.
    b. She taught me to bake a cake, and that I couldn't do before.
    c. She taught me to bake a cake, which I couldn't do before.
(65) We read *Tom Sawyer,* and we had never read *Tom Sawyer* as children.

---

[2] This formulation is slightly inaccurate. Exactly what gets preposed will be described more carefully below.

[3] The order of these two rules will be reviewed below.

a. We read *Tom Sawyer,* and read *Tom Sawyer* we had never done
    as children.
b. We read *Tom Sawyer,* and that we had never done as children.
c. We read *Tom Sawyer,* which we had never done as children.

Sentences such as (64) and (65), when considered with certain other sentence
types, provide evidence for two related hypotheses.

The first, advanced by Ross, is that activity verbs are associated at some
level with the "primordial" action verb, *do.*[4] I understand him to be claiming that this *do* is present in the underlying representation of all activity
sentences. Because its occurrence is entirely predictable, I would choose not
to view it as present at this level, but as inserted into activity sentences early
in their derivation.

The second hypothesis which sentences such as (64) and (65) provide
evidence for is that the *do* in such sentences has as its object an NP. According to Ross, the NP in question is the underlying object of *do,* and it is an
entire sentence:

(66) Frogs produce croaks.

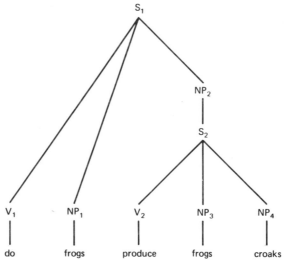

Aside from the fact that there seems to be no evidence for NP_3, that is a
second underlying occurrence of the surface subject, the evidence which
indicates that the *do* must take an NP object indicates that it is not an

---

[4] I cannot fully appreciate Ross's position since I have access to it only in the very sketchy
form of a handout from his paper, "Act," presented at the July 1969 meeting of the
Linguistic Society of America in Urbana, Illinois. From this handout, and from reports
on the paper, I believe that the points which I have attributed to Ross are accurately
stated here.

underlying NP that we are concerned with here at all, and that it is not a sentence. Let us consider this evidence. In a sentence like

(67) I realized that Art had visited the Dean, which I should do too.

we are tempted to declare that the *which* replaces an NP, since we know that in restrictive relative clause sentences and in Type I NR sentences, *which* always replaces an NP. However, this is not a very strong argument, since in questions, *which* can replace a demonstrative:

(68) Which book did you steal? I stole this book.

But the argument that *which* replaces an NP becomes more convincing when we consider the immediate source for (67), namely:

(69) I realized that Art had visited the Dean, and that I should too.

Beyond these NR sentences, no examples of *that* replacing anything but an NP come to mind. Further support comes from a paraphrase of (67):

(70) I realized that Art had visited the Dean, (which is) something I should do too.

Something is the NP pro-form *par excellence,* and it is clearly the object of *do.* But what it is coreferential with is not the sentence:

(71) Art had visited the Dean.

since what underlies sentences (67), (69), and (70) is not

(72) *I realized that Art had visited the Dean, and I should Art visit the Dean too.

What underlies (67), (69), and (70) instead is

(73) I realized that Art had visited the Dean, and I should visit the Dean too.

In other words, somehow the phrase *visit the Dean* must be an NP before the rules changing this phrase to *that* apply.

Ross has suggested that pseudo-cleft sentences provide additional support for the hypothesis that phrases like *visit the Dean* must be NP's:

(74) What I should do is visit the Dean.
(75) Art did what I should do: visit the Dean.

What examples (67) through (75) show is that the NP which the NR and pseudo-cleft rules, and certain other rules, must refer to need not be an S at any level.

Further evidence that the NP referred to by these rules is a surface NP rather than an underlying NP can be found in the fact that what follows surface *be* must also be an NP. A collection of relevant examples is

(76) Nick is tall, which I will never be.
(77) Nick is tall, (which is) something I will never be.
(78) What I will never be is tall.
(79) Nick is what I will never be: tall.

Ross (1969) has used examples like these to show that adjectives must be underlying NP's. However, examples like the following show that adjectives and other post-*be* expressions must be not underlying but superficial NP's.

(80) I saw that Irma was easy to please, which I should be too.
(81) I saw that Irma was easy to please, (which is) something I should be too.
(82) What I should be is easy to please.
(83) Irma is what I should be: easy to please.

The expression *easy to please* in (80)–(83) cannot be an underlying NP, since in deep structure *easy* and *please* are not even constituents of the same S:

(84) ((One please Irma) easy).

In the examples

(85) Chinese was easily mastered by Rich, which it was not by Claire.
(86) Chinese was easily mastered by Rich (which is) something it was not by Claire.
(87) What Chinese was was easily mastered by Rich.

We can see that the phrase *easily mastered* is not an underlying complement of *be* for there is no underlying *be*; moreover, since the verb *master* is an activity verb, at some intermediate level it would actually be the object of *do*.

My proposal, then, is the following: neither *do* nor *be* is present in underlying representations. *Be* may become the main verb by any of a variety of well-known obligatory transformations. *Do* is inserted preceding activity verbs. At the point at which *do* or *be* is inserted into a sentence, the part of the VP which follows becomes an NP; its NP status is then referred to by a number of optional rules, such as those which produce the sentences we have been considering here. If none of these rules applies to separate the *do* from its object, Ross's rule of "*do*-gobbling" applies, deleting *do*'s that are directly followed by their objects.

If this analysis is in general correct, we are ready to reformulate the steps by which Type II NR's may be formed. Rephrasing the set of three rules (a)–(c) given earlier, we arrive at the following statement: Given a near-surface-level conjunction in which part of the surface VP of the second conjunct is a repetition of part of the surface VP of the first conjunct, (a) the NP "complement" of *be* or *do* may be preposed; (b) this NP may be replaced by *that*; and (c) the connector may drop, with concomitant change of *that* to *which*. This reformulation corrects two inaccuracies in the previous (a)–(c). The earlier formulation said that the portion of the second conjunct involved in these rules was the "repeated portion." This is not quite accurate, since in

(83)   Nick is tall, and I shall never be tall.

be is part of the repeated portion of the second conjunct (with tense disregarded). But clearly the *be* is not part of what is changed to *that,* or preposed:

(89)   Nick is tall, which I shall never be.
(90)   Nick is tall, and that I shall never be.
(91)   Nick is tall, and I shall never be that.
(92)   *Nick is tall, which I shall never.
(93)   *Nick is tall, and that I shall never.
(94)   *Nick is tall, and I shall never that.

What does achieve the desired results is the requirement that what is preposed or changed to *that* be an NP.

Second, the order of rules (a) and (b) is irrelevant now, since *that* can appear either after *do* or *be* or in its preposed position. Beginning with the initial sentence of (64), we derive

(95)   She taught me to bake a cake, and bake a cake I couldn't do before.

by applying (a) alone,

(96)   She taught me to bake a cake, and I couldn't do that before.

by applying (b) alone, and:

(97)   She taught me to bake a cake, and that I couldn't do before.

by applying both rules. Similarly, beginning with (80), we derive

(98) I saw that Irma was easy to please, and easy to please I should be too.

by applying (a) alone,

(99) I saw that Irma was easy to please, and I should be that too.

by applying (b) alone, and:

(100) I saw that Irma was easy to please, and that I should be too.

by applying both rules.

A final minor point: a *do* occurring right after a stressed modal may be dropped. Thus, sentences (57) and (65) have a variant form with final *do*:

(101) They said she could play the marimba, which she can (do).

In this section I have considered two types of NR sentences, showing how both are related to near-surface conjunctions, and how NR sentences of Type II provide evidence for two hypotheses, one that activity sentences have at some level *do* as main verb, and the other that only at a fairly superficial level must the phrase following *do* or *be* be an NP.

4. Summary

I have tried to present some heretofore unexamined evidence that both restrictive and nonrestrictive relative clauses must be derived from underlying conjunctions, and that this can be achieved in a grammar with certain well-motivated and fairly traditional restrictions on what aspects of the meaning of a sentence are to be represented in its underlying representation.[5]

---

[5] As this paper was going to press, Perlmutter and Ross (1970) appeared, in which it was proposed that sentences like

(i) A man entered the room and a woman went out who were quite similar.

"present the theory with a new paradox." In their words,

> Neither of these singular noun phrases can serve as the antecedent of a relative clause whose predicate (*similar*) requires an underlying plural subject, and whose verb (*were*) is inflected to agree with a plural subject in surface structure. The only possible antecedent of the relative clause in (i) would seem to be the discontinuous noun phrase *a man . . . (and) a woman*. But how can a discontinuous noun phrase be the antecedent of a relative clause? No analysis of relative clauses that has yet been proposed for the theory of generative grammar is able to account for sentences like (i).

I would like to point out that sentences such as (i) [which are indeed anomalous in a traditional embedding analysis of relative clause sentences] present no paradox at all if relative clause sentences are viewed as underlying conjunctions; the conjunction source for (i) would simply be:

(ii) (Man entered room) (woman went out of room) (man and woman were similar).

TENSE
AND TIME REFERENCE
IN ENGLISH

James D. McCawley University of Chicago

Ross (1967) has contested the celebrated analysis of English auxiliaries presented in Chomsky (1957, 1965) on the grounds that while Chomsky's analysis makes it necessary to treat auxiliaries as not within the category "verb" (and indeed, not all belonging to any one category), in fact most transformations treat auxiliaries in exactly the same way that they treat "main" verbs,[1] that is, the one known source of evidence for category membership argues that auxiliaries are really verbs and that the traditional term *auxiliary verb* is syntactically justified. Ross proposes that the deep structure of a sentence such as (1)

(1) John had been smoking pot.

is not

(2)

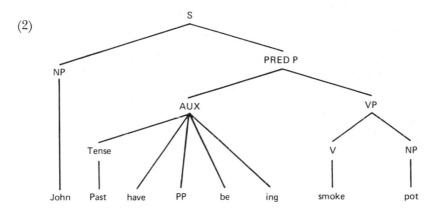

as Chomsky's proposals would have it, but rather (3), as shown on the following page.

Successive applications of the cyclic transformation known variously as "subject raising," "*it*-replacement," or "VP raising" plus application of "complementizer placement" to add PP and *-ing* to the complements of *have* and *be* respectively convert (3) into (4).

---

[1] Auxiliaries are exceptional by virtue of undergoing a transformation of "tense attraction" which combines them with an immediately preceding tense morpheme. All other transformations that might appear to treat auxiliaries in a special way (for example, subject-verb inversion) are simply transformations that follow "tense attraction" and have a structural description calling for the first verb.

(3)

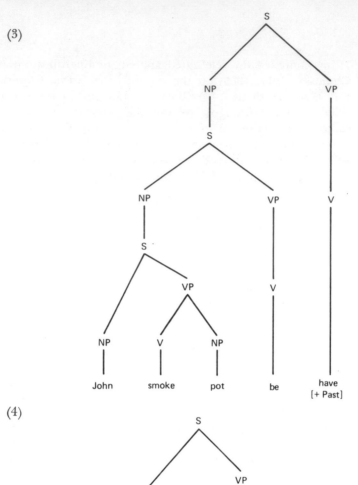

(4)

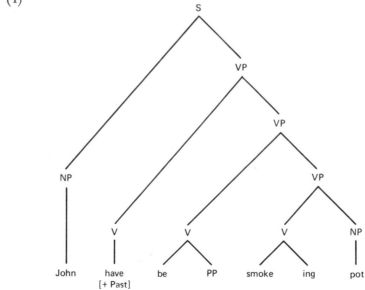

Ross notes that the resulting surface structure gives additional support for his proposal, namely that the parts of a sentence such as (1) which can be pronominalized are syntactic constituents in Ross's analysis but not in Chomsky's; for example, (5)

(5) They say that John had been smoking pot, which he had.

involves pronominalization of *been smoking pot,* thus providing evidence
that *been smoking pot* is a constituent at the point of the derivation where
this pronominalization takes place; *been smoking pot* is a constituent in (4)
but not in the surface structure that would result from Chomsky's analysis.

This paper will be devoted to refining Ross's analysis and relating it
to semantics. The refinements that I will propose in Ross's analysis relate
to tense. Specifically, I will propose that tenses are not features but are themselves underlying verbs[2] and that all occurrences of the auxiliary *have* are
underlying past tenses, so that (1) will be derived not from (3) but rather
from

(6)

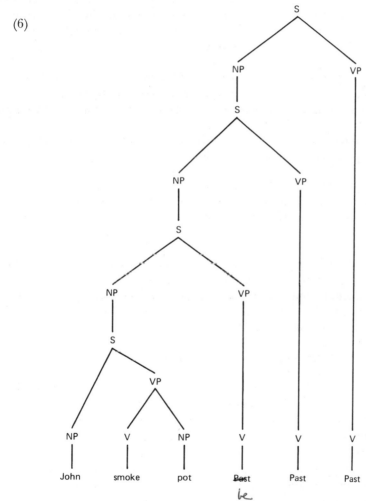

[2] I had already assumed this conclusion in footnote 1.

These refinements will add several items to the already huge list of advantages which Ross's analysis buys over Chomsky's; in particular, they will make it possible to show that the various restrictions on the co-occurrence of auxiliaries which Chomsky summarized in the celebrated formula

(7)   Aux → Tense (Modal) (have PP) (be ing)

are consequences of other more general syntactic facts, that is, Ross's analysis allows one to explain why those combinations of auxiliaries occur rather than any other set of combinations that one could summarize with a formula along the lines of (7).

The argument that *have* is an underlying past tense is based on Hoffman's (1966) observation that in certain environments the distinction between simple past, present perfect, and past perfect is neutralized in favor of *have*. For example, sentences (8)–(10):

(8)   John is believed to have arrived at 2:00 yesterday.
(9)   John is believed to have drunk a gallon of beer by now.
(10) John is believed to have already met Sue when he married Cynthia.

involve embedded clauses which would have to be in the simple past, present perfect, and past perfect if used as independent clauses:

(11) John arrived at 2:00 yesterday. (*has arrived, *had arrived)
(12) John has drunk a gallon of beer by now. (*drank, *had drunk)
(13) John had already met Sue when he married Cynthia. (*met, *has met)

A grammar will have to provide some mechanism for matching time adverbs with appropriate auxiliaries both in full clauses, where there is a four-way contrast between present, past, present perfect, and past perfect, and in infinitives and certain other structures, which allow only a two-way contrast between *have* and nothing, as in (14):

(14)   John is believed to admire Spiro Agnew.

Hoffman rightly concludes that the mechanism for getting the right adverbs to go with the right auxiliaries is the same in both the full clause and the infinitive and that infinitives thus go through a stage in their derivations in which present, past, present perfect, and past perfect are distinct, and that some later rule or rules converts that four-way distinction into a distinction between zero and *have*. A first approximation to such rules would be a rule which deletes present and turns past into *have* after *to,* followed by a rule which deletes one of the *have*'s from the *have have* sequence that the first rule would produce in past perfect cases:

(15) a. Pres → Ø ⎫
        Past → *have* ⎬ in env. *to* _____
     b. *have*$_{AUX}$ → Ø in env. *have* _____

Hoffman notes that the same neutralization takes place in other environments, for example, with the *-ing* complementizer:

(16) John's having arrived at 2:00 yesterday surprises me.
(17) John's having drunk a gallon of beer by now surprises me.
(18) John's having already met Sue when he married Cynthia surprises me.

and most importantly, after modals:

(19) John may have arrived at 2:00 yesterday.
(20) John may have drunk a gallon of beer by now.
(21) John may have already met Sue when he married Cynthia.

This last fact implies that there must be more underlying combinations of auxiliaries than Chomsky's formula allows: since the same rules govern which time adverbs go with *have* and which ones exclude *have* as in the cases discussed already, there must be a stage of the derivation at which modals can be followed by present, past, present perfect, and past perfect. The correct rule, of course, will not simply give a list of environments such as *to, -ing,* and modal as the environments where tense replacement takes place. There is a generalization which unites all these cases, namely that these are the environments in which the tense morpheme would not undergo subject-verb agreement. Thus, tense replacement can be made applicable simply to those tense markers to which subject-verb agreement has not applied:

(22) (replaces (15)a) Pres → Ø ⎫
                        Past → *have* ⎬ if agreement has not applied.

But since all occurrences of the auxiliary *have* are in environments in which subject-verb agreement would not be applicable, the generalized version of tense replacement that I have just proposed would permit one to take all underlying *have*'s as underlying past tenses.

I am now in a position to fulfill my promise to show that a refinement of Ross's analysis provides an explanation of why only the combinations of auxiliaries tabulated in Chomsky's formula occur. (a) Tense can only occur first, since tense in any other position is either deleted or turned into *have*. (b) Modals can be preceded only by tense because of their defective morphology: if modals appeared anywhere else they would have to be in an infinitive or participial form, and English modals do not have such forms.[3] (c) Progressive *be* must occur last because of the constraint that the topmost verb of its complement must be nonstative:

(23) John is acting like Harry.
(24) *John is resembling Harry.

If the auxiliaries under discussion are verbs, they are surely stative verbs; thus the same constraint which excludes (24) would also exclude (25):

(25) *John is having drunk bourbon.

(d) There could not be more than one *have* since any *have*'s in a structure not already excluded by (b) or (c) would have to be contiguous and since all but one of a string of contiguous *have*'s would be deleted.[4]

This analysis would appear to allow infinitely many sources for either a present perfect or a past perfect if something with a tense for its main verb can be embedded as the subject of a tense, as in (6), there should be no limit as to how far this could be continued, and all of the infinitely many conceivable combinations of past and present ought to be generated, for example, 37 consecutive pasts. Those combinations in which there were two or more embedded pasts would yield a past perfect by tense replacement and *have*-deletion, and those combinations having only one embedded past would yield a present perfect. For example, if 37 consecutive pasts were generated, 36 of them would become *have* and 35 of those *have*'s would be deleted, thus leaving a past perfect.

How ambiguous are present perfect and past perfect in fact? The past perfects found in sentences (26) and (27)

(26) When John married Sue, he had met Cynthia five years before.

---

[3] The attractive proposal that modals are suppletive, for example, that *can* is obligatorily replaced by *be able to* in infinitive and participial forms, probably is not feasible since the modals and their corresponding periphrastic forms are not always semantically equivalent. Note, for example, the sentences (brought to my attention by Louanna Furbee)

How can I tell you?
How am I able to tell you?

[4] One important item that I have failed to discuss is the passive *be*. I suspect that grounds will eventually be found for saying that *Max has been caught by the police* is not the passive of *The police have caught Max* but rather the present perfect of tenseless *Max be caught by the police* and that things such as *The police have caught Max* strictly speaking have no passive. However, confirmation or refutation of this conclusion will have to await an adequate account of what passive is applicable to. This conjecture, if true, would imply that no special rule was needed to get passive *be* in the right place relative to other auxiliaries.

(27) When John married Sue, he had read *Principia Mathematica* five
      times.

are reasonable candidates for analysis as the past of a past and the past of a
present perfect respectively, since the content of the main clause, if expressed
at the time when John married Sue, would require past tense and present
perfect respectively, as in (28) and (29).

(28) John met Cynthia five years ago.
(29) John has read *Principia Mathematica* five times.

Moreover, analyzing them as the past with an embedded past or present perfect allows one to explain why a past perfect allows two time adverbs: at a
more underlying level of structure, there is only one time adverb per clause,
and the past perfect would arise from an embedding structure, whose main
clause and embedded clause could each supply one time adverb.

This gives reason for setting up two sources for a past perfect, which is
far short of the infinitely many sources that I suggested. What about a third
source, the past of a past perfect? I know of no good examples of a past
perfect with three time adverbs, but there are examples of past perfects
with two time adverbs and an implicit reference to a third point in past
time, as in a discourse containing sentence (30),

(30) When John had married Sue, he had known Cynthia for five years.

which is possible only if the discourse has already mentioned some past time
which is taken as the "reference point" for *John had married Sue*; (30) could
then be analyzed as the past (the unmentioned reference point) of the past
(John's marrying Sue) of a present perfect (John has known Cynthia for
five years).[5] Thus, if a "reference point" is taken to be a tense, with or without time adverb, whose subject is an embedded sentence corresponding to
the event or state that is being described relative to that reference point,
there is some reason for allowing the potentially limitless freedom of combination of underlying tenses which my revision of Ross's analysis appears
to demand, except that the occasion would hardly ever arise for one to use
so many subsidiary "reference points" as to require tenses piled more than
three deep.

I turn now to the present perfect. The present perfect obviously is not
merely the present of a past in the same sense that the past perfect can be
the past of a past: the obvious parallel to using the past perfect for something which at a designated reference point in the past would have been

[5] Fischer (1967) points out that some varieties of French allow different forms for a "triply
past" and a "doubly past" past perfect.

reported in the past tense ought to be using the present perfect for something which at a designated reference point in the present would be reported
in the past; but since the present is the only point in the present, that characterization would amount to the absurdity that the present perfect is used
for what the past is used for. I am not going to argue that the present perfect is ultimately the present of a past but rather that through deletions it
acquires a derived constituent structure having a present as its highest verb
and past as its next highest verb, that is, what I had suggested as a deep
structure in the revision of Ross's analysis proposed above is really just an
intermediate stage in the derivation.

The present perfect in English has the following uses:

(a) to indicate that a state of affairs prevailed throughout some interval
     stretching from the past into the present (Universal):

     (31) I've known Max since 1960.

(b) to indicate the existence of past events (Existential):

     (32) I have read *Principia Mathematica* five times.

(c) to indicate that the direct effect of a past event still continues (Stative):

     (33) I can't come to your party tonight—I've caught the flu.

(d) to report hot news (Hot news):

     (34) Malcolm X has just been assassinated.

While some doubt might be raised as to whether (b, c, d) are distinct senses,
it can easily be seen that they are. For example, sentence (35) is ambiguous
and not vague between the three senses 'There are occasions on which Max
was fired', 'Max is currently out of work, having been fired', and 'Max
has been fired, which I presume is news to you', as can be seen by considering sentence (36) which can cover (a) the case of both Max and Fred on
occasion having been fired, (b) the case of both of them being out of work
as a result of being fired, or (c) the case of two pieces of hot news dealing
respectively with the firing of Max and the firing of Fred, but it could not
be used to assert that Max is out of work and that Fred, who we may assume
to have a job currently, has occasionally been fired.

     (35) Max has been fired.
     (36) Max has been fired, and so has Fred.

I will argue that all four of these senses of the present perfect correspond to semantic representations in which something that provides the source of a past tense is embedded in something that provides the source of a present tense, and that accordingly, deletions can give rise to a structure of the type proposed above.

The universal and existential present perfects appear both to involve a quantifier that ranges over an interval stretching from the past into the present and differ as regards whether that quantifier is universal or existential. I have argued elsewhere (McCawley, 1969b) that the semantics of natural languages involves not the "unrestricted quantification" found in most logic textbooks, where *All men are mortal* is transcribed '$(\text{All}_x (\text{Man}(x) \supset \text{Mortal}(x)))$', but "restricted quantification" such as would be found in a transscription '$\text{All}_{x:\text{Man}(x)} \text{Mortal}(x)$', that is, that a quantifier joins two propositional functions, one giving the "range" of the variable, and one giving the property that is being asserted of things in that range. I propose that these two propositional functions provide the sources of the two tenses that I wish these present perfects to be derived from: the range provides the present tense, since it must be an interval containing the present, and the function being asserted provides the past tense, since it is being asserted of events or times that are in the past. I assume that the tense morpheme corresponding to the range would be put in the clause corresponding to the quantifier. At some later point in the derivation, these quantifiers are deleted, leaving as traces only their tenses and such words as *ever, already,* and *sometimes,* and a time adverb describing the range, for example, *since Tuesday, during the last five years.* In many languages the universal and existential cases are not treated alike; for example, in German and Japanese, the tense of the scope in universal sentences is lost, and a simple present appears:

(37) Sie warten seit 5 Uhr. 'They have been waiting since 5:00.'
(38) Gozi kara mat-te   i-ru.
      5:00 from wait-participle   be-present

In Japanese, the existential case is treated exactly like any other existential sentence:

(39) Tanaka-san -wa   hon -o   kai-ta   koto -ga   ar-u
      Mr. Tanaka topic   book object write-past   fact subject exist-pres
      'Mr. Tanaka has written books'

One major advantage to treating present perfects as derived from a semantic representation such as I have sketched is that much of the co-occurrence restrictions between auxiliaries and time adverbs is thereby explained. For example, this treatment explains, at least for these two uses of the present perfect, why adverbs designating points in time cannot be used with the present perfect: since the time adverb of the scope of the quantifier is a bound variable which the quantifier binds, *I have written a letter yesterday would be excluded for exactly the same reason as *I talked to someone the butcher: in both cases a constant and a variable would be filling the same position.

The condition that the range of the quantifier include the present is closely connected with the question of the presuppositions of present perfects. Chomsky (1969) discusses the oddity of (40)[6] as compared with (41):

(40) [*]Einstein has visited Princeton.
(41)   Princeton has been visited by Einstein.

and states that it illustrates a principle whereby the surface subject of certain types of present perfect is presupposed to refer to someone who is alive. I contend, however, that the false proposition that Einstein is alive is not, strictly speaking, presupposed by (40) but is merely inferrable from the presupposition of (40) plus factual knowledge such as the knowledge that one must be alive to visit Princeton, and moreover, that the presupposition has nothing to do with the question of what is the surface subject. Note first that whether a sentence in the present perfect commits the speaker to the belief that the subject refers to someone who is alive depends on the rest of the sentence:

(42)   Frege has contributed a lot to my thinking.
(43)   Frege has been denounced by many people.
(44) [*]Frege has been frightened by many people.

and also depends on stress. Presumably Chomsky intended (40) and (41) to be read with primary stress on *Princeton* and *Einstein* respectively; however, (45) does not commit one to the belief that Einstein is alive, whereas (46) does.

(45) Eínstein has visited Prînceton.
(46) Prínceton has been visited by Eînstein.

This last fact suggests that topic rather than subject is directly related to presuppositions. In (45) one is talking about events of visiting Princeton, not just events of Einstein visiting Princeton, but in (46) about events of Einstein visiting. The former kind of events can still happen since Princeton still exists, but the latter cannot, since Einstein is no longer alive. Frege has to be alive for people to frighten him, but he doesn't have to be alive for

[6] I will use [*] to indicate oddity caused by the absurdity of the presuppositions that a sentence involves.

people to denounce him. Actually, strictly speaking, the property of being alive is not directly involved in the oddity of (40), since a person who believes that the dead return to haunt the living could perfectly well say (40) without contradicting his knowledge that Einstein is dead. Likewise, a person who holds both that belief and the belief that Frege is as neurotic a ghost as he was a living person could perfectly well say (44).

The presupposition in an existential present perfect thus appears to be that the range of the variable which the existential quantifier binds is a period during which the event or state designated by the propositional function in the scope of the quantifier can happen or be the case. Since the present perfect can only be used if the range includes the present, the presupposition is that the present is included in the period in which the designatum of the propositional function in question can happen or be the case.[7]

I will now give a number of illustrations of this principle.

(47)   My mother has changed my diaper many times.

Sentence (47) would be appropriate if said by a linguistically precocious 2-year-old who still wore diapers but not if said by a man who stopped wearing diapers 30 years ago. Leech (1969) points out that (48) would be appropriate only in referring to an exhibition which the speaker believes still to be running, whereas one would have to say (49) if referring to an exhibition which one believes to have already closed.

(48)   Have you seen the Monet exhibition?
(49)   Did you see the Monet exhibition?

However, a presupposition that the exhibition is still running is not sufficient to make (48) appropriate; for example, one would have to use (49) and not (48) if speaking to a person who one knows to have recently suffered an injury which will keep him in the hospital until long after the exhibition closes. Sentence (50) does not commit one to the belief that those designated by the subject are alive, nor should it, since (50) is about events of a person dying in an auto accident, which can still happen, as compared with (51) which is about events of Dennis Brain dying in an auto accident, of which there can be only one.

(50)   Many people have died in auto accidents.
(51)   [*]Dennis Brain has died in an auto accident. [ignore the 'hot news' sense],

---

[7] This must be interpreted in such a way that gaps in a discontinuous interval are ignored. The present can perfectly well fall into a gap in a discontinuous period in which something can happen, as in

Max has often gotten up at 8 A.M. (said at 10 P.M.)

Sentence (52) is again about the propositional function 'x dies in an event t of the type *auto accident*'.

(52)   Dennis Brain and many other famous musicians have died in auto accidents.

It is nonanomalous since *Dennis Brain* does not appear in this propositional function but only in the expression giving the range of the variable x.[8] Similarly with Chomsky's example:

(53)   Marco Polo and many others have climbed Everest.

One extension of this construction which I can get at least marginally is illustrated by (54):

(54)   Many people have climbed Everest; for example, Marco Polo has climbed it.

The present perfect here is repeated in a clause which provides an example of the kind of event which a preceding existential present perfect asserts to have occurred. I do not understand the details of the derivation of a sentence such as (54) nor can I characterize the range of cases in which this phenomenon can occur. I suspect that it is the same phenomenon which Chomsky (1969) observes when he writes, "It seems to me that if Hilary had just announced that he had succeeded in climbing Everest, it would have been appropriate, without the presupposition that Marco Polo is alive, to have said, 'But Marco Polo has done it too'."

The stative present perfects would presumably correspond to a semantic representation in which a description of the event is embedded in a context like 'the direct result of _____ continues', which would again involve a source for a past tense embedded in a source for a present tense, so that again a deletion could give rise to the desired present + past configuration. However, in this case I am at a total loss to find a detailed analysis which would correctly explain what effect the sentence refers to, for example, why it is that (55) refers to the effect of John's not being here (not, as is often erroneously supposed, the effect of John's being at the office), to the effect of my wife's being in jail, to the effect of my being sick with the flu, and to the effect of your being in a position to inform me regarding the whereabouts of my slippers.

(55)   John has gone to the office.

---

[8] Note that this implies that (52) cannot be derived by conjunction reduction from a conjoined sentence having *Dennis Brain* in one conjunct and *many other famous musicians* in the other.

(56) The police have arrested my wife, so we can't come to your party.
(57) I've caught the flu.
(58) Have you seen my slippers?

The oddity (noted by Leech) of *Yes, six months ago* as an answer to (58) comes from the answer assuming an existential interpretation of a present perfect that would normally be intended as a stative. Note, incidentally, that the commonly encountered description of this use of the present perfect as ascribing a state to the subject of the clause is incorrect, since in (56) it is the speaker's wife and not the police that is being asserted to be in the state in question.

In the hot news present perfect, it is clear that the status as news of the thing being reported is essential to the acceptability of the sentence. Since a person reporting hot news presupposes that his addressee does not yet know the news that he is reporting, the following possibility presents itself for relating this use of the present perfect to the existential use: one might say that the hot news present perfect is an existential present perfect in which the speaker bases the range of the quantifier not on his own presuppositions as to when the event in question might happen but on his estimate of his addressee's presuppositions: if the addressee does not know that Malcolm X has been killed, then for him the period in which Malcolm X might be killed extends indefinitely far into the future and thus includes the present. This analysis is supported by the fact that it would be normal to say things like *Kennedy has been assassinated* or *Khrushchev has been deposed* to a person who has just been rescued from a remote island where he had been marooned since 1960. However, note that this type of present perfect also occurs in questions as in (59) and in a past setting as in (60).

(59) Has there been an accident?
(60) When I arrived in New York, Malcolm X had just been assassi-
       nated.

This last example makes me a little suspicious of the cute idea that I suggested above of basing the choice of tense on the speaker's estimate of his hearer's presuppositions. Perhaps the only hope for an analysis of this use of the present perfect is to introduce a quite *ad hoc* principle that the period in which something is supposed "available for happening" is always extended forwards so as to include the time that it would take for news of its happening to get around and that in the case of a sentence actually being used to convey the news, *get around* is taken to mean 'get to the person to whom the sentence is addressed'.

It is possible for two of these senses of the present perfect to be combined, as in a hot news report of an existential present perfect:

(61)   Have you heard the news? Frank has been sleeping with Julie.

Such combinations of these senses present no new problems: if the (admittedly programmatic) analysis of the different present perfects sketched above works for the simple cases, then it will automatically handle things like (61) also. The structure underlying an existential present perfect would be embedded in the structure underlying a hot news present perfect, and the resulting present-past-present-past combination would become present-*have* by tense replacement and *have*-deletion.

I have so far thrown around the word *tense* with rather gay abandon, an abandon whose gaiety was especially unjustified when I was talking about semantic representations. The embedded pasts that I talked about were not absolute pasts but rather pasts relative to the context in which they were embedded, that is they expressed 'prior to' rather than 'past'. Of course, if one adopts Ross's (1968) proposal that all sentences arise from a structure whose topmost verb is a (often unexpressed) "performative verb," which indicates the illocutionary force (*question, command, promise, warning,* and so forth) which the sentence is intended to have, then absolute pasts also mean 'prior to' relative to the context in which they are embedded, since they are embedded in a context which refers to the time of the speech act, that is the present. However, the tense morpheme does not just express the time relationship between the clause that it is in, and the next higher clause —it also refers to the time of the clause that it is in, and indeed, refers to it in a way that is rather like the way in which personal pronouns refer to what they stand for. For example, a past tense normally requires an antecedent: sentence (62) is odd unless the prior context provides a time for the past tense to refer to; the oddity of (62) without such an antecedent for the past tense is exactly the oddity that is left in (63) when uttered in a context which has not provided any prior mention of a person for the *he* to refer to.

(62)   *The farmer killed the duckling.[9]
(63)   *He resembles Mike.

Moreover, the relation between a past tense and its antecedent satisfies Langacker's (1969) pronominalization constraint—that a pronoun must be preceded or commanded[10] by its antecedent:

(64)   Although Max was tired last night, he couldn't sleep.
(65)   Although Max was tired, he couldn't sleep last night.

[9] I am grateful to Sydney M. Lamb for bringing this interesting example to my attention.
[10] A node in a labeled tree is said to command all the nodes in the portion of the tree dominated by the lowest node labeled S which dominates the node in question, that is a node commands all the nodes which are in the same "simplex sentence" as it is in and all the nodes that are in clauses subordinate to that "simplex sentence."

(66)   Max couldn't sleep last night, although he was tired.

(67)   *Max couldn't sleep, although he was tired last night.

In addition, treating tenses as some kind of pronoun allows one to avoid having to set up two different *and*'s, one symmetric and the other asymmetric (= *and then*). Note that especially in narratives one may get several consecutive sentences or clauses which all contain past tenses but which refer not to simultaneous events but to consecutive events, each past tense referring to a time shortly after that which the preceding past tense referred to. For example, in (68), t_2 contains an implicit reference to t_1 ('shortly after t_1') and t_3 contains an implicit reference to t_2 ('shortly after t_2').

(68)   The Lone Ranger broke$_{t_1}$ the window with the barrel of his gun, took$_{t_2}$ aim, and pulled$_{t_3}$ the trigger.

If we in fact say that t_1 is the antecedent of t_2 and that t_2 is the antecedent of t_3, then Langacker's constraint explains why (67) is not equivalent to (69).

(69)   The Lone Ranger pulled the trigger, took aim, and broke the window with the barrel of his gun.

In a coordinate structure, pronouns cannot be commanded by their antecedents and therefore must be preceded by them; hence, t_1 must precede t_2 if it is to be its antecedent. Thus there is no need to say that the *and* of (68) is different from the "symmetric" *and* of (70).

(70)   John is tall and handsome.

I have argued that the past tense morpheme is an intransitive verb, that it is a two-place predicate meaning 'prior to' in the same sense in which *she* is a predicate meaning 'female', that is, that pronouns both stand for things and express presuppositions about the things they stand for. In my above examples, I treated *last night* as the antecedent of a past tense, that is, I treated the tense as being the pronominal form of a time adverb. Since a sentence like *Max was tired last night* involves both a time adverb and a matching tense morpheme but semantically only makes one reference to the time involved, my suggestion that tenses are pronominal in nature would entail having a reduplication rule which added a pronominal copy of every time adverb. There is nothing to prevent this pronominal copy from being added in predicate position, that is, the time adverb reduplication transformation could be so formulated as to create derived structures in which tenses appear in main-verb position and those constituents which will give rise to explicit time adverbs will appear in other positions than main-verb position. This proposal for English, incidentally, matches exactly Kiparsky's (1968) proposal for the history of tense in Indo-European. Kiparsky argues that in proto-Indo-European, tense morphemes were in complementary distribution with overt time adverbs and thus could be considered as belonging to the same grammatical category as them and that the development of the modern Indo-European languages from this stage involved the copying of features of the referents of time adverbs onto the verb, first optionally and later obligatorily.

I will close by commenting briefly on some important matters which I have not yet touched on. The future tense appears to present no major difficulties for the above analysis. The future tense in English differs mainly morphologically from the present and past: its marker is morphologically a modal verb rather than an affix. The future marker is deleted or replaced by the present tense morpheme in a number of environments. For example, it is deleted after *may* and *might,* as in (71) and (72), which can be interpreted as an embedded habitual present but not as an embedded future.[11]

(71) John may beat his wife.
(72) John might beat his wife.

The future marker is replaced by a present tense in conditional clauses and certain time adverbial clauses:[12]

(73) If he comes tomorrow, I'll give him some money.

There is no "mirror image" of the past perfect, that is, a combination of auxiliaries to indicate something in the future relative to a future reference point; the simple future is used in this case:

(74) When I get the money, I'll pay you within a week.

It thus appears that future is deleted when it directly follows future. There is likewise no special future analogue to the present perfect: a simple future is used to express the existence of future events or to express that something is the case through an interval starting at the present and running into the future:

(75) Max will die before he's 30.

---

[11] This deletion of the future marker is one of several transformations which are triggered by some but not all modals. If one takes uniform syntactic behavior as the criterion for setting up a syntactic category, then modals fail in a spectacular way to form a syntactic category: no two of them have exactly the same syntactic properties.
[12] I have ignored additional readings which (71) and (72) allow. (71) is at least seven ways ambiguous.

(76) I'll work here until I find a better job.

One interesting restriction on the future (called to my attention by Michael Stewart) is that a past embedded in a future may not refer to something that the speaker knows to have already happened; thus (77) is normal if the awarding of the degree is to take place between now and your seeing Max or even if it is due to take place today and the speaker does not know whether it has already taken place, but it is odd if the speaker knows that Max received the degree three days ago and you are to see him in four days.

(77) When you see Max, he'll have received his Ph.D. a week earlier.

While the analysis given above allowed in principle for presents and pasts to be embedded in one another to one's heart's content, examples of embedded pasts were much easier to come by than were examples of embedded presents; indeed, the only examples of embedded presents to be found above are the presents of embedded present perfects. Another peculiarity of the analysis given suggests that even these examples of embedded presents are spurious and that there are in fact no embedded presents. Specifically, consider the present tense that was introduced by the "range" of a present perfect. In the case where the range of something asserting the existence of past events does not contain the preesnt, the "range" does not contribute its own tense: a past tense is used rather than a past perfect, as in (78).

(78) Henry VIII got married six times.

This suggests that the rule creating the outer tense of present perfects applies only in present contexts. This in turn implies that present tense differs from past tense in more ways than it has generally been held to: it marks an absolute rather than a relative time relation.[13]

Another problem which I have not touched on and which this treatment provides no clue on is the problem of why tense is an obligatory category in English. Note that the obligatoriness of tense is the only aspect of Chomsky's auxiliary formula which does not follow from the refinement of Ross's analysis which I presented. I suspect that the obligatoriness of tense must be described by an output condition, but I must leave the proof or refutation of that conjecture to another time and perhaps another linguist.

[13] It is actually an overstatement to refer to the present tense as 'absolute', since certain 'world-creating' contexts (see G. Lakoff, 1970a) have their own present time, for example:
(i) I've just seen a movie in which someone steals the crown jewels.
Note that this is one of the few contexts in which a nonhabitual present tense is possible in English.

If's, And's,
and But's
about Conjunction*

Robin Lakoff   The University of Michigan

* This is a considerably revised and extended version of a paper delivered at The Ohio
State University Spring Semantics Festival, April 1969. Much of the work was done while
I was working for the Language Research Foundation during the year 1968–1969, and
I would therefore like to acknowledge with gratitude the support of the TEC Co. and
the LRF. I should also like to thank the following people for their insightful comments
and criticism of various aspects of this paper: Adrian Akmajian, Bruce Fraser, Georgia
Green, Larry Horn, George Lakoff, Jim McCawley, Jerry Morgan, Paul Neubauer, and
John R. Ross.

Introduction

This paper does not pretend to be a thorough examination of the mechanisms of conjunction. Rather, it is an attempt to examine some of the properties of conjunction, to see if they can be described or explained according to recent theoretical work in the field. Therefore, there will be more discussed than accounted for. No attempt is made here to provide a 'theory of conjunction'.

Moreover, I am not interested here in what happens to conjoined sentences or noun phrases after they are conjoined: that is, I will not be dealing, except perhaps incidentally, with phenomena such as reduction or gapping. I will confine the bulk of my discussion to the three coordinate conjunctions *and, or, but* and will not deal with the corresponding subordinate conjunctions *(since, although, while, when, for, because)* except very briefly and peripherally. Perhaps future work can deal with these problems in a fuller and more satisfying way: this is only the first exploration of these questions.

1. *And*: Symmetric

Gleitman (1965) claims that *and* may be used to join any two sentences. She gives as an example of an acceptable[1] sentence with *and* the following:

---

[1] The use of terms like *ungrammatical, inappropriate, strange, unacceptable,* and so forth, may be confusing throughout the paper if their special, semitechnical use is not made clear here at the outset. As Chomsky pointed out first in *Syntactic Structures,* the linguist must distinguish between grammaticality and meaningfulness: there is more than one reason why a speaker might not use a sentence, or might reject one. But straddling the line between these two concepts there are a number of others, less clearcut, yet necessary, I believe, if one is going to talk sensibly and accurately about language use by real speakers.

Let us try to reserve the term ungrammatical (as I may not consistently do in this paper) for anomalies that arise out of violations of syntactic rules alone: *John and Bill is here.* More often, we will be considering sentences that are syntactically well formed, but semantically deviant for one reason or another. Perhaps they are used in a (previously-defined) situation in which they are *inappropriate* (though in another context, they might be perfectly acceptable); perhaps they force the speaker or hearer to assume the existence of a situation that he knows cannot exist in the real world; perhaps they suggest a relationship between two things that it is illogical or unreasonable to consider related. These sentences will be judged odd, or unacceptable, by speakers although superficially their structure conforms perfectly to the rules of syntax. Cases like these will be considered anomalous whatever language they are translated into (as opposed to purely ungrammatical sentences, which may vary from language to language), unless their inappropriateness arises out of special cultural assumptions. Yet sentences like the ones I have starred in this paper are much more readily intelligible, and deviant in a different sense, from sentences which are bad because selectional restrictions, and so forth, are violated: *Colorless green ideas sleep furiously.* Linguistic theory should incorporate within it the means to describe and discriminate among all these types of anomaly: all are within the province of language use.

115

(1) My grandmother wrote me a letter yesterday and six men can fit in the back seat of a Ford.

It seems to me, and to the majority of people I have spoken to about sentences like this, that a sentence like (1) is very odd indeed. While each of its parts individually is perfectly intelligible, the sentence as a whole causes confusion: and there is nothing overtly present in that sentence that can be pinpointed as the cause of the confusion. My feeling is that such a sentence is marginal at best.

Sentences like (1) seem to rank near the bottom of a hierarchy of acceptability as conjunctions. A hierarchical ranking of possible conjoined sentences, in order of decreasing acceptability, appears below.

(2)   John eats apples and John eats pears.
(3)   John eats apples and his brother drives a Ford.
(4)   ?John eats apples and many New Yorkers drive Fords.
(5)   ?John eats apples and I know many people who never see a doctor.
(6)   ??Boys eat apples and Mary threw a stone at the frog.
(7)   *John is a strict vegetarian and he eats lots of meat.

Sentence (2) is somewhat strange in the form in which it is given because conjunction reduction is normal in case of identical subjects. But this is not relevant: the point is that the two sentences themselves are freely able to conjoin, and with the least amount of difficulty or perplexity on the part of the hearer of all the sentences on this list. It is true that Wierzbicka claimed (1967) that sentences like (2) were not the source of sentences like (8):

(8) John eats apples and pears.

But it seems to me that the assumption that (2) and (8) have separate sources denies that (8) has a place in the hierarchy above, which it seems to have: namely, that of (2).

Continuing in this list, (3) is a perfectly normal sentence, but in order to understand it as one, the speaker must make an assumption, or presupposition: in this case, admittedly, a rather trivial one: that one's brother is related to one, has something to do with one. The same is true for (4), where the presupposition is a little more difficult: to understand this sentence as a proper conjunction, we must assume that John is a New Yorker, or is somehow related to New Yorkers. If we happen to know, in (4), that John has never been to New York, and has nothing to do with anyone there, this sentence will become much stranger. In (5), the assumption is of another kind: to interpret this sentence as grammatical, we must be aware of the proverb "an apple a day keeps the doctor away." If we know this, then (5) is acceptable—in fact, probably better than (4), in which the connection between the two parts in any case is rather tenuous. But knowledge of the proverb is specific to Anglo-American culture, and someone who came from a different society, one in which apples were unknown or not regarded as particularly healthful, would find this sentence odd. That is, (4) is good provided you know something about John, which is likely for anyone if he is to say or hear (4) at all. But for (5) to be acceptable, one must have at his disposal information about the assumptions made in a particular culture, independent of and in addition to what is known about John, apples, doctors, and other overt elements in the sentence. Therefore this sentence is more capable of causing confusion than those which precede it.

A sentence like (5) has an additional peculiarity, because of its relationship with a special form of culturally-transmitted knowledge or belief, the proverb. Ordinarily, in a conjunction the acceptability of which depends upon knowledge common in a culture, any wording that expresses this knowledge is sufficient to ensure the acceptability of the conjoined sentence. But with proverbs, the exact form of the wording is crucially important— a proverb will not be recognized if any but the least important words in it are omitted, changed in order, or replaced by synonyms. Therefore compare (5), which is probably acceptable, with something like the following, which is very nearly identical in meaning, and thus should involve precisely the same cultural assumptions, yet is far less acceptable: *John eats apples and I know many people who never see a physician.

Sentence (6) is a close parallel to (1), and seems to me to be equally bad. If, however, we had a sentence like (9) instead of (6), the situation would be much improved.

(9)   John eats apples and Mary throws stones at frogs.

The chief problem with sentences like (6) and (1), then, is not so much the fact that the subjects, or the objects, are unrelated, as that the verbs are of different categories, the first in (1) being a verb that refers to specific time, the second a generic that describes a state true for all time. In (6) this order is reversed. Similarly, although I think a sentence like (10) is better than (6), because at least the subjects are similar in form and meaning, it's much worse than (9), because the verbs do not match in genericity.

(10)   ?Six men are throwing stones at a frog just now and seven men can fit in a Ford.

Sentence (7) is much worse than any of the others: it is impossible, I think, to imagine a situation in which it could be appropriately used. This is of course because it contains two contradictory statements. Similarly, two tautologous statements will not conjoin.

(11) *John is rich and he has 80 million dollars.

As these facts suggest, there are additional conditions on what can be conjoined, beyond the ones we have already mentioned. Two sentences may
be conjoined if one is relevant to the other, or if they share a common topic.
But, as these examples show, the common topic is not necessarily, or even
usually, overtly present and identifiable in the sentences; nor is this a sufficient condition, though it is necessary. Sentences (1), (6), (7), (10) and (11)
all have either implicit or overt elements that might be interpretable as
items in common, under at least one interpretation, and yet none of these
sentences is acceptable even with this interpretation.

These, then, are the two principal problems we are facing in trying to
decide when conjunction is possible:

1. What does the notion of "relevance" or "common topic" involve?
    More specifically, when do two sentences share a common topic? If
    the common topic is not explicit in the superficial sentence, how can
    one tell what it is, or whether it is there?
2. In those cases where the presence of a common topic is not enough,
    what else must one know?

In sentences like (2), the answer to the first question is easy. The common topic is that part of each conjunct of the sentence that is identical. If
the identity extends to the lexical item itself—that is, if an item in the two
conjuncts is the same in form as well as meaning—conjunction reduction
or gapping may occur: compare (2) and (8). If, on the other hand, identity
is provided by lexical items that are coreferential or synonymous without
being identical, it is assumed that reduction cannot occur, or the deletion
would not be recoverable. In cases like these, as pointed out by G. Lakoff
(personal communication), the identity may be one of sense or reference or
both. For example:

sense: Bachelors eat Wheaties and unmarried men enjoy their break-
             fast.
reference: Nixon watched the football game, and then the President
             played checkers.

But in (3), (4), and (5), there is no overt identity present, nor is there identity
by any obvious sort of synonymy. In (3) we can say that, since *John* and *his*
are understood as coreferential, the common reference constitutes the common topic (thus contrast (3) with an otherwise identical sentence in which
Harry's is substituted for *his*: it becomes much less acceptable). But in the
other sentences, we cannot do this. To understand them at all, the hearer
must supply, from his experience or knowledge of the world, or from prior

discourse he has participated in, additional facts that link something in one conjunct to something in the second. That is, he must make *presuppositions* about the overt elements in the sentence, and the presuppositions he makes, though they have no overt form in the superficial structure of the sentence, very definitely affect the acceptability of sentences. Further, the speaker or hearer often must do still more, in order to understand what appears to be relatively normal instances of conjunction: given the two conjuncts, and any of several presuppositions, one may not yet have enough information to figure out why the two sentences have been, or may be, conjoined: one must then, in addition, perform deductions based on these presuppositions and their relationship with the overt elements of the sentence. Not much will be said here as justification for this notion of deductions as part of the equipment needed for understanding and explaining conjunction. The reader is referred to G. Lakoff (1971) for full discussion. I will discuss a few examples here, however, to show how different possibilities of presupposition and deduction allow one to understand sentences that might be impossible to assign meanings to otherwise; or allow one to have two interpretations of a single sentence, though the sentence is not one that would be considered ambiguous under any normally-accepted definition of this term.

The simplest type of presupposition illustrated here is that of identity, in (2): the first instance of *John* refers to the same person as the second. This does, of course, involve the speaker's or hearer's knowledge of the world, but once he knows the two individuals are the same person, he need do no more. In (3), he must know that *John* = *he* (*his*). In (4), the hearer's work gets harder. He must know from external sources that John is a New Yorker. Then he can make the presupposition of (partial) identity: *John* (and *New Yorker*) is automatically included in the set of (all) *New Yorkers*. This partial identity, or identity by inclusion, is apparently sufficient. In (5), we must make presuppositions as well. Here a set of presuppositions, plus two deductions based on them, appears to be necessary.

a. There is a proverb, "an apple a day keeps the doctor away."
b. This proverb means that if you eat apples you will not need to visit doctors, because you will be healthy.
c. By this reasoning, if you believe the proverb, people who never see doctors are (or may be) people who eat apples.
d. John eats apples = people eat apples.

Of this series of statements, the first two are presuppositions. The third and fourth are clearly deductions based on the presuppositions plus the overt elements in the sentence. The main point, in any event, is that this sentence is harder to understand and less likely to be universally acceptable than the foregoing sentences because the process of figuring out the relationship of identity is much harder and depends as well on special, albeit widespread, knowledge. As an example of a sentence that is acceptable to a smaller group, or generally harder to understand, because of even more specialized knowledge being involved in the deductions, consider (12):

> (12) John wants to make Peking Duck, and I know that the A&P is having a sale on hoisin sauce.

This sentence is not immediately intelligible, I think, unless one knows that Peking Duck is typically served with a sauce consisting largely of hoisin sauce. Moreover, the sentence will be better for a person who does not know this, but knows that both are items of Oriental cuisine, than for someone who does not even know this much. Therefore, those people who find (12) intelligible and acceptable would cease to find it so if *hoisin sauce* were replaced by *ketchup*. A sentence like (12) is intelligible on at least two levels: one may make either of two alternative sets of presuppositions + deductions with (12) to arrive at the conclusion that it is satisfactory. Thus, for the first situation, where the hearer knows about the direct relationship between Peking Duck and hoisin sauce, work need only be done on the right-hand side:

1. (presupposition): Hoisin sauce is the usual accompaniment to Peking Duck.
2. If there is a sale, it is a good opportunity to buy what is on sale.
3. Therefore, now would be a good time to make Peking Duck.
4. to make Peking Duck = to make Peking Duck

    I am not sure that it is right to claim that this sentence is understood as involving a deduced identity relationship, but certainly the two contain a great deal in common.

In the other case:

1. Peking Duck is an item of Chinese cuisine.
2. Hoisin sauce is an item of Chinese cuisine.
3. item of Chinese cuisine = item of Chinese cuisine

And here again there is deduced identity.[2]

---

[2] In a sentence like this—actually not very uncommon in use—we come to grips with a conflict involving the definition of *ambiguity*. Typically, in the literature of transformational theory, ambiguities were considered to be of either of two types, both involving some element or elements present in the superficial structure of the sentence.

   In one type, the relationship between the immediate constituents in surface structure, without recourse to labeling, was sufficient for disambiguating the sentence (like *They don't know how good meat tastes*); in the other, the constituents had to be labeled, with

With respect to these facts, the behavior of subjects presented with hierarchies like (2)–(7) is noteworthy. Virtually everyone accepts (2)–(5) without much question. But at (6), the more ingenious speakers of the language have a chance to show their mettle. It is at this point that certain speakers say things like, "Well, you might get this sentence if you assumed. . . ." The fact that people can sometimes assign meanings to sentences like (6) should not be considered as a counterexample to this analysis. In fact, the behavior of those who do find interpretations is striking evidence that there is a real difference between (6) (and, to a lesser extent (5)), and the other sentences. If the presuppositions and deductions are straightforward, fairly few in number, and culturally widespread rather than idiosyncratic, no one will feel the need for interpretations. Thus, if I gave a subject (2) and asked if he found it grammatical, I would be quite surprised were he to say, "Yes, presuming that John in the first part is identical to John in the second." Only a quibbler would even think of such things. No one needs to be particularly ingenious to imagine a situation in which John = John. A little more complex because it depends on knowledge of the world, but basically the same as (2) is (13):

(13)   Cassius Clay eats apples, and Muhammad Ali drives a Ford.

But with sentences like (1) and (6) the likelihood of finding an interpretation is really quite unlikely, except as an asymmetrical conjunction (see below). With (2)–(5), speakers will differ in their ability to find an inter-

---

different labelings disambiguating the sentences (as in *Visiting relatives can be a nuisance*). But in both recourse to some form or other of the superficial tree would distinguish between the readings. Consequently, if a hearer was uncertain which of the two ambiguities was intended, he might attempt to make the speaker clarify the matter by paraphrase, with one paraphrase for each possible tree: 'Do you mean, Relatives who visit, or If one visits relatives?' (Or, in somewhat more sophisticated terminology, 'Is Visiting relatives dominated by NP or S?') But in a sentence like (12) none of this pertains, yet there are, at least, two alternative readings of this sentence, as has been shown. The superficial trees are identical in every respect, and in fact they are identical throughout their derivational histories, except for the presuppositions that one invokes (which are not a part of the constituent structure proper). This must differ from a sentence that can be understood only in terms of one possible set of presuppositions and deductions, or a sentence that has many more such possibilities. Yet we cannot call such a sentence ambiguous in the usual sense: note that a hearer, faced with such a sentence and uncertain as to what was meant, reacts in a rather different way from a hearer in an analogous situation with a true ambiguous sentence, who paraphrases. In this case, there is no possible paraphrase: rather, what one does is attempt to get a clearer definition of the relationship, to see why the speaker used *and*: he will attempt to provide the situation in which one or another reading is appropriate: 'Do you use hoisin sauce in making Peking Duck?' for the first type; 'Is Peking Duck an item in Chinese cuisine?' for the second. We can call this *situational* or *contextual*, as opposed to *structural* ambiguity, to indicate that this sort of thing partakes of some of the problems of the other types of ambiguity, but behaves differently. It is worthy of note, however, that unless we include presupposition and deduction as items in our semantic representation somewhere we will be unable to discuss this type of ambiguity at all, much less relate it, formally or otherwise, to structural ambiguity.

pretation, as well as in the interpretations they find. In fact, it seems true that the harder it is to find an interpretation, the more numerous the possibilities speakers discover will be.

Thus it seems that, for sentences to have a common topic, it must be possible to combine overt items, common presuppositions, and deductions to get a statement of identity as a result involving at least one of the items in each member of the conjunct. The sentence will generally be better the commoner the presuppositions and the fewer in number they are.

Let us turn now to the second question posed above. The criteria just given would appear to predict that sentence (14) was better than (2), and (15) better than (13).

(14) John eats apples and John eats apples.
(15) Cassius Clay eats apples, and Muhammad Ali eats apples.

This is clearly ridiculous, as these sentences are tautologous and therefore very bad. (In fact, most speakers will undoubtedly not even attempt to assign meanings to them, once they have been warned not to try the intensive sense of conjunction: *John ran and ran,* and so forth.) Similarly, sentence (7) is bad, a contradiction, though it obviously has identical elements in the two conjuncts. Sentence (6) no more obviously lacks a common topic than does (9), yet (9) is much better than (6). How are we to deal with these cases?

If we match each constituent in one member of a conjunct with its corresponding constituent in the other members of a conjoined sentence, in theory any pair may reduce to identity or complete synonymy, and therefore, in theory, all pairs might. Now clearly this theoretical possibility does not occur in English, and undoubtedly not in any natural language. If there are *n* paired conjuncts in two conjoined sentences, the largest possible number of identical pairs we can expect to find, and not be dealing with a redundant sentence, is $n - 1$. This will be true whether the identity in question is lexical and superficially obvious (*John = John*), whether synonyms are employed (*bachelor = unmarried man*), or facts that lead to deduced or presupposed synonymy are to be taken into account (*apples = fruit, Cassius Clay = Muhammad Ali*). These facts are merely the reverse of the coin discussed earlier: that at least one set of paired constituents must be reducible to partial or complete identity, in one of these ways, for a conjunction to be appropriate. That is essentially what is meant by *common topic,* and further implied by this name is the notion that, if only one pair is identical, this cannot be just a random pair, but, in some sense, the identity must involve that pair of constituents in the two conjuncts that are *what the sentence is particularly about.* This, I think, is the normal way in which conjoined sentences are interpreted. For this reason, the sentences (16)–(20) are odd: there are too many identical constituents in each.

(16) *John eats apples and John eats apples.
(17) *John eats apples and John eats fruit.
(18) *Cassius Clay eats apples and Muhammad Ali eats fruit.
(19) *John eats apples and John eats fruit in the yard.
(20) *Cassius Clay eats apples at 9:00 and Muhammad Ali eats fruit at
     3:00 in the yard.

It is not evident at this point whether any adverbial is to be thought of as a
matching constituent for any other adverbial, or whether matches may only
be made between two identical types of constituents. It would seem that the
first is the better solution because of the unacceptability of (21), which is as
bad as (20):

(21) *Cassius Clay eats apples at 9:00 and Muhammad Ali eats apples
     in the yard.

Related to the question of the nature of redundancy in conjunction is its
opposite, the nature of contradiction. The solution, or partial solution,
given above to prevent redundancy conjunction will not help with this, of
course. For a sentence like (7) obeys the rule that $n - 1$ of the paired constituents and no more will be identical (actually, only one pair is identical,
by any of the means of achieving identity), and yet the sentence is bad. The
rule here is something like this: if the paired constituents that compose the
common topic are identical, and all other pairs are similarly identical,
overtly or by deduction, except for one; and this pair is such that, if one
member is A and one B, $A = \sim B$, again explicitly, or by deduction, the
conjunction will be contradictory. The effect of a situation like this will
be that the second conjunct denies an assertion or presupposition made in
the first. Of course, if one of the nonopposite pairs is not identical, then
contradiction need not result, as in (27). I feel that this definition is subject,
no doubt, to numerous counterexamples, and seems to be too simple to
account for so complicated a phenomenon. I offer it more as a start towards
a solution, than a solution in itself. I think, however, that it serves as a
way to classify the sentences (22)–(29), which range from complete acceptability (29) through acceptability in certain highly special readings (28) to
completely unintelligible utterances (22). Sentence (28) is perhaps of especial
interest here: it will be grammatical if *can* means here, 'is allowed to' (for
example, for medical reasons); or 'can tolerate them' (again, for medical
reasons). But it will not be good if *can* is used in the literal sense of 'is
able' (physically): thus, if he cannot eat apples because the entire world
crop was destroyed by locusts, or he has no teeth, or no stomach, or the
like. *Can't* in the sense 'not be permitted to' is not counterfactual: it does

not presuppose that its complement will not take place. But *can't* meaning 'be unable to' is counterfactual in this sense.

(22) *John eats apples and John doesn't eat apples.
(23) *John eats apples and John doesn't eat fruit.
(24)   John eats apples and he doesn't eat pears.
(25)   John eats apples and he doesn't buy apples.
(26) *John eats apples in the kitchen and he doesn't eat apples.
(27)   John eats apples in the kitchen and he doesn't eat apples in bed.
(28)   ?John eats apples and he can't eat apples.
(29)   John eats apples and Bill doesn't eat apples.

There is another point that should be noted with reference to the appropriateness of conjunction with *and* under various circumstances. In normal discourse, one will not say something that is already assumed to be known to the other participants in a conversation: although doing so will not produce a false sentence, nor deny explicitly any presuppositions, it will still be avoided. So for example, I will not ordinarily say, in the course of a discussion about the weather, "It is winter here now," even though it is true and perhaps relevant as well: it is also empty, in the sense that it gives the hearer no information he is not already in possession of.

The fact that such constraints figure in language use helps to account for the fact that certain conjoined sentences with *and* are odd although a common topic is present and neither conjunct denies any presupposition made by the other. Consider sentences like the examples below:

(30)   John has a Ph.D. in linguistics and he can read and write.
(31)   Felix is a cat and he has four paws.

The odd thing about sentences like these is analogous to that in the conversational situation discussed above, with one exception: in the case above, the oddness was brought about because of presuppositions arising from the knowledge of the world held by participants in a normal conversation; but in (30) and (31) the oddness arises out of the conjunction itself: the first part involves certain presuppositions that make the second part empty. The strangeness of sentences like these, then, involves a combination of explicit linguistic information and knowledge of the world. Thus, to say of someone that he has a Ph.D. involves a chain of deduction, part of which contains the idea that he has completed a course of study, therefore, presumably, has been forced to do reading and writing as a prerequisite for earning the degree. Hence the additional information in the second conjunct is, by virtue of the prior statement of the first conjunct, already one of the assumptions the hearer is expected to make about John. Contrast with this (32):

(32)   John has a Ph.D. in linguistics and he can't read or write.

With the normal sense of *and*, this sentence is now odd in a way complementary to the oddness of (30): The second part of the conjunct denies the
presupposition made by the first, yet *and* is used. In (30), by contrast, the
second conjunct expressly states a presupposition made in the first, and it
is odd for that reason. That is, a sentence like (14) is really just the limiting
case of a conjunction that is out on the grounds of redundant information;
since the two conjuncts are perfectly identical, every presupposition made
in the first is expressly reflected in the second. It should also be pointed out,
with respect to cases like these, that it is redundancy of semantic information
that makes these sentences bad, rather than (as might appear true from a
mere examination of the superficial structure) phonological noneuphony
brought about by too great similarity in sound. Thus, although (33) sounds
worse than (34), the latter is really just as anomalous (if in both the two
subjects are assumed to be coreferential).

(33)   The bachelor saw a movie and the bachelor saw a movie.
(34)   The bachelor saw a movie and the unmarried man watched a flick.

There is one more nonobvious type of bad conjunction. This is the situation seen in sentences like (1) and (10), where there may be a common
topic, or at least it is theoretically no more difficult to deduce a common
topic in sentences like these than in many other cases we have examined
that are perfectly acceptable. Yet these sentences are far worse than they
ought to be, if the presence or absence of a common topic were the single
relevant factor governing the grammaticality of conjoined sentences. The
problem with sentences like these lies purely in the tense, or perhaps we
should say aspect, of the verb: in one member of the conjunct it is generic,
and true for all time; in the other, it is specific, and refers to a particular
point in time. How are we to account for this? It could easily be solved in an
ad hoc manner, by requiring that verbs in conjoined sentences match in the
feature [+ stative], or something similar. This would describe correctly one
set of impossible conjunctions, but it would not explain why they are impossible: whether we are dealing with contradictions in features or whether
the difference in the semantic structure of the verb precludes the establishment of a common topic. I would opt in favor of the second suggestion: these
sentences do not sound contradictory to me: rather, the feeling I am left with
is, 'What has the first member to do with the second?' (since they describe
such different types of things). But this raises the notion once again of what
can be a topic, let alone a common topic, of a sentence or set of sentences.
Ordinarily this name is reserved for something dominated at some point
in the derivational history by a NP: this will work, obviously, for subjects,

objects, and prepositional phrases, and rather less obviously, but quite likely, for verbal elements, according to recent analyses of VP's as degenerate S's, which are in turn complements of higher sentences, and therefore in turn at some level of analysis NP's. But here we are dealing with what had been thought of as a *feature* in the lexical entry of a verb, and no theory I can imagine would identify a feature as an NP. Then either we must redefine the notion of *topic,* or redefine our verbal system, so that what had been considered a feature [+ stative] will be something that can be analyzed as dominated by NP, on the basis of independent, non-*ad hoc* analyses. Since recent work has suggested an analysis of tenses as verbs, taking main verbs as parts of their complements, perhaps it is time to consider aspectual distinctions in this light. The facts presented here would be most amenable to a treatment of this sort: this does not imply, of course, that they constitute proof of, or even evidence for, any such view. Meanwhile, it should be pointed out that a conflict in stativity does not preclude asymmetric conjunction, as will be discussed in the following section.

2. *And*: Asymmetric

It had been assumed until relatively recently that there were two, more or less homonymous, *and*'s: one of which simply linked two or more sentences, and the other of which imposed an order of priority on the sentences it linked. This second, asymmetric *and,* was thus equivalent to *and then,* in either a temporal or a causal sense.

Lakoff and Peters (1966) claim that asymmetric *and* is reducible to symmetric *and* plus *then.* But their justification for this claim rests on a somewhat improbable assumption, that *and then = and after it S,* where S = the first sentence. The problem here is that *after* is not a fully analyzed notion, and itself involves aspects of the meaning of *and,* so that the argument is circular. Further, they made this claim in order to support their hypothesis that phrasal conjunction could only be symmetric, now acknowledged to be false.

A more serious claim to the same effect is made by McCawley (1971). McCawley relates asymmetric *and* (through *and then*) to the tense verb. He concludes that (35) and (36) are bad for the same reasons.

(35) *The Lone Ranger rode off into the sunset and mounted his horse.
(36) *John leaves for New York tomorrow, and left for Chicago yesterday.

This is perfectly reasonable. The only point with which I would take issue is that, again, *then* (the notion of temporal-causal priority) is itself not basic. If you explain away asymmetric conjunction by reducing it to *and then,* you must then explain the meaning of constraints on the use of *then.* It would also be useful, though it has never been done and will not be done here, to discuss the relationship between temporal and causal priority, since they share so many syntactic properties, as well as use much the same vocabulary (*when, after, then, since* may all refer either to time or cause).[3] Let us turn now to an examination of asymmetric conjunction, to see how it differs from, and what it has in common with, symmetric conjunction.

Symmetric conjunction freely allows for any number of conjuncts in a sentence. It is of course possible to combine more than two conjuncts asymmetrically, but there is a tendency, when this is done, to interpret the whole sentence as consisting of one main pair, the members of which themselves are broken up into conjuncts. Compare a sentence like (37), which is symmetric, with (38), which is asymmetric.

(37) What a night we had last night: The fuzz came in during the party, and the cat kept dropping the kittens into the punch bowl, and Mary screamed when Bill tried to abduct her, and the strobe light never did arrive.

(38) Well, the story is as follows: The police came in, and everyone swallowed their cigarettes, and Bill choked on his, and they had to take him to the hospital, and his mother just about went frantic when she heard, and I had to placate her by lending her my copy of *Portnoy's Complaint*.

In a symmetric conjunction like (37) the members may change their respective order without changing either the grammaticality or the meaning of the sentence. This is not true with asymmetric conjunction. Compare (39) and (40), of which the first is symmetric, and the second not. Their reversals are (41) and (42) respectively.

(39) Mary is eating toast and Fred is chasing the aardvark.

(40) The police came into the room and everyone swallowed their cigarettes.

(41) Fred is chasing the aardvark and Mary is eating toast.

(42) Everyone swallowed their cigarettes and the police came into the room.

If (42) is good at all, either it is as a symmetric conjunction, or it makes very different assumptions about causality than does (40). In other words, (39) is essentially synonymous with (41) as symmetric conjunctions, but as

---

[3] A possible explanation for this similarity, found in English as well as many other languages, has recently been suggested by G. Lakoff (1970b). In this work Lakoff discusses specifically the identical form of prepositions of place and of time (for example, *in that year, in the garden, from the store, to the house, from 3:00 to 10:30*), and suggests that this identity may be due to the fact that the corresponding temporal and locational concepts share certain axioms. The same might be said of temporal and causal priority.

asymmetric conjunctions, (40) and (42) are not synonymous. We must assume therefore some difference in underlying semantic representation of sentences of these types that can explain this very crucial distinction.

Another question that can be raised involves the difference in the discovery and definition of the "common topic" in symmetric and asymmetric conjunctions. In the latter, we can see that at least some of the constraints on what could be conjoined appropriately may be relaxed. For example, sentences containing one conjunct with a stative or generic verb, another with a verb of punctual time, like (1) and (6), are generally unacceptable in symmetric conjunction, as noted earlier. But under some conditions they may be acceptable and interpretable as asymmetric conjunctions. They may be interpreted this way, it seems, if the generic comes first: it will then establish a true-for-all-time condition for the causation of the second, punctual conjunct. Therefore (43) may be interpretable.

(43)   Six men can fit in the back seat of a Ford and I wrote my grandmother a letter yesterday.

This sentence is grammatical if we make a set of assumptions like the following: I made a bet sometime previous to yesterday that, if six men could fit in the back seat of a Ford, I would write my grandmother a letter. It was duly proved that six men could do this, so yesterday I did what I promised.

For obvious semantic reasons, however, a sentence like (1), with the punctual verb first, cannot be assigned an interpretation even as an asymmetric conjunction. The reason for this is that something that is eternally true can reasonably be expected to provide the conditions under which something that occurs at a specific moment may occur, but not the reverse.

Additionally, there is a difference between symmetric and asymmetric *and* with respect to presupposition. With symmetric conjunction, it seems probable to me that none of the conjuncts is presupposed, but all are asserted. With asymmetric *and,* the first member of the pair is presupposed, in order for the second to be meaningful. Thus, to return to sentence (37) above, one might object to such a statement by saying, *But the fuzz didn't come in at all,* just as one might object similarly to any of the other members of the conjunct, without creating a nonsensical situation or denying the validity of the rest of the conjunction. But in (38) if one attempts to reply in a similar way—*But the police never came in*—the result is bizarre, and renders the whole discourse somehow nonsensical, the usual result of denying a presupposition. In this way too it would appear that asymmetric *and* works quite differently from symmetric *and,* a difference that does not follow naturally from any known properties of *then.*

Symmetric and asymmetric conjunctions differ in other significant ways. A sentence like (37) is understood differently from (38): in (37), each conjunct is understood as no more closely bound to or independent of the conjuncts it precedes or follows than are any of the others: viewed from any point in the complete sentence, each conjunct retains its integrity, and none particularly adds to the meaning of any other, nor does the fact that a string of other conjuncts preceded it make a later conjunct intelligible. Taken out of context, any of the conjuncts could function as a complete sentence, with no need for any of the others. This is typical of symmetric conjunction. When teachers of composition inveigh against stringing sentences together with *and*, it is unnecessary symmetric conjunction they are against: I feel, at any rate, that stylistically (37) is more objectionable than (38), although of course they are both perfectly grammatical and normal sentences of unpolished oral English.

Sentence (38) works quite differently. Here, the whole is, in a sense, greater than the sum of its parts: besides the stringing together of a number of facts (the sum of the parts), the whole also includes the idea that each one led up to the next, and that one would not have occurred, or would not be true, except that the ones that preceded it were true. Taken out of context, the conjuncts would not retain this causal or implicational link, so that part of the meaning of the sentence would be lost. Each of the later conjuncts presupposes all the earlier ones, and in addition deduction may be necessary to see how one leads to the next; with symmetric conjunction, deduction is not necessary in this regard, though it is necessary in discovering the common topic. Notice, therefore, that (37) must have a clear common topic, in this case something like, "the horrors of last night." But (38) need not have such a clearly-delineated common topic as an introduction. In fact, some of the events in (38) might be pleasant, or neutral; this is not so of (37), unless the stated common topic is broadened. Thus, the common topic constraint either is relaxed in asymmetric conjunction, or is represented in another way.

The question raised here may be rephrased: In what way does an asymmetric conjunction resemble a symmetric one, and where do they differ? I think it would be desirable to say that asymmetric conjunction is just a special case of symmetric conjunction, being more constrained but not really different, and I believe there are reasons to say this, though the arguments are by no means self-evident. This is, of course, similar to what McCawley hypothesized; but I think the claim is better made on different grounds.

In symmetric conjunction, a common topic is necessary if the conjunction is to be acceptable. Sometimes the elements of these are sentences like (3)–(6). In sentences like these, if one cannot make the presupposition, 'x and y share property z', then one cannot arrive at the notion of "common topic," or derive a grammatical interpretation of the conjunction as a whole. For example, consider the following symmetric conjunctions:

(44)   John owns a yacht and Bill has a lovely home in Scarsdale.
(45)   Doctors are rich and lawyers marry pretty girls.

Compare with these the following:

> (46) *John owns a yacht and Harry has a $30,000 mortgage on his house.
> (47) ?Doctors are rich and house painters marry pretty girls.

How do the pairs differ from each other? Superficially they have identical structures. The difference is that, in the first two, one can quite naturally make a presupposition about each of the members of the conjoined sentence that will enable one to deduce a common topic; in the second pair, the formation of such presuppositions is far less natural, and consequently there will be much more difficulty in finding a common topic and giving a reasonable interpretation to the sentence. So, for example, a possible (not by any means the only) presupposition one might make for (44) is, "Owning a yacht is an example of conspicuous consumption, and having a lovely home in Scarsdale is too." In (46), there is no such link between the two. In (44), one can proceed from there, defining the common topic as, "cases of conspicuous consumption," or the like. But in (46), there would be no such possibility. Let us turn now to a few cases of asymmetric conjunction.

> (48)   The fuzz came in and everyone swallowed their cigarettes.
> (49)   ?The fuzz came in and everyone started eating their applesauce.
> (50)   John turned up at nine, and Harry left at ten.
> (51)   ?John turned up at nine last night, and Harry is leaving for Brazil
>   when the auditors come.

Here, again, we have two sets of cases, apparently parallel but with different claims as to relative grammaticality. In the first pair, the first seems to make a reasonable claim about causality, while the causal factor in the second is very hard to understand, if possible at all. In the second set, similarly, the notion of temporal priority is easy to see in the first, much harder in the second; there is no reason why the first member of the conjunct should be thought of as preceding the second, or temporally related to it at all for that matter. This situation is comparable to that of the symmetric conjunctions: what one does is make a presupposition about the likelihood of potential causality or temporal priority of one conjunction with respect to the other, just as one makes a presupposition of a similarity between the two symmetrically conjoined sentences. Then the common topic in the asymmetric types is the causality or temporal priority, related to but not identical with the presupposed potential causality or priority, just as the common topic of a symmetric conjunction is related to but not identical with the presupposed relationship between the members of the symmetric conjunct. One difference between the two types is that in symmetric conjunction, it is necessary for only parts of the conjoined sentences to be able to be related by the presupposition in order to insure that one can deduce a common topic; but with asymmetric conjunction, it is the two conjoined sentences as wholes that participate in the relationship, not parts of them. If this is true, then we can say that asymmetric conjunction is but a sub-species of symmetric conjunction; in the latter, the predicate of the pre-supposition can be of any class; but in asymmetric conjunction, the predicate is a member of the small class of asymmetric two-place predicate-taking verbs: *cause* and *precede* are the ones we have discussed. (Obviously, *follow from*, *come after* would be possible variants.) Therefore one might say that symmetric conjunction is a case of ordinary sentential conjunction of two presuppositions that are capable of undergoing conjunction reduction; but asymmetric conjunction comes about when the conjunction of the presup-positions takes place in the base itself, as part of the meaning of the verb, since those that have been identified are members of the class of verbs that require conjoined subjects (see Lakoff and Peters, 1966). But now notice that *similar* is a member of a closely-related meaning-class also requiring under-lying conjoined subjects. What would this mean? First, it is clear that a presupposition like 'A and B are both examples of conspicuous consump-tion' allows the further deduction, 'A and B are similar'. Then, perhaps, what one means by symmetric conjunction, and common topic in connec-tion with it, is 'possibility of reduction by presupposition and deduction to an underlying symmetric predicate', opposed by asymmetric conjunction involving reduction to an asymmetric predicate. There are interesting argu-ments for this: while *John and Bill are similar* is synonymous with *Bill and John are similar*, *John followed Bill* is not at all synonymous with *Bill fol-lowed John*. Moreover, *Bill, John and Harry are (all) similar* is grammatical; a symmetric predicate can take any number of conjuncts. But **Bill followed John followed Harry* is not. This (admittedly inconclusive) evidence suggests that symmetric and asymmetric conjunction with *and* must be considered subcases of the same phenomenon.

3. *But*

But has some of the properties of *and,* plus some complexities of its own. Like *and, but* requires a common topic. Further, there are two possible sorts of general situations in which *but* is appropriate, but as with *and,* and the interpretation of the notion 'common topic' is different in each. First of all, the two members of the conjunct joined by *but* must be related to one another, in some way. Again, the relationship is based on semantic rather than purely lexical similarity.

(52)   John has a yacht, but Bill has a $30,000 mortgage on his house.
(53)   ?John has a house, but Bill has a sore toe.

(54)   John is a Republican, but you can trust Bill.
(55)   ?John is a Republican, but Bill voted for Nixon in 1968.
(56)   *John is a Republican, but Bill will take the garbage out for you.

Several things can be said about the acceptability of these conjoined
sentences. First, the connection need not—in fact, as I shall discuss more fully
later, cannot—be as close between two sentences conjoined with *but* as it
must be with *and*. Thus, having a yacht is similar in various ways to having
a mortgage on one's house, though not as similar as (in a sentence like
(44)) are owning a yacht and owning a house: in both cases, property owner-
ship is involved, though in the first member of the conjunct we are thinking
of this possession as advantageous to the owner, in the second, as disadvan-
tageous. This combination of similarity and difference is what allows the
use of *but,* and in fact forces *but* rather than *and*. In (53), the dissimilarity
is present, all right; but what is odd, or jarring, about the conjunction is
the lack of similarity: having a yacht is not, despite superficial lexical identity, at all the same thing as having a sore toe: this is not one's property,
nor does it result from a conscious and purposeful act of acquisition, but is
inflicted upon one. Sentence (54) is one that is somewhat more problematical;
some speakers of English may not accept it, or may accept it only under
protest. The acceptability of this sentence, however, does not stem from
necessarily inherent properties of Republicans, but rather from the speaker's
feelings about Republicans, based on personal prejudice. If he feels that
trustworthiness is a trait typical of Republicans, he will reject (54), on the
grounds that the dissimilarity implied by *but* is not present; if he feels otherwise, he will accept (54), feeling that there is a dissimilarity between being
a Republican and being trustworthy. In (55), on the other hand, we find a
sentence that will be unacceptable to virtually anyone with any knowledge
of American politics: the problem here is not like that of (53), lack of similarity, but rather lack of dissimilarity. *And* would be appropriate in (55),
but not (except as a joke) in (53). And finally, in (56), it is hard to find an
appropriate interpretation, due to the difficulty of assuming any logical
connection between the two members of the conjunct: while it is possible
and perhaps normal to associate certain traits of character with membership in one or another political party, it is not natural to assume an association between the latter and willingness to take garbage out. (Of course,
if the speaker has known many Republicans, and none would take the garbage out, while members of other political parties in his experience generally would, then a sentence like (56) would be just as good for him as is
(54) for someone who thinks Republicans are not to be trusted. More will
be said on these topics below.)

There is more than one appropriate use of *but,* and the constraints on
its occurrence are somewhat different in the two cases. Compare sentences
like the following:

(57) John is tall but Bill is short.
(58) John hates ice cream but I like it.
(59) John is tall but he's no good at basketball.
(60) John hates ice cream, but so do I.

In each of these sentences, we can begin by asking precisely where the "difference" lies that allows the use of *but*. In the first two, it is apparently present overtly, in two of the lexical items in each sentence, which form a pair of antonyms in each case. There is no relationship, implicit or otherwise, between the two parts of the sentence except that the subjects of the two sentences are directly opposed to each other in a particular property: there is no reason to assume that, since the first part of the sentence is true, the second should be false; no conclusion about the second member of the conjunct is derivable from the first, insofar as we know from the sentence itself. Let us call this, then, the semantic opposition *but*. In the last two sentences, however, there are no pairs of words that are opposed: in fact, in (60), the same lexical item (*hates*) is apparently contrasted with itself. Here *but* is used without any notion of semantic opposition. But there is clearly a difference implied between the two members of the conjunct: it is significant that in these cases, using *and* instead of *but* would produce a greater change in the meaning of the conjoined sentence as a whole than that change of conjunction would produce in the first two sentences.

In a sentence like (59), there is a presupposition implicit which has no counterpart in the first two sentences. This sentence is composed of an assertion plus a presupposition, and the two functioning together are what condition the use of *but*. The conjunction as a whole is asserted: *John is tall and he's no good at basketball*. What is presupposed is the connection made by the speaker, or the world in general, between being tall and being good at basketball: If someone is tall, then one would expect him to be good at basketball. The presupposition involves a general tendency or expectation: if, on the other hand, it were stated, as, *Someone who is tall is good at basketball*, (59) would be contradictory. We shall refer to this use as the denial of expectation *but*. Sentence (60) is similar. The assertion is *John hates ice cream, and so do I*. The presupposition is: *One would expect* (for whatever reason) *that anything John hated, I would like*. Clearly, the speaker and hearer must be in possession of some special knowledge about John's relationship to the speaker in order for such a sentence to be meaningful (as is not true, for instance, of (59)).

In some sentences, the decision as to which *but* is involved is clear: thus, in (60), denial of expectation is the only possibility. In other sentences, depending on the circumstances, either interpretation might be appropriate. For example, this is true in (61):

(61) John is rich but dumb.

Such a sentence might be appropriate in any of several contexts. For example, if a mother is urging her daughter to marry John, on the grounds that he is rich (a good thing), the daughter might use (61) as a semantic opposition *but*: 'Being rich is a good thing, but being dumb is a bad thing (so it might not be such a good idea to marry him)'. If, on the other hand, one had for whatever reason acquired the notion that rich people were usually smart (without necessarily feeling that smartness was a virtue), one might use (61) as a denial of expectation *but*: 'I have been trying for years to find a rich man to invest in my treacle well. But I've had no luck: most rich men are smart, dammit. Then I met John, and lo and behold! John is rich but dumb'. Therefore, a sentence like (61) is to some extent ambiguous, in that it may be derived from either of two quite disparate types of underlying structures, though it is not ambiguous in the classical sense, in that any part of the assertion may be derived from either of two sources.

As with *and,* sometimes a simple presupposition alone will not suffice to account for the use of *but,* or for the fact that the two conjoints are conjoinable. In these cases, one needs a presupposition in addition to deductions derivable from this presupposition plus the assertion. Since G. Lakoff (1971) discusses these cases at length, there is no need here to belabor the point further. The point here is roughly that made about *and* and deductions previously.

It should be noted, of course, that the meaning of the semantic opposition *but* is not unrelated to the presence of presuppositions. But in this type of sentence the presupposition is a part of the lexical item that is contrasted, rather than residing in the speaker's knowledge of the world, and therefore his expectations. The presupposition here is just that of antonymy: that A and B share all semantic features but one. (That is, an antonym of a word is not one that shares nothing with it, but rather something that is not far removed from being a synonym.) Here is not the place to discuss what distinguishes a near-synonym formally from an antonym: both would differ by one feature only from a complete synonym.[4] And it is also true that, as sentences like (61) show, the notion of antonymy must be extended considerably in applying it to the semantic opposition use of *but*: clearly, *rich* and *dumb* are not antonyms. When true antonymy is present, the subjects of the two conjuncts cannot be identical.

(62) *John is rich but poor.
(63)   John is rich but Bill is poor.

---

[4] As an example of this problem, consider how one would represent in the lexicon the difference between *hot* and *cold,* as well as the difference between *hot* and *warm*. If we considered *hot* and *cold* as differing in that one was [+temperature] (or some such notion) and the other [—temperature], we could explain their opposition, as well as many of their properties with respect to each other. But *hot/warm* will also differ in one essential property: perhaps [±intensive]. Possibly some way can be found to distinguish the properties that are antonym-creating from those that merely distinguish between closely related words. I bring this up here merely to point out that the solution is not self-evident.

If *rich* and *poor* share most semantic features, except for a binary split on 'have money', or something similar, as seems a possible way to look at antonyms, it is hard to say offhand how this situation would be formally distinguished from that of *rich/dumb,* where though many features are not shared, the only reason that *but* may be used in the sentence is the fact that *rich* and *dumb* share one semantic characteristic, and share it in that one is "+" for it, the other "−". (That is, the reasons (61) is appropriate are (1) richness and dumbness are alike in being able to be the objects of approbation or disapproval: good thing/not good thing; (2) richness and dumbness differ in that one is [+good thing], the other [−good thing].)

In our discussion of *and* we identified two types, symmetric and asymmetric. Since *but* involves *and* as one of its components, it would be interesting if we could discover whether one, or both, of these uses of *and* is identifiable in the two uses of *but.* Although the evidence is not as clear as with *and,* I think one can make a case for a symmetric and an asymmetric use of *but.* Consider, first, sentences like the following, with *and*:

(64) Fords can go fast, and Oldsmobiles are safe.
(65) Fords can go fast, and Harry just got a ticket for speeding.

The first of these is the symmetric *and*: the two clauses are reversible, with no significant change in meaning. The common focus involves, 'Good things about various types of cars'. But the second is asymmetric, and involves both a presupposition (the sentence is pointless unless we assume Harry has a Ford) and the notion of causation: being able to go fast may cause you to speed; if you speed, you may get a ticket. In (65), the order of the conjoints cannot be reversed keeping the sentence meaningful.

(66) *Harry just got a ticket for speeding, and Fords can go fast.

Now let us change *and* to *but* in these sentences.

(67) Fords can go fast, but Oldsmobiles are safe.
(68) Fords can go fast, but Harry will never get a ticket for speeding.

The first of these is a case of semantic opposition: two virtues of cars, one a different sort of virtue than the other; or, reasons for choosing a particular make of car, with Fords having one + and Oldsmobiles another. The second, however, is a denial of expectation, along with a set of presuppositions and deductions; (i) Harry drives a Ford, (ii) One would expect that, if you can go fast, you will do so, (iii) If you do so, you may be arrested for speeding. The expectation is combined (in (ii)) with the idea of causation implicit in the asserted *and* conjunction that underlies a sentence with *but.* Therefore, because of the similarity in meaning and use of (64) and (67), and of (65) and (68), we might tentatively identify semantic opposition *but* with symmetric *and,* and say it was composed of symmetric *and* + presupposition of difference in meaning; and similarly identify denial of expectation *but* with asymmetric *and.* One reason to suppose this might be that, if one takes a sentence that is clearly a symmetric *and,* and changes *and* to *but,* the result appears to be a semantic opposition *but;* and similarly with asymmetric *and* and denial-of-expectation *but.* Moreover, the semantic opposition *but* has at least one of the properties of symmetric *and*: it is reversible, as noted above, while denial-of-expectation *but* is not, as (69) and (70) illustrate.

(69)   Oldsmobiles are safe, but Fords can go fast.
(70)   *Harry will never get a ticket for speeding, but Fords can go fast.

If there is a meaningful interpretation of (70), it is in any case quite different in meaning, and in the conditions under which it would be appropriately used, from (68). Thus, it seems likely that the two types of *but* are closely related, semantically and syntactically, to the two types of *and.*

There remain a few odd uses of *but* that do not appear to fall under the generalizations given above. First, we find sentences like the following:

(71)   Bill murdered Alice, but he was caught.
(72)   Bill murdered Alice, but he got away.

Sentence (72) appears to be a relatively straightforward case of denial-of-expectation: if you murder someone, it is expected (in an ideal world, perhaps) that you will be caught. But then why is (71) just as normal a sentence? It does not appear to be a semantic opposition *but,* as it is not reversible. Note that only (73), the analog of (71) is normal with *and.* Sentence (74) might have a grammatical reading, if one is talking about, say, crime in the streets and the need for law and order; but one must first make the presupposition (for whatever reason), 'criminals are expected to get away with their crimes'.

(73)   Bill murdered Alice, and he was caught.
(74)   ?Bill murdered Alice, and he got away.

This suggests that being caught does not run counter to expectations about what happens to someone who commits murder. One distinction between (71) and (73) is that the latter involves straight reportage, as in a newspaper story: the former is more likely to be used if the speaker's emotions (either for or against Bill, or murder, or Bill's being caught) are aroused. It is not clear how this is related to the normal asymmetric *but,* since expectation is not involved; but asymmetric it is, as it cannot be reversed. It may be another type of asymmetric *but*: just as there is a causal or implicational asymmetric *and* (the normal counterpart of asymmetric *but* contrasting with the equally-asymmetric *and* of temporal priority), this seems to be a *but* whose asymmetry derives from temporal priority, rather than causal-related denial-of-expectation.

The second set of problematic cases is this:

(75)   John wanted to be a doctor, but he failed chemistry.
(76)   *John managed to be a doctor, but he failed chemistry.
(77)   John thought he would be a doctor, but he failed chemistry.
(78)   *John realized he would be a doctor, but he failed chemistry.
(79)   John would be a doctor today, but he failed chemistry.

One interesting fact about these is that they differ syntactically from more usual *but*'s in that they cannot be replaced by *although*. Semantic opposition *but*'s tend to be a little strange with *although*, but nowhere near as bad as these.

(80)   ?Although John is rich, Bill is poor.
(81)   Although John is rich, he is honest.
(82)   *Although John would be a doctor today, he failed chemistry.

Compare also:

(83)   John is a doctor today, but he failed chemistry.
(84)   Although John is a doctor today, he failed chemistry.

The latter illustrates the normal denial-of-expectation case: One would expect that, if someone is a doctor, he would not have failed chemistry. But in the sentences of (75)–(79), this expectation is not present. Possibly this should be classified as a special type of semantic-opposition *but* with ellipsis: John would be a doctor today, but he failed chemistry = If John hadn't failed chemistry, he would be a doctor today. Hence the subjunctive with *would be*. But in sentences like (75) and (77), which are semantically similar to (79), there is no such paraphrase. Therefore it would seem that there is no argument for deriving these *but*'s from *if*-clauses (or vice versa).

Related to these odd uses of *but* is an odd use of *and*, which matches in many ways the usual meanings of *but*.

(85)   Moishe married a Gentile—and him a nice Jewish boy!
(86)   John ran off with Linda—and after everything I've done for him!

These *and*'s express surprise that the conjunct that follows them could have taken place, given the facts in the preceding conjunct. In this way, it is equivalent to a denial-of-expectation *but*. However, if one attempts to recast these sentences using *but,* one finds that this can be done naturally only by reversing the order of the conjuncts (and making various other changes).

(87) *Moishe married a Gentile, but he is a nice Jewish boy.
(88)   Moishe is a nice Jewish boy, but he married a Gentile.
(89) *John ran off with Linda, but I did everything for him.
(90)   I did everything for John, but he ran off with Linda.

The starred sentences above are bad in the way that rearranged asymmetric *and*-containing sentences, or denial-of-expectation *but* sentences are bad. When they are reversed, as in (88) and (90), they show the same relationship between the expectations entailed by the first conjunct to the facts stated in the second conjunct, as the original sentences with *and* contain, only in reverse order. (For example, in (85) and (88): One would expect that a nice Jewish boy would not marry a Gentile.) Syntactically these are odd, in that what follows the *and* must be an exclamation, rather than a declarative.

(91) *Moishe married a Gentile—and he is a nice Jewish boy!
(92) *John ran off with Linda—and he did it after everything I've done for him.

(A sentence like (91) is good, of course, spoken as an excuse by another nice Jewish boy who intends to marry a Gentile. But in this case, of course, there is no denial of expectation involved, and the sentence cannot be reversed and *but* inserted, keeping this meaning.)

Finally consider one more use of *but* that does not fall under the general rules stated earlier, in any obvious way:

(93)   John likes Peking Duck, but who wouldn't?
(94)   Mary is a lexicalist, but so is everyone at that school.

These sentences are also severely constrained. The second conjunct must contain, overtly or implicitly most of the semantic material in the first conjunct. By "implicitly," I mean that either it may be deleted under normal rules for deletion (as in (93)), or pronominalized to *so* (as in (94)) or something similar, or else the material in the first conjunct must be able to be deduced from what appears in the second, as in these examples:

(95)   George likes Peking Duck, but all linguists are fond of Chinese food.
(96)   Smith is untrustworthy, but all politicians need careful watching.

Contrast these with:

(97) *Smith likes Peking Duck, but all linguists are fond of Chinese food.

(98) George likes Peking Duck, but all linguists are fond of curry.

(99) ?George likes hamburgers, but all linguists are fond of Chinese food.

Sentence (95) is intelligible only if one makes several assumptions:

1. George is a linguist.
2. Peking Duck is an item of Chinese cuisine.

Compare this with a more ordinary use of *but,* as in (98), where the same two assumptions must be made, but the *but* is that of semantic opposition (*Chinese food* vs. *curry*). But in (95), if we make the same two assumptions, we find no semantic opposition, nor a denial-of-expectation, in the overt sentence. All we find is *Chinese food = Chinese food,* a situation in which *and* is, according to the rules we have formulated, more appropriate.

Another thing true of these sentences is that the focus of the first conjunct (which we can very informally think of as, 'the thing the speaker is interested in talking about') must be logically included in the focus of the second. Thus, if George is a linguist, George is logically included in the set of all linguists. In (93), the rhetorical question *who wouldn't?* really means *everyone does,* and again, *John* is included in *everyone.* This inclusion must either be necessary (as with *all*) or extremely probable (as with *lots of, virtually everyone*). Thus compare:

(100)   John will eat mudpies, but so will lots of lexicalists.

(101)   Bill likes Harry, but he can tolerate virtually anyone.

(102) *John will eat mudpies, but so will some lexicalists.

It is true that (102) has a grammatical reading, but only if John is excluded from the class of lexicalists, precisely the opposite of what must be done to interpret (100): in this case, of course, we have a semantic opposition *but*: *John* versus *lexicalists,* which of course is not the case in (100). There is a noticeable difference in intonation pattern, too, between (100) and (102): which in (100) receives no stress (as expected in an anaphoric expression), is stressed in (102) (as is normal in nonanaphoric expressions). Therefore it is all the more apparent that there is no semantic opposition going on. Yet, unlike some of the other nonopposition uses of *but* discussed above, these cannot be replaced by *and,* and preserve their meanings:

(103) *George likes Peking Duck, and all linguists are fond of Chinese food.

(104) *Bill likes Harry, and he can tolerate virtually anyone.

Therefore we must conclude that there is some opposition somewhere, if this is not to be considered a total anomaly—to the rules of both *but* and *and*. In fact, I think there is one, but not evident from the superficial structure of these sentences.

An explantion is possible, given the assumption that, as advocated by Ross (1968) and others since then, every declarative sentence is dominated by a higher sentence, and a normal declarative sentence has above it the structure (approximately), 'I (speaker) declare to you (hearer) that S'. A logical first assumption under this theory is that underlying (95) is a structure like (105):

(105)

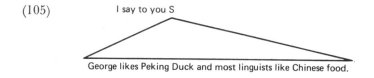

George likes Peking Duck and most linguists like Chinese food.

But this underlying structure tells us nothing about the makeup of sentences like these. It is entirely probable that most uses of *but* and *and* emanate from structures that look like this at some stage in their derivation (what their deepest structure is, of course, is a much more difficult problem, but it seems fairly clear it is not much like (105)), with the necessary presuppositions and deductions present elsewhere in the semantic representation, which will, among other things, provide the environment for the later change of *and* to *but*. But if we adopt this as the structure underlying sentences like (95) along with other more typical uses of *but,* we will have failed to give any account of what these sentences actually mean.

An accurate paraphrase of (95) entails bringing into discussion a number of elements that have no superficial representation in this sentence: a likely candidate is a sentence like (106).

(106) I say to you that George likes Peking Duck, but I really don't have to say this, because all linguists are fond of Chinese food.

The other sentences of this type are also reducible to similar paraphrases. In fact, if someone says, *George likes Peking Duck,* a second speaker can say, as a rejoinder, *But all linguists are fond of Chinese food.* The purpose of his rejoinder, in its normal conversational use, is to ask politely why the first speaker bothered to say anything, rather than to contradict anything the first speaker said. (Compare another possible reply: "But he refused to

eat any at the restaurant last week.") The paraphrase (106) can be assigned
the underlying structure schematically represented by (107):

(107)

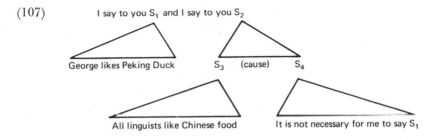

Thus, the *but* that occurs superficially in (95) is actually the product of the
and that conjoins two instances of the performative verb of saying, plus
presuppositions involving these verbs of saying. What are these? We can
identify this *but* as either a semantic-opposition or denial-of-expectation use.
Either *I say* is semantically opposed to *It isn't necessary for me to say*—
positive versus negative statement—or *I say S* implies *It is necessary for me
to say S*, or at least, *It is not necessary for me to say S*. [Since one usually
says things only when there is some need to say them. (Compare Grice's (1968)
concept of "conversational implicature.")] I think the second is somewhat
more likely (that is, the denial-of-expectation), particularly in view of the
fact that *but* here is quite easily replaceable by *although,* which is not generally the case with semantic-opposition *but.*

(108)   Although I say that George likes Peking Duck, I really don't
         have to, because all linguists like Chinese food.

In any event, by including the performative verb in the underlying structure, and relating the conjunction to the performative verb, it becomes
possible to account both for the meaning and for the uses of this *but.*

As has been noted briefly at several points, only certain uses of *but* are
replaceable by *although.* In particular, the denial-of-expectation *but* seems
to lend itself most naturally to this change. When the semantic-opposition
but is replaced by *although,* one finds that, if the sentence is still meaningful, one has inadvertently assumed a denial-of-expectation interpretation.

(109)   John is poor but Bill is rich.
(110)   *Although John is poor, Bill is rich.
(111)   John is a Republican but he voted for Humphrey.
(112)   Although John is a Republican, he voted for Humphrey.

In our discussion of *and,* it was suggested that with the symmetric *and,* the
first conjunct did not appear to be presupposed by the second, whereas it

did with the asymmetric *and*. If the semantic opposition *but* is to be identified with symmetric *and,* and denial-of-expectation *but* with asymmetric *and,* perhaps this behavior of *but* and *although* becomes explicable. For subordinate conjunctions like *although* appear to presuppose the conjunct in which they occur as part of their meaning. If *although* were used with a statement asserted rather than presupposed, it might well be expected that anomaly would result. The semantic opposition *but,* on the other hand, is replaceable by *while,* at least in colloquial speech.

(113)   John is poor, while Bill is rich.

The denial-of-expectation *but* sounds worse when *while* is substituted:

(114)   While John is a Republican, he voted for Humphrey.

This may suggest that when *while* is used, the first conjunct is not presupposed by the second. If this is true, *while* differs radically from other subordinating conjunctions. Of course, these facts do not constitute conclusive evidence.

4. *Or*

Or is in some respects like *and* in its behavior, in others like *but,* and in still others, different from both. *Or* is like the other two in that it requires a common topic between the two conjuncts, and in that this common topic may be overtly present or derivable by presupposition and deduction.

(115)   Either John eats meat, or Harry eats fish.
(116)   Either tigers live in Mongolia, or Hrothgar is a llama.
(117)   *Either John eats meat, or Hrothgar is a llama.

(Sentence (117) may have a grammatical interpretation, of course, if we assume, for example, prior discourse like: John will eat meat only in case it turns out that Hrothgar is not a llama. But this is a rather unnatural set of assumptions.) In (115), the common topic is asserted: in (116), we must presuppose (i) that a llama is not a tiger and (ii) that Hrothgar lives in Mongolia. In both types, we must further assume that one of the two conjuncts is true, and the other therefore is not. Natural language is in this respect different from symbolic logic: except for a very few possible exceptions, *or* must be exclusive. Thus, (115) is equivalent to a combination of both of the following propositions:

(1)   If John doesn't eat meat, Harry eats fish.
(2)   If John eats meat, Harry doesn't eat fish.

Thus, the conjunction is in effect offering a choice between two possibilities, one and only one of which must be true.

Or is in some sense like *but,* in that if one of the propositions is true, one expects the other not to be. But in the case of *but,* this is the result of a presupposition, while in *or,* the choice is asserted. With all the foregoing mention of choice as a factor in the use of *or,* it is tempting to think that perhaps some element like *choose* figures in the underlying structure of *or.* There is not much evidence in favor of this: one small reason for possibly proposing such a representation for at least some kinds of *or* is this: that sentences containing *or* are frequently ambiguous, in that the choice is either assumed to be that of the speaker, or is left up to the hearer, or the participant(s) in the action of the sentence, or some unspecified other person. If we assumed that a real verb *choose* underlay these sentences, we could predict which of the interpretations to expect in a given case according to the assignment of one noun-phrase or another as the subject of *choose.* For example, consider two of the possible uses of (115):

  (i) Either John eats meat, or Harry eats fish. (Which is it? All those pieces of wrapping paper in the kitchen would appear to indicate one or the other, but I don't know which: Only one ever takes place, as far as anyone knows.)
  (ii) Either John eats meat, or Harry eats fish. (Alternately—sometimes one, sometimes the other. When John and Harry get home at night, they look in the refrigerator, and depending on what they find and what each feels like eating, they reach a decision. Both happen, but at different times.)

In (1), the speaker may be asking the hearer to choose, or may be indicating that he himself is trying to reach a decision, and wants more evidence. In (2), the decision is up to John and Harry, not the speaker or hearer: *they* must do the choosing. This provides some exceedingly tentative evidence on which to begin to develop a theory of the underlying structure of *or.*

Like *and* and *but, or* may be used either symmetrically or asymmetrically. For an example, contrast (115) with (118):

  (118)   Either little Seymour eats his dinner, or his mother complains to the neighbors.

This sentence is similar in structure to asymmetric *and* and *but.* In (115), as in the symmetric types of the other conjunctions, the connection between the two conjuncts was in parts of the respective sentences: similarity or contrast in the meaning of lexical items. But in the asymmetric types, like (118), the connection is causal, between the whole of the first conjunct and the second. The difference between asymmetric *and* and asymmetric *or* is that with *and* the relationship between S_1 and S_2 is causal: $S_1 \supset S_2$; while with *or* it is adversative: $\sim S_1 \supset S_2$. Unlike the symmetric *or*, both possibilities are not taken together in these cases: The only paraphrase with *if* appropriate for (118) is equivalent to the first of the two choices given for the symmetric *or*: If little Seymour doesn't eat his dinner, his mother complains to the neighbors. There is of course no implication that if little Seymour behaves properly, his mother will refrain from complaining. As with the other asymmetric conjunctions, *or* as used in (118) is irreversible. This is also the *or* seen in threats:

(119)   Eat your oatmeal or you'll be sorry!
(120)   Don't leave or I'll shoot!

Also asymmetric are what might be called "rhetorical disjunctions," in which the choice offered is no choice at all, much like threats although there is no threat involved. An example is the familiar (121):

(121)   Give me liberty or give me death!

On uttering a sentence like this, the speaker does not mean to imply that death would be an acceptable alternative to liberty. In fact, sentences like these are only intelligible in this way if the second choice is so unlikely that it is obvious no one would seriously choose it over the first.

(122)   ?Give me liberty or give me a salami sandwich!

Further, if the hearer replies to (121) by whipping out a gun and making as though to shoot the speaker, this response will be considered inappropriate. Additionally, of course, these are irreversible. Moreover, they appear not to be subject to reduction, as true choice disjunctions generally are.

(123)   *Give me liberty or death!
(124)   Give me a hot dog or a salami sandwich.

There are several uses of *or* that offer insight into other areas currently in dispute. Consider first of all the behavior or modals and negatives with *or*.

(125)   Either I can answer the question or not.
(126)   I can either answer the question or not.

For some speakers of English, one or both of these sentences will be ambiguous; for others, each will have only one reading (of the two I will be discussing here). The dialectal difference depends on the freedom with which *either* can be moved, but is not of importance to the question I want to discuss here. In the dialect in which *either* cannot move freely, (125) can be paraphrased: Either I am able to answer the question or I am not able to answer the question. (The choice here is not up to the speaker, but up to some unspecified external forces.) Sentence (126) can be paraphrased: I am able to do whichever of the following I wish: either answer the question or not answer the question. Now, leaving aside the presently insoluble problem of the underlying nature of the conjunction itself, the difference between these two readings is reflected in a difference in the underlying structures we can set up for them. (For (125)):

(127)

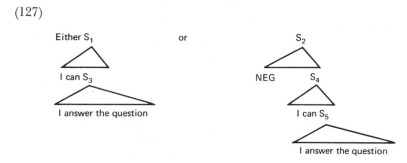

Sentence (126) has the following underlying structure:

(128)

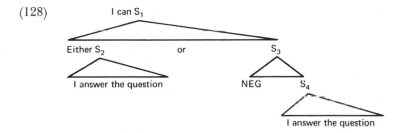

The difference between these two structures is reflected in the differences in meaning and the reasons for them. The significant differences in both cases are in the positions of the modal, the negative, and *or* relative to one another. It should therefore be evident that only a theory in which modals and negatives are verbs that take the "main" verbs of their sentences as parts of their complements can capture these facts in this intuitively satisfying way. In G. Lakoff (1969b), an explanation for the behavior of modals relative to negatives and *either-or* is discussed, and it is shown that this fact is but another consequence of constraints on the movement of quantifiers under certain conditions. This in turn suggests that these conjunctions are, perhaps, at some deep level, similar to quantifiers: hence it would be expected that they share syntactic and semantic properties. McCawley (forthcoming) has in fact given reasons to adopt such an analysis: he identifies

and with the universal quantifier ∀, 'for all', and *or* with the existential
∃, 'there exists'. Aside from logical representation, there are arguments,
noted by Ross, McCawley and myself, for assuming that there is a relationship between *and* and *all, or* and *some*. For example, *and* occurs in the same
sorts of imperative sentences in which *all* is found; in other types of imperatives, *some* and *or* both occur.

(129)   Everybody get the hell out of this room!
(130)   John, Bill, and Clara, get the hell out of this room!
(131)   *Somebody get the hell out of this room.
(132)   *John, Bill, or Clara get the hell out of this room!
(133)   Somebody bring me my glasses.
(134)   John, Bill, or Clara, bring me my glasses.
(135)   *Everybody bring me my glasses.
(136)   *John, Bill, and Clara, bring me my glasses.

But a detailed analysis of conjunctions that shows how they and quantifiers
can be derived from the same underlying source is lacking, especially in
view of the fact that quantifiers themselves are poorly understood in many
ways.

I have made use of the abstract performative verb of declaring at several points in my discussion. Because I believe that overwhelming evidence
has been presented elsewhere in favor of its existence, I have not tried to
justify it here. Along with the assumption of a declarative abstract verb,
generative semanticists assume the existence of several others, including an
imperative and an interrogative, on the basis of similar sorts of evidence as
Ross presented for the declarative. One otherwise inexplicable use of *or*
involves an argument in favor of an underlying interrogative performative
abstract verb; or perhaps it is more accurate to think of questions as introduced by a somewhat more complex abstract underlying structure, 'I request
that you give me information so that I can learn/know whether S', or something similar. The evidence involves sentences like the following:

(137)   Did John leave, or didn't you notice?

This sentence is quite different in its use from others that resemble it superficially in form:

(138)   Did John leave, or did Mary come in?
(139)   Did John leave, or am I dreaming?

Sentence (137) really is not a disjunction between the two overt elements
joined by *or*. Rather, it can be paraphrased, 'Can you tell me the answer
to the question Did John leave, or (because you didn't notice) are you unable

to give me this information?' Otherwise, a sentence like (137) violates the constraint we have already noticed that there must be a common topic between the two conjuncts: the first, as overtly stated, has nothing to do with the second, nor is there any natural reason, judging from only the superficial elements of the sentence, why the two conjuncts should be separated by a disjunction: there is no reason why John's leaving precludes my noticing, or vice versa. But as expanded, the use of *or* turns out to be normal. Also, there are constraints on this use of *or* that are not found elsewhere. The following are rather odd:

(140) ?Did John leave, or didn't Bill notice?
(141) *Did John leave, or didn't I notice?
(142) *Did John leave, or did you notice?
(143) *Did John leave, or will you notice?
(144) *Did John leave, or didn't Nixon get elected?

That is, the elements of the second part of the disjunction are severely constrained, if the sentence is to be interpreted in this way. (140) is perhaps possible, on the condition that the person replying to it is able to speak for Bill, and assumed to be doing so. In a dialogue in which Bill's report of a situation is being discussed, and the person replying to (140) himself is not in a position to ascertain whether in fact John left, this sentence is appropriate, otherwise not. It corresponds in use to what is called "informal indirect discourse" in Latin and other languages. In (141), however, there is no possibility of even this interpretation: if the speaker must ask at all, he obviously didn't notice, so the question is empty. Similarly, (142) is bad because, when we attempt to discover its paraphrase, we find ourselves faced with a contradiction: 'Can you give me the information, or can you not give it to me, because you noticed?' If someone has noticed, then it is assumed that he is able to give the information, rather than otherwise. Alternatively, the sentence may be bad because there is no opposition between the elements of the disjunction, if there is no contradiction: 'Can you give me the information, or can you, because you noticed?' Either interpretation of the sentence is absurd, so the sentence is out. In (143), the sentence is bad because the respondent, in order to be able to give the desired information, has to have already done the noticing, rather than leaving it for the future. And finally, (144) is out, with this interpretation, because Nixon's failure to get elected does not, in any normal situation, prevent the respondent from being able to give the information. (If one can conceive of a situation in which it could, then perhaps this sentence might have a grammatical interpretation based on this situation.) The point here is that both the meaning and use of sentences like (137), and the constraints on what can occur in them, arise automatically, and can be explained, if we assume that an interrogative abstract expression underlies these sentences and figures in both their syntactic and semantic properties. Otherwise I do not think there is any way of accounting for these facts.

Although as we have seen *or* shares many of the properties, syntactic and semantic, of the other coordinate conjunctions, it differs from them significantly in one way, which appears to be a natural outcome of its meaning. With both *and* and *but,* at least in their asymmetric senses, the first element of the conjoined sentence was generally presupposed in order for the second, and therefore, the sentence as a whole, to be correctly interpreted. Therefore there were in both these types corresponding subordinate conjunctions, which made the presupposition of the first conjunct even more obvious. But with *or,* the truth of the first member of the conjunct is never presupposed: if anything, its negative is, if the second member is to be considered true or possibly true. Therefore it is not surprising that *or* should have no subordinate counterpart.

This concludes what I have to say on the subject of coordinate conjunction in English. Obviously not all the problems that could be discussed have been; still more obviously, I have terminated the analysis at a fairly superficial level, stopping before what is probably the most interesting and significant question could be dealt with: what are conjunctions semantically? Although I have failed to come to grips with this issue, I hope that the discussion here may clarify some of the problems, and bring the ultimate solution a little closer. With this aim in mind, then, let me summarize what I believe to be the main points of my discussion.

1. For all conjunction, a common topic is necessary. This may be overtly present in the superficial structure of the sentence, or may be derivable by more or less complex combinations of presuppositions + deductions. In any event, to account for the kinds of superficial structures that are amenable to conjunction, we need to incorporate the concepts of presuppositions and deductions in our grammar.

2. There is a "hierarchy of naturalness" of the presuppositions and deductions: certain ones are universal, or at least assumed to be widespread within a culture; others are confined to a subclass, or are idiosyncratic with the speaker. The more widespread the presupposition, the more likely that the conjunction itself will be accepted by hearers. Hence some sentences that are, apparently, syntactically well formed are unable to be understood; and others, which ought to be ambiguous, have only one usual reading.

3. All coordinate conjunctions occur in symmetric and asymmetric uses, exhibiting different syntactic and semantic properties. In the latter, the first element of the conjunction is typically presupposed in order for the second to be true, though its negation is what is presupposed in the case of *or.* Hence, for *and* and *but,* we find the corresponding subordinate conjunctions *since, although* in these meanings.

4. Aside from these fairly typical uses of the conjunctions, we find numerous "odd" uses that, judging from the superficial forms of sentences alone, are not amenable to the rules we have given. These are commonly subject as well to severe constraints on meaning and co-occurrence. Judging from superficial syntax alone, these constraints would have to be stated arbitrarily. We find, however, that if we adopt some of the proposals independently motivated elsewhere in a theory of generative semantics, or abstract syntax, many of these apparently aberrant cases can be included under the rules, and the constraints become natural and explicable on independent grounds. Some of these proposals, for which evidence has been given here to a greater or lesser extent, are:

a. The existence of abstract performative verbs of declaring and questioning.
b. Modals as main verbs that embed the sentence containing the superficial "main verb" in them as their complements.
c. (For which very little evidence has been given here, but more is building up elsewhere) conjunctions as underlying predicates: more specifically, the universal and existential quantifiers of symbolic logic.

AN ANALYSIS
OF "EVEN"
IN ENGLISH*

Bruce Fraser   Language Research Foundation and Harvard University

* The work reported here was supported in part by a contract from the TEC Company, Tokyo, to the Language Research Foundation, Cambridge, Massachusetts. I thank Steve Anderson, Adrian Akmajian, Robin Lakoff, Mike Harnish, and John R. Ross for suggestions they have made during the course of the research.

Introduction

In a recent paper Chomsky (1969) raises the question whether any level of representation other than deep structure is relevant for determining the semantic interpretation of the sentence. In particular, he questions whether facets of the semantic interpretation such as topic, comment, focus, presupposition, and scope of logical elements can be determined solely on the basis of the information present in the deep structure. He concludes that both deep structure information as well as some information arising from the application of transformations and the rules of the phonological component play a role in determining a complete interpretation—a position I will refer to as the *interpretivist position*. Certainly, before this conclusion can be substantiated, some crucial questions must be answered, not the least of which is the definition of the *semantic interpretation* of a sentence. For example, should notions of focus, entailment, and presupposition be included? Equally crucial is a careful examination of the facts of language which putatively support the claim that surface structure is relevant for semantic interpretation. Only when these facts are clarified and their implications presented can their relevance be determined.

I will be concerned in this paper with examining one of the elements suggested by Chomsky (1969) as supporting the interpretivist position: the adverbial *even*. The *even* under investigation is illustrated in (1). (The scope of *even* has been italicized.)

(1) a. *Harvard will* even *hold a pep rally tonight*. (the entire sentence is the scope)
   b. Even *John* failed the exam. (the subject noun phrase is the scope)
   c. The boys even *destroyed the glass door*. (the verb phrase is the scope)
   d. Harry threw even *the newspapers*. (the object noun phrase is the scope)
   e. We can even see *Long Island*. (the object noun phrase is the scope)
   f. You shouldn't even *try* the toadstools. (the verb is the scope)

I acknowledge in advance that I have approached this investigation with a fair amount of skepticism concerning the appropriateness of interpretivist position for accounting for the facts of *even*. This skepticism holds, in fact, for all logical elements, for example, negation, quantifiers, *only, even, both, also,* and so on. (See the papers by Jackendoff (1969a) on negation, and Partee (1970) on *both*.) The orientation of this paper will be one of attempting to examine the facts of English concerning *even* carefully and then

151

attempting to determine to what extent they really force one to assume the interpretivist position.

The paper is organized in the following way. In Section 1, a general approach for the interpretation of *even* is presented and examples of various English constructions are used to illustrate the approach; in Section 2, the introduction of *even* into the deep structure is discussed. Section 3 examines a number of rules and their restrictions to move *even* from the position immediately preceding its scope to alternative positions; Section 4 presents some potential problems for the position adopted in Section 2; Section 5 contains some suggestions on how the notion of a protected environment can be relevant in preventing unacceptable sentences containing *even*; Section 6 presents a brief summary.

1.   Interpretation of *Even*

1.1   The occurrence of *even* in an English sentence does not alter the basic proposition as does *not,* for example. Rather it introduces two new aspects to the interpretation of the sentence. To see the effect of *even* on the constituent functioning as its scope, let us consider the sentence in (2).

(2)   Even *Max* tried on the pants.

There are at least three parts to the interpretation of (2); these are presented in (3).

(3)   a.   Max tried on the pants.
       b.   Other people tried on the pants.
       c.   The speaker would not expect or would not expect the hearer to expect Max to try on the pants.

The first part of the interpretation, (3)a, is clearly the main assertion of the sentence in (2) and remains unaffected if the *even* is not present. The second part, (3)b, has been labeled a presupposition of (2) (see Fraser, 1969a), but I believe this to be an incorrect analysis. If we accept the notion of presupposition to be the following:

(4)   Some proposition P presupposes a second proposition Q just in case the following conditions obtain:
       a.   If P is true, then Q is false.
       b.   If P is false, then Q is true.
       c.   If Q is false, then P has no truth value; that is, P is then said to be neither true nor false.

we can see that if (3)b is to be taken as a presupposition of (2), then (3)b must be true whether or not (2) is true, and if (3)b is not true, then (2) cannot be either true or false. Now consider the situation where someone utters (2) and is then informed that no one other than Max tried on the pants. Can we say that because (3)b is false that (2) has no truth value? I think not. I certainly agree that there is something very strange about (2) if Max turned out to be the only one to try on the pants, but I think we can still assert that (2) is either true or false depending on the empirical evidence. Thus, rather than assign to (3)b the status of a pre-supposition, I suggest it is an implication of (2), in the sense discussed by Austin (1962). We can say that from (2) one can reasonably infer (3)b; alternatively, (2) implies (3)b.

The effect of *even* on the subject noun phrase *Max* in (2) permits the hearer to make the inference that the referent of *Max* must be viewed as a member of a set of similar tokens with which it (the referent) can be con-trasted within the context of the remainder of the sentence. We will not discuss the notion of similarity of tokens here, but a reasonable estimate would be that tokens with which the scope of *even* is contrasted must share at least the same co-occurrence restrictions. That is, it must be at least semantically possible for the other members of the set to be substituted for the contrasted constituent (the scope of *even*). It follows from this analysis that the sentences in (5) are unacceptable since the scope of *even* in each does not permit a contrast with another token of the same type. (The con-stituent functioning as the scope of *even* is italicized in these and all sub-sequent examples.)

(5) a. *Even *someone* has already arrived.
     b. *Even *who* likes dogs.
     c. *I can't find George even *anywhere*.
     d. *We want to see even *everybody*.

In addition, it follows from this analysis that parts of an idiom cannot be the scope of *even* because, by definition, an idiom is an expression whose meaning is not a compositional function of its parts. (See Fraser, 1970.) Only the idiom taken as a unit can be said to have an interpretation—this is the *sine qua non* of an idiom. For example, in the expression *kick the bucket,* in what sense does bucket have an interpretation or referent? Similarly, in what sense can we say that someone who has kicked the bucket has per-formed a transitive action such as kicking? The sentences in (6) illustrate some unacceptable cases that arise when the scope of *even* is extended to include part of an idiom.

(6) a. *We shot even *the breeze* last night.
     b. *Even *tabs* were kept on John by the F.B.I.

    c. *They have a computer even *at their disposal*.
    d. *You should let off even *some steam*.

Using the same sort of argument, we can show that the third part of the interpretation of (2), (3)c, is not a presupposition as has often been suggested, but an implication. If someone utters (2) and then is informed that Max tries on pants for a living, can we say that (2) is without a truth value? Again, I think not. One problem here is that it is usually not clear whether it is the speaker or hearer who is supposed to be surprised. For example, in uttering (2), the speaker could be expressing his amazement at what he believes to be the case: that Max tried on the pants. It might be that the speaker believes that Max doesn't like pants, is hesitant about trying on pants after others, was sick that day, and so forth. On the other hand, the speaker might very well know that Max really likes trying on pants but believes that the hearer believes the contrary. Thus, the speaker would then be using *even* (as opposed to *also*) to emphasize to the hearer the unexpected nature of the act. There are some sentences such as *Bill dreamt that he had caught a mermaid and that even her tail was green* where it appears that the *even* is a reflex of Bill's surprise at the dream, not the speaker or hearer's state. However, these cases are the exception.

Rather strange sentences arise when the effect of *even* is to imply the contrary of what is generally believed. The examples in (7) illustrate this point.

  (7) a. Einstein solved even *that easy problem*.
       b. Even *God* is omnipotent.
       c. The Boston Patriots lost to even *the New York Jets* in 1969.
          (where in 1969 the Patriots lost to everybody and the Jets beat
          everybody at least once)
       d. It snows even *in Lower Slobovia* in January.

Note that if we suddenly were informed that Lower Slobovia was in the Southern Hemisphere, sentence (7)d would seem far less strange since "summer" would occur in January.

Negation has a systematic effect on a sentence containing *even*: it simply negates the three parts of the interpretation, where the negation of a negative implication is interpreted as a positive implication. The negation of (2) is (8) and the corresponding interpretation is stated in (9).

  (8) Even Max didn't try on the pants.
  (9) a. Max didn't try on the pants.
       b. Other people didn't try on the pants.
       c. The speaker would expect or would expect the hearer to expect
          Max to try on the pants.

1.2 Having presented a general outline for the interpretation of *even* when it occurs in English sentences, I would now like to turn to a number of constructions and examine the effect of *even* on their interpretation.

1.2.1 Comparatives

Comparatives provide a rather interesting example of the interpretation of *even* beyond the simple sentence case. Consider the sentences in (10).

(10) a. Even *Bill* is taller than John.
      b. Bill is even taller than *John*.
      c. Bill is taller than even *John*.

The interpretation of each of these example sentences follows from the model given above in 1.1; for example, (10)a would have the interpretation in (11).

(11) a. Bill is taller than John.
      b. Other people are taller than John.
      c. One would not expect that Bill is taller than John.
          One would expect that Bill is not taller than John.

However, as Fillmore (1965b) observed, there is an additional piece of information expressed in a sentence like (10)a, namely, that relative to the people with whom Bill and Tom might be compared for height, they are both relatively short. Note, for example, that given our knowledge of Tom Thumb and Wilt Chamberlain, the sentence *Even Bill is taller than Tom Thumb* is acceptable while the sentence *Even Bill is taller than Wilt Chamberlain* is very strange. But I think this additional information can be inferred in a systematic way from the interpretation given in (11). Notice that (11)c states that one would not expect the assertion of (11)a to be the case. Why not? The most obvious answer to this question is that Bill is not tall relative to the compared group. And from this we can easily infer that John is relatively short, since the main assertion of the sentence was that Bill was taller than John.

The interpretation of a negative comparative is obtained in exactly the same way. The interpretation of (12) is that in (13).

(12) Bill is not even taller than *John*.
(13) a. Bill is not taller than John.
      b. Bill is not taller than other people.
      c. One would expect that Bill would be taller than John.

By asking why (13)c should be the case, we get the following answer: we would expect Bill to be taller than John because John is relatively short. There could be no other reason, given that we are focusing on John. From this fact, we can infer that Bill is also relatively tall.

1.2.2 Clefting

Cleft sentences provide another case, for no noun phrase functioning as the scope of *even* can be clefted. The sentences in (14) illustrate this.

(14) a. *It was even John who shot James.
      b. *It was even a table she repainted.
      c. *It was even at 5 P.M. that the bell chimed.

The reason for this was pointed out to me by S. Kuno (personal communication): the clefted noun phrase is being placed into prominence in the sentence with the interpretation that it is unique. By clefting the noun phrase the speaker is implying that the rest of the sentence holds for this and only this noun phrase referent. Thus, note the unacceptability of the sentences in (15).

(15) a. *It was Max who lost a dime and Harry did too.
      b. *It was George who he called up and I did too.

But of course the uniqueness requirement conferred by the clefting of the noun phrase directly violates the second part of the interpretation of the sentence when this same noun phrase is functioning as the scope of *even*. For example, for a sentence such as (14)a, we would have as part of the interpretation, the statements in (16).

(16) a. Only John shot James. (due to clefting)
      b. Other people shot James. (due to *even*)

Clearly these two statements are in conflict; thus, the unacceptability of (14)a. Notice, however, that an *even* may occur in a nonclefted part of a sentence.

(17) a. It was the lawn mowing that even *I* objected to.
      b. It's that girl to whom I wanted to give even *a second kiss*.
      c. It was John that we must see even *in San Francisco*.

(An *even* with a sentence scope cannot occur in a cleft sentence.)

Interestingly, the class of noun phrase which cannot function as the scope of *even* (for example, *no one, anyone, someone, all, everyone, each,* and so on) cannot be clefted. This is predictable, for in both cases a function of the construction is to single out the noun phrase in contrast to others. Since this class of noun phrases consists of indefinite noun phrases, a definite referent is impossible to single out.

1.2.3 Conjunction

Conjunction poses numerous problems, especially in stating the constraints on *even*, most of which I do not understand. I can find no examples of the first member of a conjunct functioning as the scope of *even* (for example: *Even *John* and Mary will come tomorrow). The restrictions for *even* on the noninitial member are complex as the following sentences illustrate.

(18) John slept and
    a.   even *Harry* rested.
    b.   *Harry even *rested*.
    c.   ?even *Harry* worked.
    d.   *Harry even *worked*.
(19) Harry rested and
    a.   *even *John* slept.
    b.   John even *slept*.
    c.   *even *John* worked.
    d.   John even *worked*.

The unacceptability of (18)b appears to reside in the relative intensity of *sleeping* and *resting*; notice the acceptability of (19)b in which the order has been reversed. I am at a loss to explain the unacceptability of (18)d, (19)a and (19)c.

We observe that noun phrases formed through sentence reduction may function as the scope of *even*. It is just these cases of sentence reduction that normally may be preceded by *both* (see Partee, 1970). However, *even* and *both* cannot co-occur as the examples in (20) illustrate.

(20) a.   Even
     b.   Both
     c.   *Even both   } Joe and Jane yelled.
     d.   *Both even

Here again I have no satisfactory explanation for these facts.

1.2.4 Concessive Conditionals

Another case involves sentences such as those in (21) which are often referred to as concessive conditionals.

(21) a. Mary will leave even *if John stays.*
      b. Even *if you'd been there,* I would have given up.
      c. Can they succeed even *if Harry helps them?*

While these sentences have the general appearance of conditional sentences, they have no conditional force. The *if* is preceded in each case by an *even* which neutralizes the hypothetical force of the following *if*-clause. The result is a concessional clause, a clause which plays no role in determining the truth conditions for the main clause of the sentence.

We note in passing that there are various constructions such as those in (22).

(22) a. (*Even) If I only had a dime.
      b. (*Even) If you wish, you may stay here.
      c. I wonder (*even) if John will arrive today.
      d. I remember the party as (*even) if it were yesterday.

which resemble conditionals in that they contain the subordinate conjunction *if,* but do not function as such. The sentence (22)a is a wish paraphrased as 'I wish I had a dime', while (22)b is a polite form of giving permission with no conditionality implied. In (22)c the *if* is an alternative form for *whether* as is shown by the fact that optionally it may be followed by *or not.* The *as if* form in (22)d clearly indicates that the following clause is contrary-to-fact; but here also, there is no conditionality involved. We will not be concerned with such cases, and as the examples indicate, none of them permit an *even* to precede the nonconditional *if.*

I will assume without presenting any evidence that the underlying position for all subordinate clauses, in particular the *if*-clause, is following the main clause of the sentence. Thus, in terms of the model for the analysis of *even* presented in Section 1, we would predict the interpretation of a sentence such as (2)b to be that in (23).

(23) a. Mary will leave if John stays.
      b. Mary will leave if other things happen.
      c. One would not expect that Mary would leave if John stays.
          One would expect that Mary would not leave if John stays.

This is exactly the interpretation of such concessive sentences. The parts of the interpretation, when taken together, permit the correct inference that Mary will leave no matter what happens; that is, that there is no conditional here at all. (23)c conveys the information that it would be very unlikely for Mary to leave if John stays. Thus we see that no special type of conditional sentence need be postulated for such concessive conditional sentences: they can be accounted for in a straightforward way within the general framework of *even* already presented.

From the examples discussed thus far, one might reasonably suppose that any conditional sentence may have the conditional clause neutralized by the introduction of a preceding *even,* with the resultant sentence becoming a concessive conditional. This, however, is not the case, and I will now present some exceptions to this general hypothesis.

The first involves conditionals having the main clause as a question.

(24) a. Can they succeed if Harry helps them?
      b. What could I do if John were to pass the exam?
      c. How should Mary travel if it rains tomorrow?

Each of the sentences in (24) is asking for information under the particular conditions specified by the following *if*-clause. There appear to be no syntactic constraints between the form of the questioned main clause and the conditional except various sequences of tense restrictions. There does seem to be some preference for the *if*-clause to follow the main clause, but this appears to be only a matter of style.

There are, however, some very unexpected constraints if the conditional is made concessional. The sentence (24)a is as acceptable as (25):

(25) Can they succeed even if Harry helps them?

but the predominant (and perhaps only) answer to the question is the negative, *no.* That is, (25) resembles a rhetorical question, in that the question implies 'They cannot succeed', not 'They can succeed'.

If an affirmative answer to such a question is possible, it must be with a following qualifying or contrastive clause, for example *Sure they can, if they begin early enough* or *Yes, but there must be clear skies all day.* In light of the approach given above to account for sentences containing even, we would predict the interpretation of (25) to be (26).

(26) a. I want to know if they can succeed if Harry helps them.
      b. I want to know if they can succeed if other things happen.
      c. One does not expect that they can succeed if Harry helps them.
          One expects that they cannot succeed if Harry helps them.

It is the third part of the interpretation, (26)c, that provides the explanation for the negative expectation associated with (25)—the expectation is that they cannot succeed under the condition of Harry helping them. And this follows directly from the approach discussed in Section 1.

A sentence such as (27),

(27)   What could I do even if John were to pass the exam?

if acceptable at all, is certainly related to (24)b but, similar to (26), the expectation associated with the main clause is negative—one expects that I should do nothing. In general, any *wh*-question for which there is a negative form for the questioned constituent (for example, *no one, nothing, nowhere, never*) can occur in question concessive conditionals, although the conditions for acceptability appear to be rather complicated. I find the remaining *wh*-questions unacceptable when made concessional.

(28)   a.   *How should Mary travel even if it $\begin{cases} \text{doesn't} \\ \text{does} \end{cases}$ rain tomorrow?

b.   *Why could Jason figure out the answer even if he had (hadn't) been to school?

It is worth noting here that we cannot predict the unacceptability of the sentences in (28) on the basis of unacceptable declarative form. This is illustrated in (29) where the questioned part of (28) is italicized.

(29)   a.   Mary should travel *by car* even if it (doesn't) rain tomorrow.

b.   Jason could have figured out the answer *because he is smart* even if he had(n't) been to school.

A second restriction on concessive conditions involves the pseudo-imperatives illustrated in (30).

(30)   a.   If you talk I'll shoot Max.
b.   Talk and I'll shoot Max.
c.   Don't talk or I'll shoot Max.

The three sentences are synonymous, and in each case, the first part states the condition under which the second part will hold. (We assume here that (30)b and (30)c are derived from the deep structure underlying (30)a by the deletion of the *if you* and the appropriate adjusting of the negative marker and coordinate conjunction.) But notice that *even* introduced at the beginning of each sentence causes the synonymy to disappear.

(31)   a.   Even if you talk I'll shoot Max.
b.   Even talk and I'll shoot Max.
c.   Don't even talk or I'll shoot Max.

Sentence (31)a is clearly a concessive conditional as discussed above; it states that 'I'll shoot Max no matter what happens—even if you talk'. (31)b, however, has the interpretation that 'I'll shoot Max no matter what you do, even if you talk, walk, or dance'. And (31)c has the interpretation that 'I'll shoot Max but only if you do anything, the most likely thing being to talk'.

There are, in addition to the restrictions just discussed, a number of other, less interesting ones. We briefly mention some of them now. Unfortunately, I can suggest no real explanation for these facts.

First, in generic conditional sentences like (32) the *if* is functioning as an alternative form of *whenever*.

(32)   a. If John comes on time, I leave on time.
   b. If it rains before lunch the game is cancelled.

The sentences in (32) are synonymous with the corresponding ones in (33).

(33)   a. Whenever John comes on time, I leave on time.
   b. Whenever it rains before lunch, the game is cancelled.

However, *whenever* can never be preceded by *even,* though *when* can.
Second, we find conditional sentences like

(34)   a. You will succeed if you really try.
   b. John has enough money for the trip if he is prudent.

where the *if* has the interpretation 'so long as'. The sentences in (34) are not acceptable in the concessive conditional form with the same interpretation.

Third, it is often argued that *unless* is equivalent to *if . . . not* and that the sentence pairs like those in (35) are synonymous.

(35)   a. Unless you leave today, I'll fire you.
    If you don't leave today, I'll fire you.
   b. Unless Henry fixes the bike, we won't be able to go.
    If Henry doesn't fix the bike, we won't be able to go.

Clearly both variations in (35) are conditionals; yet only the second of each pair permits a preceding *even* so as to form a concessive conditional.

(36)   a. *Even unless you leave today, I'll fire you.
    Even if you don't leave today, I'll fire you.
   b. *Even unless Henry fixes the bike we won't be able to go.
    Even if Henry doesn't fix the bike we won't be able to go.

Fourth, a variation of the *if*-clause of a conditional can be formed by deleting the *if* and inverting the subject and the auxiliary, as in forming a *yes-no* question.

(37)   a.   If I had known the facts, I wouldn't have gone.
            Had I known the facts, I wouldn't have gone.
       b.   If he were here now, you could talk to him.
            Were he here now, you could talk to him.

1.2.5   Subordinate Clauses

Another construction involves subordinate clauses of which the concessive conditional just discussed is one case. Observe that there are a number of subordinate conjunctions including *if, after, before, as, though, while,
when,* and possibly *until* which permit a preceding *even,* while *since,
although, for, because,* and *however* (all *even* cases) do not. The sentences
in (38) illustrate such cases.

(38)   a.   John didn't go home even after it was dark.
       b.   I won't agree even if you promise to pay me.
       c.   Mice shouldn't play even while the cat's away.
       d.   Max could play poker even before he was married.
       e.   *Mary took a swim even since it was warm.
       f.   *We didn't try the door even although we knew it was open.

The *even* here has the effect already discussed in Section 1. We note that
there are synonymous alternatives which result when the negation of the
main clause has been extracted, introduced before the *even* and the resultant
not-even clause preposed to the sentence-initial position, with concomitant
subject-verb inversion.

(39)   a.   Not even after it was dark did John go home.
       b.   Not even if you promise to pay me will I agree.
       c.   Not even while the cat's away should the mice play.
       d.   Not even before he was married could Harry play poker.

(See Klima, 1964, for some remarks on negative-attraction of this sort.) However, what is particularly interesting about these cases is that only in preposed concessive conditionals may no negation be present in the *if*-clause.

(40)   a.   Not even after he hadn't reported for six weeks did she worry
            about him.
       b.   Not even while Jack isn't at home does his wife use the phone.
       c.   *Not even if John hasn't called will I go.
       d.   *Not even if John hadn't told me to go would I have stayed any
            longer.

Moreover, this restriction on concessive conditionals appears to be an output condition (see Ross, 1967) in view of the fact that the more basic order (with the subordinate clause last) permits a negated *if*-clause.

(41) a. I wouldn't have stayed any longer even if John hadn't told me to go.
b. Tulips can't be planted in spring even if the flower shop doesn't agree with me.

1.2.6 Pronominal Reference

Another case involves the pronominal reference between the main clause of the sentence and a subordinate clause in which the coreferential noun phrase is the scope of *even*.

(42) a. *If even John could have tried, he could have succeeded.
b. *John leaves on time after even he is sick.
c. *Before Mary found even the red pencil, it had been hidden from view.
d. *Max must begin preparing now because even he can't leave until 5 P.M.

I have no explanation for these facts; similar sentences containing a noun phrase functioning as the scope of *also* are also unacceptable.

2. Introduction of *Even* into Sentence Structures

Kuroda (1965) suggested that *even* (analogous to the Japanese particle *wa*) is permitted only once in a sentence. He claimed that *even* was subject to a global constraint, similar to negation, and suggested that one *even* be optionally introduced into the deep structure. This *even* would be associated with a single constituent, its scope, at some point in the derivation. This is, to my knowledge, the first published suggestion of what is today referred to as the interpretivist theory. Kuroda is certainly correct that an arbitrary number of *even*'s cannot occur in the surface structure of a sentence but I find that there are many sentences in which at least two *even*'s may occur, especially if a negative element is present.

(43) a. Even *I* even gave *a book* to Mary.
b. Jones won't even wave *good-bye* to even *his sister*.
c. Even *words* give trouble to even *linguists*.

    d. Even *an idiot* couldn't even *refuse that offer.*
    e. Even *Henry* won't even *lift a finger* around here.

Although the acceptability of the sentences in (43) is questionable in some cases, the interpretation is usually clear. Analogously, we find cases of double negation such as *No one hasn't kissed Mary* which, in some dialects, are questionable. McCawley has argued (McCawley, 1969c) that the occurrence of a single negative marker in the surface structure of a sentence is an output condition, and I would argue here that the same holds true for *even*. This position—that one *even* per sentence in surface structure was an output condition—was first brought to my attention by W. Watt (personal communication) who pointed out that sentences with two *even*'s appear to be perfectly acceptable semantically, albeit difficult to unravel. Thus a sentence such as (43)c can be paraphrased as (44).

(44) Many phenomena give trouble to people and, surprisingly, words give trouble; moreover, words, unexpectedly, trouble linguists.

The issue here is this: should *even* be introduced into the deep structure associated with the constituent which serves as its scope in surface structure before any syntactic transformations apply; or should *even* be associated with its scope at some (much) later point in the derivation, perhaps even after the phonological component has applied? I shall assume for the sake of argument (and also because I think it is the correct solution) the former position and assume that an *even* is introduced immediately before a constituent (its scope) in the deep structure. The following questions arise and must be answered satisfactorily if this position is to be maintained: (i) can the grammar account for the various positions which *even* may take in a sentence by moving the *even* from its deep structure position; (ii) are there constituents in surface structure arising from the application of syntactic transformation which can function as the scope of *even*; and (iii) are there advantages to this approach over the interpretivist position? We discuss these three questions in the following three sections.

However, before turning to these points, I would like to indicate that some unacceptable sentences containing *even* arise because of a conflict between the interpretation of *even* and some other part of the sentence. I find this to be the case with the sentences in (45).

(45) a. *Even *John* melted her last ice cube.
    b. *Even *only Max* will be there tonight.
    c. *The tallest man in the world is even *very tall.*
    d. *At this very moment, I am even speaking *French.*
    e. *My favorite dessert is even *ice cream.*
    f. *Even *I* hereby concede the election.

In (45)a, there is a conflict between John melting her last ice cube and other people doing it—only one group could possibly be responsible for such an act. (45)b provides a conflict between *only,* which entails that Max and no one else but Max will be there tonight and *even,* which implies that Max and other people will be there. (See Horn, 1969.) The conflict in (45)c arises because one has to expect the tallest man in the world to be relatively tall— on what other basis could tallness be decided? In (45)d, the time adverbial *at this very moment* restricts the action of the verb to one particular time; one cannot be speaking more than one language at a given moment. Perfectly acceptable, however, is the sentence "I am even speaking *French* these days." In (45)e, only one referent can qualify as a favorite dessert, since this adjective denotes a single set of objects. And in (45)f, the sentence cannot be a performative (see Ross, 1968) with the subject *I* as the scope of *even,* because only the speaker can be performing the act of concession when speaking the sentence. Others cannot be simultaneously conceding the election. Thus all the sentences in (45) are ruled out on the basis of the fact that they have an implication which conflicts with some other aspect of the interpretation of the sentence. These cases appear to be but the tip of the iceberg and will remain a formidable challenge, irrespective of which approach to the solution one selects.

3. Position of *Even*

In general, *even* occurs immediately before the constituent functioning as its scope. In addition, there is a requirement that the intonation center (see Chomsky, 1969) must occur within this constituent. Given the function of *even*—to contrast the constituent functioning as its scope with other possible tokens of the same type—the requirement that the primary stress of the clause fall within the scope of *even* is not surprising; contrast in English is normally indicated by a heavy stress. The examples in (46) show a variety of scopes for *even,* the position of *even* relative to the scope, and the location of main stress (indicated by upper-case letters).

(46)   a. *Harvard will* even *hold a PEP RALLY.* (sentence scope)
       b. Even *JOHN* failed the exam. (subject noun phrase scope)
       c. The boys even *destroyed the glass DOOR.* (verb phrase scope)
       d. Harry threw even *the NEWSPAPERS.* (object noun phrase scope)
       e. We can even see *Long ISLAND.* (object noun phrase scope)
       f. You shouldn't even *TRY* the toadstools. (verb scope)

Since the normal position for the intonation center in a declarative sentence is the verb phrase final position, the example in (46)a and (46)c–e require no movement of the normal main stress position. Notice that (46)c and (46)e are ambiguous with respect to the scope of *even*, since it is unclear from the verb phrase final stress whether it is the direct object, noun phrase, the entire verb phrase, or the entire sentence which is functioning as the scope. Sentence (46)d has only one interpretation. The main stress in (46)a and (46)f has been attracted to the scope of *even* (the subject noun phrase *John* and the verb *try*, respectively). However, even though it is generally the case that *even* occurs immediately before the constituent serving as its scope, there are a number of interesting exceptions to this rule and we will now consider them.

I can find no cases in which *even* precedes a sentence which is functioning as its scope. Rather, the *even* usually occurs immediately before the verb phrase as the sentences in (47) illustrate.

> (47) What happened in 1969 that was so exciting? Brady was finally located! Men landed on the moon! Tiny Tim got married! Why,
> a. Harvard even held a pep rally.
> b. The Mets even won the World Series.
> c. John even got a haircut.

In some dialects of English a sentence-final *even* which has sentence scope is permitted; the sentences in (48) illustrate this.

> (48) a. *John went home on time,* even.
> b. *We ought to find out for him,* even.
> c. *Max burped,* even.

I have been unable to find any direct evidence that the *even* having sentence scope should be introduced in the sentence-initial position, from which it must be obligatorily moved to either the verb phrase-initial or sentence-final position. I find that whenever *even* is sentence-initial, it is always interpreted as having the subject noun phrase as its scope.

We have already used examples such as (46)e in which the *even* having an object noun phrase scope has been moved to the left to the verb phrase-initial position. Leftward movement is restricted, at least in my dialect, to just immediately before the verb phrase. An *even* having a direct object or indirect object noun phrase as its scope can move to the verb phrase-initial position but no further. Leftward movement to an auxiliary-initial position (for example, *She even can pick up mushrooms with her toes*) or to the subject noun-phrase-initial position (for example, *Even she can pick up mushrooms with her toes*) both force another interpretation of the scope of *even* for me. Moreover, as *even* having an indirect object scope cannot move leftward to a direct object-initial position without causing a change of scope. Note that no stress change is required when *even* moves leftward in these cases, since the primary stress will automatically go on the verb phrase-final position.

Rightward movement of *even* having a noun phrase scope may occur to the position immediately following the noun phrase. The *even* in these cases must be set off by intonation pauses in order to distinguish its scope from the constituent immediately following it, and the noun phrase often receives an extra heavy stress. However, when the noun phrase in question is sentence final, the rightward movement of *even* will result in an ambiguity of scope for those dialects which permit sentence-final *even*. The sentences in (49) illustrate these points.

(49)   a.   *John,* even, will try out.
        b.   He gave *the book,* even, to Mary.
        c.   You should throw *the ball,* even.

In sentences containing a nonnegative adjectival predicate, an *even* having the subject noun phrase scope is often found in the adjectival-initial position, following the verb *be*. Moreover, there appears to be no emphatic stress in these cases although the intonation rises in the subject-final position. The sentences in (50) are representative.

(50)   a.   *That John is here* is even obvious. (other things are obvious too)
        b.   *The man* is even sad. (the woman is sad too)
        c.   *The fact that the U.S. is bankrupt* is even true. (so is $2 + 2 = 4$)

It is possible to make the adjectives in (50) function as the scope of *even,* but this requires emphatic stress.

Approximately the same comments made in Section 3.2 about noun phrase scope are applicable for prepositional phrases; we will not present them here.

As we mentioned earlier, since the verb is not the intonation center of the verb phrase—unless the verb phrase consists only of the verb which is then in the verb phrase final position—*even* having a verb scope requires that the verb receive primary stress. I will offer no suggestion concerning the best way to assure that the primary stress is correctly assigned to the verb in these cases since the answer depends heavily on the approach one chooses. Neither leftward nor rightward movement is possible for an *even* having a verb or verb phrase scope.

A particularly interesting case of leftward movement of *even* is one which is analogous to negative transportation (see Fillmore, 1963; R. Lakoff, 1969a). With certain nonfactive verbs such as *believe, think, figure, expect* (see Kiparsky and Kiparsky, 1968) the sentence pairs in (51) are synonymous on one of the readings of the second sentence.

(51)   a. I believe that Hubert isn't going to run.
           I don't believe that Hubert is going to run.
       b. They expect no one to begin on time.
           They don't expect anyone to begin on time.
       c. I believe that even *Hubert* will run again.
           I even believe that *Hubert* will run again.
       d. They expect us to even *begin* on time.
           They even expect us to *begin* on time.

All verbs which permit negative-transportation permit *even*-transportation. There are constraints which I do not understand that govern the interaction of negative and *even*-hopping, but I will present no more examples here.

The question arises whether *even* movement obeys the same movement constraints as other constituents. In particular, can it move leftward out of relative clauses, a violation of the complex noun phrase constraint (see Ross, 1967b)? At issue is the putative synonymy of sentence pairs in (52) and (53) on *any* of their readings.

(52)   a. I saw the man who can solve even *that problem*.
       b. I saw even the man who can solve *THAT problem*.
(53)   a. A student who even *votes* is rare.
       b. Even a student who *VOTES* is rare.

I find no identical readings. For example, in (52)a, one man is seen with the unexpected ability to solve many problems including a particular problem; in the second, many people were seen including, unexpectedly, the man who can solve a particular problem. If these and similar sentence pairs are synonymous, as has been claimed (Anderson, 1969), the introduction of *even* in the deep structure associated with its scope, with subsequent possible left and right movement, is cast into question. There are other issues involved here, which I will discuss in the next section.

A related question is whether two separate constituents can simultaneously function as the scope of *even*. Anderson (1969) has argued for this and claims a sentence like (54)c is a combination of (54)a and (54)b.

(54)   a. John can't sell even *whisky* to Indians.
       b. John can't sell whisky to even *Indians*.
       c. John can't even sell *whisky* to *Indians*.
       d. John can't sell even *whisky* to even *Indians*.

I am in basic agreement with this claim, but I suggest in addition that (54)d is acceptable. The occurrence of multiple *even*'s in a sentence has already been discussed in Section 2.

To summarize, we have indicated a variety of positions that *even* may take for the various constituents which may serve as the scope of *even*. Taking the position that the *even* is introduced immediately preceding its scope in deep structure, we have seen that it must move rightward for sentence scope, may move rightward and leftward for noun phrase and prepositional phrase scope, and cannot move at all for verb and verb phrase scope. For the cases presented, there appears to be no advantage to either the deep structure approach or the interpretivist approach. We will see in Section 4, however, that there are more controversial cases.

4. Cases of Transformationally Derived Constituents

By taking the position in Section 2 that *even* is associated with its surface structure scope at the level of deep structure, we are in the position of having to answer the following question: are there constituents in the surface structure which arise through the application of syntactic transformation, which can function as the scope of *even*? To answer this question, let us first consider the examples in (55).

(55) a. The dog even *bit* the man.
          The man was even *bitten* by the dog.
      b. Sam will throw out even *the ice box*.
          Even *the ice box* will be thrown out by Sam.
      c. Even *that idiot* can solve that problem.
          That problem can be solved by even *that idiot*.

In all three sentence pairs, we have an instance where the scope of *even* was not affected by the operation of the passive transformation. The second sentence in each pair is acceptable and the interpretation is unaltered except for the effect caused by the topicalization of the object noun phrase. It is with sentences like those in (56) that the question is relevant.

(56) a. ?The statue was even *photographed by the King*.
      b. ?The answer was even *known by Mary*.
      c. ?Sheila has even been *wooed by that student*.

I find them unacceptable. However, there are many native speakers of English who find these sentences acceptable when the scope of *even* is the derived verb phrase. Within the model for the interpretation of *even* presented in Section 1, the interpretation of (56)a, for example, would be (57).

(57) a. The statue was photographed by the King.
      b. The statue was otherwise treated as well.

    c. One would not expect the statue to be photographed by the King.

    One would expect the statue to be not photographed by the King.

I cannot accept (57)b as part of the interpretation of (56)a, if one actually exists, since I can't understand what it would mean for the statue to be otherwise treated—or whatever expression one wants to choose. I interpret (57)c as asserting that the negative expectation is either about the entire action (*The statue was photographed by the King*) or the statue's having been photographed by the King. I cannot convince myself that it is the derived verb phrase over which there is surprise. A more convincing sequence of sentences, (58) was pointed out to me by S. Anderson (personal communication).

(58)   a. *Naked Came the Stranger* was written by a group of writers.
      b. It was published by a reputable firm.
      c. It was even *reviewed favorably by the foremost critics.*

The issue is whether (58)c is acceptable with the scope of *even* taken as the derived verb phrase.

    This sort of example is most important in deciding whether *even* may be introduced into the deep structure as proposed in Section 2 or whether the interpretivist position is more appropriate. If, in the opinion of most native speakers, the verb phrase scope in sentences like (56) is acceptable, the interpretivist position is strongly supported. For here is an optional transformation—the passive—creating a scope for *even* without the deep structure reflecting this fact. Associating the *even* with the deep structure verb phrase and determining the interpretation of the sentence in terms of this scope clearly produces an incorrect result. One way out would be to make the passive transformation obligatory, thus providing an indication at the deep structure level that the scope of *even* would be a derived verb phrase. However, this is merely an *ad hoc* solution at the present.

    One final caveat concerning the sentences in (56): it is important in determining their acceptability to avoid assigning the scope of *even* to the agent noun phrase (even though the *even* is in the pre-verb phrase position), or to the verb alone. A sentence such as "The book was even *thrown*" must, under our analysis, have the verb *throw* as its scope, and may not have as its scope the derived verb phrase which has had the unspecified subject noun phrase deleted. However, there is presently no way to make a distinction in such a case.

    One possible way to show that the acceptability of sentences like (56) is only illusory involves sentences like those in (59),

(59)   a.   *The statue was even *photographed by someone.*
   b.   *The answer was even *known by someone.*
   c.   *Sheila has even been *wooed by someone.*

which are unacceptable since the intonation center is on the verb phrase final position. As we discussed in Section 1, an indefinite noun phrase like *someone* cannot function as the scope of *even*; consequently, when the main stress of the clause is on the *someone,* the only possible scope for *even* must be the entire (derived) verb phrase. But the sentences in (59) are unacceptable in just this case. Note that there is no difficulty in having a verb phrase scope for *even* with an indefinite noun phrase in verb phrase final position as the sentences in (60) illustrate.

(60)   a.   Tom even *talked to someone.*
   b.   The boys even *toasted all of us.*

A second case of a possible derived scope of *even* occurs in sentences like (61).

(61)   a.   ?That man is even *easy to please.*
   b.   ?Jones was even *certain to win.*
   c.   ?Frank was even *smarter than I thought.*

Again the issue is this: can the scope of *even* be the derived verb phrase (for example, *easy to please, certain to win, smarter than I thought*)? I find the answer to be *no*. In (61)a, for example, *easy* can function as the scope as can *please; easy to please* as the scope seems to be out. Note that these cases would not be unacceptable simply because the attribute follows the verb *be*, since we find perfectly acceptable sentences like, *She is not only intelligent, she is even beautiful* and *The dictator isn't even wealthy, to say nothing of being intelligent.*

  The facts are not clear on this issue and native informants differ with respect to the acceptability of the crucial cases such as (56) and (61). If clear evidence can be found which shows that the derived constituent does function as the scope of *even*, the interpretivist position must be credited with an extremely strong argument.

5.   The Notion "Protected Environment"

  In Section 3 we discussed the possible positions for *even*, given its scope, and in Section 4, some possible counterexamples to the claim that the scope of *even* should be a function of the deep structure representation of a sentence. In this section we will look at certain transformations which move constituents out of the scope of *even* (whereas in Section 4 the examples involved moving constituents into the scope). In particular, I will argue that the scope of *even* becomes a "protected environment"; a constituent from which no subpart may be extracted by a syntactic transformation. The thrust of the following examples will be to illustrate how the concept of a protected environment (PE) prevents the derivation of certain unacceptable sentences while permitting acceptable ones.

5.1   Negative Transportation

Fillmore (1963) and later, R. Lakoff (1968) argued for a rule of negative transportation to account for the synonymy of one reading of (62)a with the reading of (62)b. That is, they claimed that the negative marker originally in the embedded sentences in (62)a has been moved up into the higher sentence in (62)b.

(62)   a.   I suppose that John didn't leave until after midnight.
     b.   I don't suppose that John left until after midnight.

Assuming the existence of such a rule, consider the following sentences.

(63)   a.   I suppose, even, *that John left at midnight.*
     b.   I suppose, even, *that John didn't leave until midnight.*
     c.   *I don't even suppose *that John left until midnight.*
     d.   *I don't suppose, even *that John left until midnight.*

We are taking the scope of *even* in (63) to be the direct object noun phrase, that-S; the requirement that *even* must be set off by pauses (shown by commas in the examples) is a problem in anyone's approach and is not relevant here. What is important is the fact that (63)c and (63)d are unacceptable although negative transportation is acceptable [see (62)b], as is *even* transportation: "I even suppose *that John left at midnight*" is synonymous with (63)a on one reading. But note that the unacceptability of (63)c and (63)d can be easily accounted for if the object noun phrase (the scope of *even*) is treated as a protected environment, thereby blocking the application of the negative transportation rule.

5.2   Clefting

Now consider the sentences in (64).

(64)   a.   John reads girly magazines.
     b.   It's girly magazines that John reads.

    c. John even *reads girly magazines.*
    d. It's girly magazines that John even *reads.*

The object noun phrase, *girly magazines,* has been clefted in (64)b and
(64)d. However, the scope of *even* in (64)d is acceptable only if the scope of
even is just the verb *reads.* But of course, the interpretation of this sentence
is different from (64)c. The interpretivist might argue that the *even* is
associated with the verb *read* only after the object noun phrase has been
clefted. However, every analysis I know of which purports to account for
cleft sentences and pseudo-clefts as well, for example, Akmajian (1970),
designates the to-be-clefted noun phrase in deep structure. Therefore, it
should be possible to assign the scope of *even* at the level of deep structure
(or at least before any syntactic transformations apply). The PE constraint
will then prevent the extraction of an object noun phrase from a verb
phrase scope; for example, it will block the derivation of (64)d from (64)c.
(64)a will be derived from a deep structure in which the scope of *even* is
the verb alone. The point is not that the PE constraint is required here;
rather, that its application leads to no difficulties.
    A set of similar examples is presented in (65).

(65) a. He talks about politics during dinner.
      b. It's politics that he talks about during dinner.
      c. He even talks *about politics* during dinner.
      d. *It's politics that he even talks *about* during dinner.

The prepositional phrase object, though not its preceding preposition, has
been clefted in (65)b and (65)d. The scope of (65)d could be simply the verb
talk and this could be handled as discussed above for (65)d. However, the
scope in (65)d cannot be the sequence *talk about* (which is not a constituent)
nor the preposition *about.* The first restriction is a general one which
requires that the scope of *even* be a single constituent (although this constituent may consist of a sequence of subordinate constituents). The second
restriction is automatically handled by the PE constraint if the scope of
even (the prepositional phrase *about politics*) is determined at the level of
deep structure. Of course, if the preposition *about* could be contrasted in
this context (for example, *talk to* is *talk about*) we would find (65)d acceptable. Its derivation would then require the assignment of *even* to the
preposition at the deep structure level. The point here is that the scope
of *even* cannot be split up and the PE constraint appears to account for
this in a simple way. Note that the unacceptability of sentences like (65)d
cannot be predicted just because both a clefted noun phrase and *even* are
present, as the examples in (66) illustrate.

(66) a. It's John who reads even *girly magazines.*
      b. It's Max who talked about even *politics* during dinner.

Pretransformational knowledge of the to-be-clefted noun phrase is relevant for another reason: to prevent the generation of sentences like those in (67).

(67) a. *It's even *girly magazines* that John reads.
      b. *It's even *that girl* to whom I wanted to give a book.
      c. *It was even *John* that we saw in San Francisco.

There is a rather straightforward reason (suggested by S. Kuno, personal communication) for the unacceptability of sentences such as (67). The result of clefting a noun phrase is to single out its referent as being a unique item, given the context of the remainder of the sentence. Thus, from (67)a we can reasonably infer that the only thing John reads is girly magazines. A sentence like *It's girly magazines that John reads and he also reads "Fortune"* is very strange. The interpretation of *even* permits one to infer that its scope (*girly magazines*) is just one token of a type (here, reading material) to which we are calling special attention. There appears to be a conflict of inferences: the clefting requires a unique interpretation of the clefted noun phrase; the *even* requires a contrast of this noun phrase with other, similar noun phrases. Similar comments apply to pseudo-cleft sentences like those in (68) and we will not go into them here.

(68) a. John threw the garbage can.
      b. What John threw was the garbage can.
      c. John even *threw the garbage can.*
      d. *What John even *threw* was *the garbage can.*

5.3 Idioms

Idioms, taken here to be phrases for which the semantic interpretation is frozen, that is, is not a compositional function of the interpretation of its constituent parts, characteristically resist the application of syntactic transformations. (See Fraser, 1970.) However, the less frozen idioms do permit the application of certain rules such as the passive transformation (for example, *The riot act was read to the noisy children.*) The sentences in (69) illustrate the result of applying the passive transformation to a sentence, in which the scope of even is the verb phrase idiom, *make reference to.*

(69) a. Someone else made reference to our proposal.
      b. Reference to our proposal was made by someone else.
      c. Someone even *made reference to our proposal.*
      d. *Reference to our proposal was even *made* by someone else.

The unacceptability of (69)d can be explained in light of the fact that the sentence *Someone even made reference to our proposal* is also unacceptable. (This fact supports the claim that the verb *make* has no independent semantic interpretation and that the sequence *make reference to* is indeed an idiom.) The application of the PE constraint to the verb phrase scope in (69)c will prohibit the application of the passive transformations and (69)d will not be derived from (69)c. The fact that verb scope in (69)c (*Someone even *made* reference . . .) is unacceptable accounts for the fact that (69)d is unacceptable. This analysis, however, leaves unexplained the fact that the noun phrase *reference* may function as the scope of *even,* as in "He even made *reference* to our proposal."

5.4   Extraposition

Consider now the sentences in (70).

(70) a.   Evidence of his innocence was presented.
      b.   Evidence was presented of his innocence.
      c.   Even *evidence of his innocence* was presented.
      d.   *Even *evidence* was presented *of his innocence.*

In (70)c a complex subject noun phrase consisting of noun phrase-prepositional phrase sequence functions as the scope of *even.* An unacceptable (or highly questionable) sentence results when the prepositional phrase is extraposed. We might expect (analogous to the clefting cases) that the scope of *even* has been reduced from *evidence of his innocence* to simply *evidence,* and that the contrast is now between evidence and some other abstract noun phrase such as *suggestions, thoughts, ideas,* and so forth. On the contrary, (70)d remains unacceptable no matter what one takes as the scope of *even* or how emphatically one stresses *evidence* or any other constituent(s) in the sentence.

A second case of extraposition involves relative clause movement, as illustrated by the examples in (71).

(71) a.   The men who arrived yesterday are sleepy.
      b.   The men are sleepy who arrived yesterday.
      c.   Even *the men who arrived yesterday* are sleepy.
      d.   *Even *the men* are sleepy *who arrived yesterday.*

Sentence (71)d, in which part of the scope of *even* has been extracted, remains unacceptable no matter what scope is assigned to *even* or how the constituents are stressed. The interpretivist cannot account for the unacceptability of (71)d by restricting the scope of *even* from noun phrases like *evidence* and *the men* since these may function as the scope in other cases. What will be necessary here is some requirement that the scope of *even* can be a noun phrase only if some part of the noun phrase has not been extraposed. But of course this will require a knowledge of the deep structure of the sentence and its derivational history before the *even* can be associated with a noun phrase. No such problem arises if *even* is associated with the complex noun phrase before extraposition from a noun phrase if the PE constraint is applied.

A third case of extraposition from the scope of *even* is illustrated by the sentences in (72).

(72) a. It-that John was early didn't impress me.
      b. That John was early didn't impress me.
      c. It didn't impress me that John was early.
      d. Even *it-that John was early* didn't impress me.
      e. Even *that John was early* didn't impress me.
      f. *Even *it* didn't impress me *that John was early*.

If we take the position that (72)a underlies (72)b and (72)c, and (72)d underlies (72)e and (72)f, we find that the PE constraint permits the generation of the acceptable (72)e because the *it* of the underlying deep structure P-marker has not been extracted, but deleted. However, the PE constraint does apply in the derivation of (72)f, since it is the *that*-S which has been extraposed while the underlying *it* and the *even* are left behind. The interpretivist might argue here that the *even* does not get assigned until extraposition has occurred. This may or may not be correct but certainly sentences with an anaphoric *it* as the scope of *even* are acceptable (for example: What did you think of his last speech?—Even *it* didn't impress me) and thus it will be necessary to determine whether or not the *it* in question is the anaphoric one, or the expletive one as in (72)f. This will require a knowledge of the deep structure of the sentence and thus seems equivalent to introducing the *even* with its scope in deep structure and apply the PE constraint.

5.5 The Inapplicability of Existing Constraints

I think one can argue that the sequence *even*-[X] is itself a constituent of type C_i. For example, the sequence *even John* consists of *even* followed by the noun phrase *John*; I would claim this sequence is itself a noun phrase. If this is correct (a claim I will not attempt to justify here), then one might expect that some notion like the A-over-A principle or the island constraint would be relevant.

The A-over-A constraint was stated by Chomsky (1962) as follows:

(73)   If the phrase X of category A is embedded within a larger phase
       ZXW which is also of category A, then no rule applying to the
       category A applies to X (but only to ZXW). (p. 520)

In his dissertation, Ross (1967b) argues that this principle (73) is both too
weak (it fails to prevent unacceptable sentences like *Handsome though I
know a boy who is, I'm going to marry Fred*) and too strong (it blocks acceptable sentences like *It was the blond girl that we all knew that John wanted
to kiss*). In an attempt to rectify this difficulty, Ross presents the concept of
an *island*, a constituent which is immune to certain syntactic operations.
More recently, Ross (personal communication) has suggested a revision to
the A-over-A principle which goes beyond that suggested in his dissertation.
This revision, stated in (74) is referred to as the *island constraint*.

(74)   If some constituent X of category A immediately dominates some
       constituent Y, also of category A, then no constituent Z of any
       category type whatever, which is dominated (not necessarily im-
       mediately) by X may be moved from under the domination of X.

The initial impetus for this principle and its revision involved the movement of a noun phrase in an embedded sentence, itself dominated by a
noun phrase (for example, to explain the unacceptability of sentences like
**It was the man who I spoke to the girl who likes*). If the island constraint
were satisfactory, we could expect it to be applicable to the scope of *even,*
and thus render the PE concept unnecessary. Unfortunately, it is not. For
example, the constituent structure of the noun phrase, *the men who arrived
yesterday* is certainly a noun phrase followed by some constituent, perhaps
REL (for relative clause) or S (for sentence), or whatever. But notice that this
following constituent can be extraposed as in (73)b, a direct violation of the
island constraint. Similarly, for the other extraposition cases in Section 5.4,
neither the A-over-A principle nor its revision, the island constraint, will
account for the unacceptability of sentences like (63)d, (65)d, (68)e, (69)d,
(70)d, (71)d, and (72)f.

6.   Conclusion

Basically, this paper has been descriptive, attempting to characterize
the general nature of the adverbial *even* in English. In Section 1, I have
attempted to provide a general schema for the interpretation of *even* and
then indicate how the interpretation in a variety of syntactic constructions
followed from this general notion. Section 3 contains some general statements about the possible positions of *even* in terms of its scope, recognizing

of course that speakers will differ on the acceptability, especially in sentence final position. Section 2 posed the only theoretical question of the paper: where and when should *even* be introduced into the derivation of a sentence—at the level of deep structure or in some preferred position? I have assumed the deep structure position introduction of *even* and in Section 5 have presented the notion of protected environment which appears to handle many facts of *even* which otherwise would have to be handled in an *ad hoc* way. However, in Section 4 I have presented two types of possible counterexamples to the deep structure position which, if they represent actual counterexamples, suggest that the deep structure position must be abandoned in any strong (and thus interesting) sense. I think this issue is fairly clear. It will be resolved by speakers whose intuitions about the sentences in question are sharper than mine, which have been blunted by frequent worrying about these cases.

On
The Surface Verb
"Remind"

Paul M. Postal   Thomas J. Watson Research Laboratory, IBM

* I am indebted to G. Lakoff and J. R. Ross for many important improvements of content in this work, and to the latter for innumerable improvements of style. The whole would, no doubt, have been superior had I taken more of their advice. Remaining inadequacies are, of course, entirely the author's responsibility.

Introduction

In the present paper I analyze the syntactic properties of one reading of the surface structure English verbal element *remind*. It will be shown that there is an elaborate array of evidence indicating that this element has a transformational derivation from a complex underlying source in which there is no single verbal element corresponding to *remind*. Instead, there are two elements, one a main verb with properties like those of the verb *strike* which occurs in sentences such as:

(i)   Harry strikes me as being incompetent.
(ii) Margaret struck Pete as having a grudge against Lucy.

the other the verbal of a complement sentence which has properties like the verbal/adjectival forms in sentences like:

(iii) Max is like my brother.
(iv)   Pete resembles his father.
(v)   That suggestion is similar to Max's idea.

It is shown how the necessary analysis of *remind* is incompatible with the standard view of deep structure in transformational grammar, a view which, in effect, assumes a rather strict correspondence between the lexical items of surface structure and the elements of deep structure. It is argued that the properties of *remind* cast great doubt on the existence of a special set of interpretive projection rules specifying part of the relation between semantic representations and surface structures. Conversely, these properties provide considerable support for the view of this relation assumed in so-called "generative semantics," as described recently by Bach, Gruber, Lakoff, McCawley and others. The latter follows since the structure required as a syntactic basis for *remind* clauses is isomorphic in crucial ways with the properties which must be assumed to characterize the relevant semantic representations of these clauses.

I.   Aspects of *Remind* Clauses

A.   Identification

There are really several verbs in English whose phonological shape is *remind*. The one to be considered here is illustrated by such examples as:

(1) a.   Harry reminds me of Fred Astaire.
    b.   Johnson reminded Betty of an Argentinian admiral.

181

From the surface structure point of view, one is then dealing with a verbal element which requires three nominals (NP):

(2)   a.   *Harry reminds me
       b.   *Harry reminds of Fred Astaire
       c.   *Reminds me of Fred Astaire

The meaning of this verbal element involves a perception or recognition of similarity between entities. It will be convenient to have names to refer to the three NP occurring in *remind* examples. I propose, as a purely conventional terminology, with no hidden or subtle implications, to refer to them in left-to-right order (in simple declaratives) as subject (S), indirect object (IO), and object (O).

In all cases, the verb under discussion must be kept distinct from a homonym which means roughly 'cause to remember'. This verb is illustrated in:

(3)   a.   Harry reminded Betty to visit her sick uncle.
       b.   Lucille reminded me of a party (I was supposed to attend).

Some of our examples are ambiguous over "perceive similar" versus "cause to remember" interpretations, and if examples are said to be ill formed, I will be referring necessarily only to the fact that they are ill formed on the former kind of reading. It can be observed that the "perceive similar" *remind* is a stative, or nonactive, element, while the "cause to remember" *remind* is active. Hence, for example, the latter forms imperatives, while the former does not:

(4)   a.   *Remind me of your brother
       b.   Remind me to visit your brother.

B.   Initial Peculiarities of *Remind* Clauses

On the face of it, *remind* is a rather strange verb. While verbs which take three NP are found in English, for instance, those like *give, throw,* those like *steal, borrow,* those which occur with *about* phrases, and such, *remind* falls into none of these classes and is, from the point of view of its choice of NP types, unique. In particular, observe that while there are verbs like *convince, warn, inform,* which occur in structures that could be represented schematically as:

(5) NP_1 Verb NP_2 of NP_3

just as those of *remind* could, the contrast between these verbs and *remind* is sharp. For example, in the NP_3 position of structures like (5), there must be an abstract NP with any of these verbs. Animate NP are totally barred.

(6) a.   I convinced John of that.
     b.   I warned John of the danger.
     c.   *I convinced John of the dog.
     d.   *I warned John of your mother.
     e.   *I informed John of Bill's parakeet.

No such restriction holds for the post-*of* NP of *remind* clauses. Just so, verbs like those in (6) are *active,* form imperatives, and so on (see Section II.B(2) below), while the *remind* being discussed is *stative.* Similarly, the verbs in (6) have the subject NP as their *agent,* while the stative verb *remind,* of course, has no agent NP. It follows that in no significant sense is *remind* in a class with verbs like *warn, convince,* and so forth. It appears to be a unique element.

One of its most important peculiarities is that in well-formed *remind* clauses S and IO cannot be presupposed coreferents:[1, 2]

(7) a.   *Harry reminds himself of a gorilla.
     b.   *Johnson reminds himself of an Argentinian admiral.

In reading examples like (7) and further similar ones, it is important that in all cases the reflexive forms do *not* have contrastive stress. With this feature, some of the examples are well formed. I am discussing throughout forms without contrastive stress. This is not an arbitrary restriction, since observe that in sentences like:

(8)   *I reminded myself of a gorilla.*

[1] Since I will only consider presupposed coreferents throughout this study, the adjective will henceforth be omitted.

[2] Many of the arguments throughout this paper are based on facts of considerable subtlety. Many may also be based on properties subject to a good deal of dialect and idiolect variation. I have throughout utilized my own judgments. The reader may thus find that, on at least some of the topics discussed, he has conflicting judgments. Before attributing too much importance to this, he should observe the following. The conclusion which I seek to establish is supported by the validity of any reasonable subset of the overall class of arguments given. Hence, before the reader concludes on the basis of some disagreements that the point is not established, he might make a list of the total set of arguments given, comparing this with the subset for which the facts as described in the text do not correlate with his own judgments. If, as I suspect, the majority of arguments go through for everyone, the residue of undoubted variation can be seen in its proper perspective, that is, as having no real bearing on the validity of the analysis under discussion.

the *underlined* NP are *not* understood as *presupposed* coreferents but rather as *asserted* coreferents. That is, (8) is understood as an essential equivalent of:[3]

(9)   *The one who I reminded of a gorilla was mysélf.

(9) is ill formed in my dialect, for reasons discussed extensively in Section II.B(5) below. However, (9) has a clear interpretation in which the IO of *remind* is asserted to be a coreferent of the nominal which follows *was*. Thus both (8) and (9) are interpreted in such a way that they involve the *presupposition*:

(10)   X (I) reminded someone$_i$ of a gorilla.[4]

and they contain, semantically at least, the assertion that:

(11)   Someone$_i$ is X (myself).

Consequently, the restriction illustrated by (7) is a restriction on presupposed coreference, which correlates with weakly stressed reflexive forms.

Another peculiarity of *remind* clauses is that the S cannot be a coreferent of O:

(12)   a.   *Harry reminds me of himself.
       b.   *Johnson reminded Betty of himself.

An additional feature is that sentences with O and IO coreferents are not well formed either:

(13)   a.   *Harry reminded me of myself.
       b.   *Harry reminded Barbara of herself.

Thus *remind* clauses are well formed only if *none* of the three NP is a presupposed coreferent.

Let us consider now the meaning of *remind*. It seems to involve conceptually a perception of similarity between two entities, one represented by the S NP, the other by the O NP. The IO NP then represents the entity which perceives the similarity. One might represent this schematically as

---

[3] The reason for this is, I believe, that (8)-like structures are transformationally derived from (9)-like ones. For brief discussion and justification of such a derivation, see Postal (1968, Chapter 19).

[4] Here and throughout I use words with identical subscripts as a gross, merely literary device for representing coreference.

follows, postulating a two-place predicate of perception holding between an individual and a state of affairs described by a proposition involving similarity, and a two-place predicate of similarity, holding between entities:

(14)

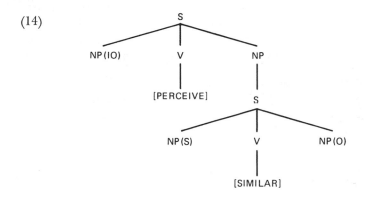

Here I use the device of bracketed, capitalized inscriptions to represent schematically elements of meaning, that is, predicates. This kind of meaning representation indicates that sentences like (15):

(15)   Larry reminds me of Winston Churchill.

are propositionally complex, conceptually. Schematically:

(16)

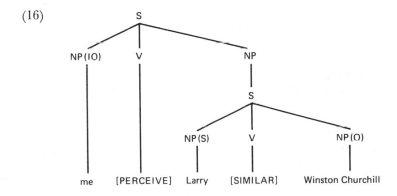

One proposition, the "main" one, states a perception relation between an individual and a state of affairs defined by a proposition involving similarity. An analysis like (14) of *remind* clauses claims that these should be paraphrases of sentences with *perceive* main verbs and complements involving assertions of similarity. Hence, for instance, (14) claims that (15) should be an essential paraphrase of:

(17)   I perceive that Larry is similar to Winston Churchill.

(14) also claims that, just as (18)a is contradictory, so is (18)b:

(18)   a.   I perceive that Larry is similar to Winston Churchill although
            I perceive that Larry is not similar to Winston Churchill.
       b.   Larry reminds me of Winston Churchill although I perceive
            that Larry is not similar to Winston Churchill.

The essential correctness of these predictions from (14) suggests that (14) is
indeed a basically right analysis for *remind* clauses semantically.
    Consider then propositional representations of the form:

(19)

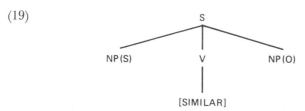

It is the NP terms of this expression which show up in sentences like
(12) as not having the possibility of being coreferents. However, propositional structures like (19) can also be realized as simple sentences:

(20)   a.   Harry is similar to Ben.
       b.   Jack is like Tommy.
       c.   Your mother resembles my aunt.

And, strikingly, such sentences manifest a coreference constraint:

(21)   a.   *Harry is similar to himself.
       b.   *Jack is like himself.
       c.   *Your mother resembles herself.

    The natural suggestion at this point is that one can *explain* the S-O
constraint in sentences with the surface verb *remind* if they are derived from
underlying structures containing embedded sentential structures with *those
properties that are common to sentences like (20)*. This assumes that the
coreference block in such sentences is attributed to some set of syntactic-
semantic features common to predicates like *similar, resemble, like*.[5] Let us

---

[5] Actually, the blockage is a function of an even more general principle governing predicates which are logically reflexive or irreflexive. Observe:
   (i) *Harry is next to himself.
  (ii) *Harry is related to himself.
 (iii) *Harry is distinct from himself.
  (iv) *Harry is identical to himself.
   (v) *Harry is married to himself.
  (vi) *Harry is more intelligent than himself.

refer to a predicate with the common properties of *similar, resemble,* and *like* as a *similarity predicate.*[6] Among other things, such predicates are logically reflexive, symmetrical, and nontransitive. Support for the proposal to derive *remind* sentences from underlying structures containing similarity predicates is that such a structure provides part of the basis for a correct account of the general meaning of such sentences, as indicated by the representations in (14) and (16).

The proposal is, therefore, that deriving *remind* clauses from structures with embedded similarity predicate clauses explains the S-O coreference blockage of *remind* clauses. It explains it in the sense that it reduces it to the independently required blockage of similarity predicate clauses. This suggestion has so far explained nothing about the S-IO coreference restriction manifested by *remind* sentences. It is noticeable that surface-complex sentences like:

$$(22) \quad \text{Jack perceives that Bill} \left\{ \begin{array}{l} \text{is like} \\ \text{is similar to} \\ \text{resembles} \end{array} \right\} \text{Tony.}$$

do *not* manifest restrictions of the sort that would explain the S-IO constraint of *remind* clauses, even if structures underlying sentences like (22) were taken to underly *remind* clauses. Sentences like:

(23)   Jack$_i$ perceived that he$_i$ was like Bill.

are well formed. The basis of an explanation of the S-IO restriction lies, I believe, in the existence of verbs whose meaning is quite close to that of *perceive* in (23), but whose grammatical properties are rather different. In particular, consider the verb *strike* of such sentences as:

(24)   It struck Jack that Betty was like Bill.

At first glance, it is not clear how such a verb provides an advance over one like *perceive,* since sentences like (25)a do *not* manifest a coreference constraint appropriate to explain that in (25)b:

(25)   a.   It struck Jack$_i$ that he$_i$ was like Bill.
        b.   *Jack$_i$ reminded himself$_i$ of Bill.

[6] Observe that, as defined, similarity predicate does not cover forms like *different, distinct, differ,* and so on. Clearly, there is some natural class containing similarity predicates, these last three forms, together with those like *identical, equivalent, equal, equals,* and so on. In fact, several of the regularities discussed below as characterizing similarity predicates are in fact valid for this wider class.

However, *strike,* unlike *perceive,* participates in the process of *complement subject raising.* That is, there exists a rule, which I will call *raising,*[7] which, with certain main verbs, has the effect of turning the subject of the complement sentence into a derived main clause object. This rule can be seen at work in the infinitival cases of:

(26) a. Joe believed Bill to be a vampire.
     b. Bill was believed to be a vampire by Joe.
     c. Joe believed that Bill was a vampire.
     d. *Bill was believed (that) was a vampire by Joe.
     e. Joe believed himself to be a vampire.
     f. *Joe believed (that) himself was a vampire.

The fact that the complement clause subject undergoes main clause passivization as in (26)b, and reflexivization, as in (26)e, are among the clearest indications that raising has taken place.

In describing raising above, I said that it produced a derived object. This is not, however, necessarily a remark about surface structures, since, as (26)b, for example, shows, subsequent rule applications may alter the situation. This is crucial, because the operation of raising with verbs like *strike* is intertwined with another, poorly known, operation which I have referred to (Postal, 1971a) as *psych movement.* Psych movement has the effect of interchanging subject and object NP with certain "psychological" verbs and adjectives.[8] That is, as far as nominal-verbal ordering is concerned, its operation is exactly parallel to the more well-known rule *passive.* That is, I claim that in sentences like (24), *Jack$_i$* is the underlying "subject," and *that Betty was like Bill* the complex abstract "object." Hence a remote structure of (24) would be:

(27)

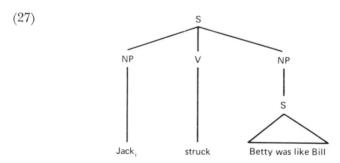

[7] This term is due to Kiparsky and Kiparsky (1968). For discussion of this rule see Postal (1969b), McCawley (1970).

[8] I ignore in this discussion McCawley's (1970) recent, important demonstration that English has underlying verb-subject-object constituent order. Consequently, there is really a rule of subject formation which provides all subjects, and rules like psych movement simply effect the relative positions of NP within a constituent. They do not make subjects into nonsubjects and vice versa.

The similarity between (27) and structures entered into by the verb *perceive* is crucial here. The difference between *strike* and *perceive* is largely that the former undergoes one or both of the rules raising and psych movement, while the latter undergoes neither. This contrast is roughly parallel to that between *seem* and *think* in such sentences as:

(28) a.   I think that vampires have large livers.
     b.   It seems to me that vampires have large livers.
     c.   Vampires seem to me to have large livers.

Compare:

(29) a.   I perceive that Max has a large liver.
     b.   It struck me that Max had a large liver.
     c.   Max struck me as having a large liver.

When psych movement operates on (27), the result is:

(30)   That Betty was like Bill struck Jack.

which is turned into:

(31)   It struck Jack that Betty was like Bill.

by the well-known rule of *extraposition,* a rule which throws clauses to the end of the next higher clause.[9] But (31) is (24). However, in the derivation of (24) = (31), the rule raising has *not* applied. If it had, it would have operated at the point (27), before psych movement had a chance to apply.[10] The result, assuming for convenience concomitant shift from *that*-clause to infinitival complement form, would be:

(32)   Jack struck Betty to be like Bill.

At this point, psych movement applies. Now, however, as a result of the functioning of raising, the object of *struck* is no longer the whole complement sentence, but only its old subject. Consequently, only the new, derived object, *Betty,* is placed in subject position, the result being:

[9] For this rule see Rosenbaum (1967) and Ross (1967b).

[10] I assume in this discussion that raising is cyclical and ordered *before* psych movement. For discussion of these features see Postal (1969b). In the light of recent developments, I rather doubt that the ordering is necessary, a special case of my feeling that transformational rules in grammar may turn out in general to be subject to other kinds of derivational constraints than extrinsic ordering. The ordering argument for psych movement and raising, just as for passive and raising, depends on assumptions about the cross-over principle which I now think are unacceptable.

(33) Betty struck Jack to be like Bill.

Obligatory operations of a sort that need not concern us require such structures to be mapped onto surface structures of the form:

(34) Betty struck Jack as being like Bill.

with *as* instead of the ordinary infinitival sequence *to be* and with obligatory presence of the progressive form of *be*.

In the previous paragraph, I considered the analogue to the derivation of (24), the difference being the occurrence of the application of raising, which was not applied in forming (24). Consider then the analogous derivation of a sentence differing from (25)a in the utilization of raising. The remote form would be:

(35)

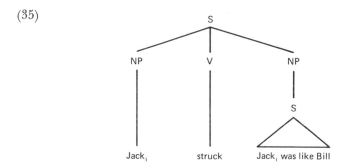

Application of raising yields:

(36)

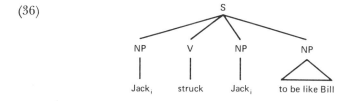

At this point, psych movement should apply, exchanging the positions of the subject of *struck* and the new derived object, which are coreferents in this case. In our notation, the result would be indistinguishable from (36). Placing the result in a properly pronominalized form[11] would then yield the reflexive output:

---

[11] That is, by replacing our expository representations of coreference by their appropriate surface structure realizations.

(37)   *Jack struck himself as being like Bill.

But (37) is ill formed (recall that the reflexive form must be read *without* contrastive stress). This is not, however, an isolated fact. There is *no* case where psych movement operates on coreferential subjects and objects. In Postal (1971a), I argued that this was a function of a general principle prohibiting transformational reordering rules from *crossing* coreferent NP under certain, quite complex conditions. I argued in particular that the restriction in (37) is exactly analogous to the restriction in reflexive passives without contrastive stress on the reflexive word:

(38)   a.   *Jack was stabbed by himself.
       b.   *Louise was criticized by herself.

It is not necessary for present purposes to accept the cross-over explanation of the restriction in (37). Indeed, I no longer believe that the explanation in terms of crossing is adequate. What is crucial is that in those cases where raising applies, sentences based on the verb *strike* do manifest a coreference constraint of the sort illustrated in (37).

Return now to *remind* clauses like:

(39)   *Jack reminds himself of me.

which arc ill formed, due to the constraint that S and IO cannot be coreferents. Suppose the underlying structure of all *remind* clauses is taken to involve a main verb with the properties of the *strike* which undergoes raising. Suppose, that is, that the remote structure of the sentence:

(40)   Jack reminds me of Bill.

were essentially:

(41)

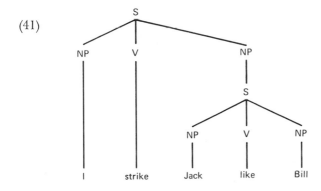

and the derivation proceeded in part as:

(42)

a. (41) RAISING

b.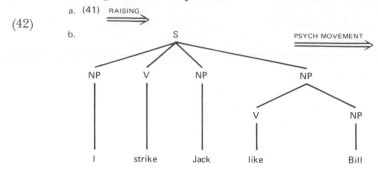

c.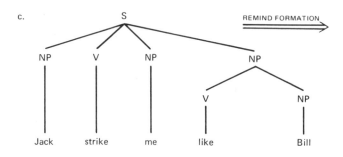

d.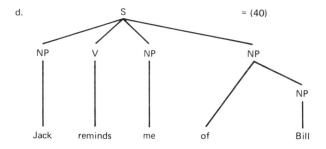

The rule *remind formation* mentioned in this derivation would involve the formation of a compound main verb out of the main verb *strike* and the complement verbal, which is a similarity predicate. I discuss this rule in greater detail below in Section III.

If (42) gives the derivation for (40), the derivation of a sentence like (39) would necessarily have to be:

(43)

a.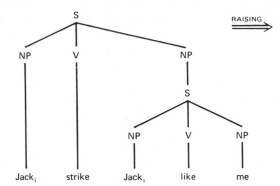

b.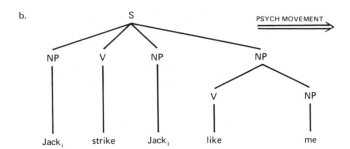

c. = b.  PRONOMINALIZATION

d.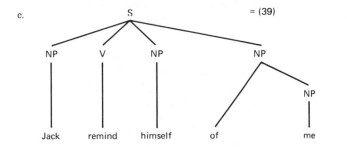

c. 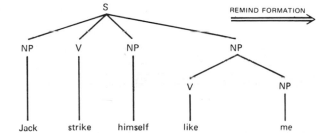 = (39)

The crucial point, then, is that a derivation like (43) must involve the application of psych movement in such a way that coreferent subjects and objects are interchanged. But as was observed in discussing sentences like (37), this is never possible.

Consequently, the derivation of *remind* sentences by way of underlying structures including a verb like *strike* as main verb reduces the peculiar S-IO coreference blockage of *remind* sentences to the independently required constraint of sentences like (37), a constraint which is, moreover, valid generally for psych movement sentences, and which can be shown to be the same as that in passive reflexives like (38). Clearly, then, the constraint is a function of some general principle, even if the cross-over hypothesis is not, as I think now, the correct reconstruction of this principle.[12]

It is thus clear that two of the three coreference peculiarities documented so far for *remind* sentences are an automatic function of derivation from underlying propositionally complex structures of the form:

(44)

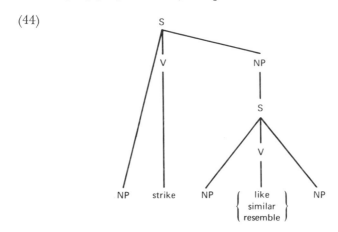

where the *strike* in question is one which undergoes raising and psych movement. I shall henceforth refer to the proposed structure in (44) as *the strike-like analysis*.

What then of the third coreference restriction, the fact that *remind* sentences with coreferent IO and O are ill formed, although possibly not to the extent of coreferent S-IO or S-O sentences:

12 One could propose an analysis of *remind* clauses such that they had psych movement but no other transformation in their derivation. This would account for the S-IO coreference constraint in terms of the principle just noted without assuming any complex, embedding analysis for *remind* clauses as in (43). It will be seen later that this approach is incompatible with other facts relating to the psych movement behavior of *remind* clauses, in particular with their behavior with respect to the extractability constraint discussed in Section II. B(5). Here we can observe that since it is not clear that application of psych movement can be predicted without *ad hoc* lexical markings, reduction of its application to *remind* to that of its application to *strike* represents a small saving in any event. But see Section V. C.

(45) a. *Harry reminded Mary of herself.
      b. *That nurse reminded Jack of himself.

Here also the restriction seems to follow from structures like (44). For me, sentences such as:

(46) a. ?It struck Mary$_i$ that Harry was like her$_i$.
      b. ?It struck Jack$_i$ that that nurse was like him$_i$.

are a bit unnatural and strained if interpreted in such a way that the unstressed pronoun is a coreferent of the postverbal NP. The unnaturalness perceived in (46) is quite subtle. However, when one takes examples in which raising has applied:

(47) a. *Harry struck Mary$_i$ as $\begin{Bmatrix} \text{resembling} \\ \text{being like} \end{Bmatrix}$ her$_i$.

      b. *That nurse struck Jack$_i$ as $\begin{Bmatrix} \text{resembling} \\ \text{being like} \end{Bmatrix}$ him$_i$.

the degree of deviance is much more marked on the coreferential readings. It seems to me that the deviant character of the anaphoric connection in sentences like (47) corresponds to the degree of deviance perceived in sentences like (45). Consequently, there are good grounds to suggest that the analysis of *remind* sentences in terms of structures like (44) also reduces the IO-O coreference constraint of *remind* clauses to an independently required statement in the grammar, namely, to the facts of sentences like (47).

Moreover, the argument from IO-O coreference constraints for deriving *remind* clauses from underlying structures with a main verb *strike* is even stronger than appears so far. This follows because apparently the properties of the sentences in (47) are not *ad hoc* features of *strike*, but follow from some relatively general principle. Notice first that they are typical of other psych movement verbals which undergo raising. Hence compare *strike* with *seem* and *appear*:

(48) a. It appeared to Louise$_i$ that Tony recognized her$_i$.
      b. *Tony appeared to Louise$_i$ to recognize her$_i$.[13]
(49) a. It seemed to me that Jack knew me.
      b. *Jack seemed to me to know me.

---

[13] Ross (personal communication) points out that for some speakers at least the choice of embedded verb is relevant to this restriction. Hence for him (i) is much better than (ii):

   (i) Tony appeared to Louise$_i$ to recognize her$_i$.
   (ii) Tony appeared to Louise$_i$ to be cruel to her$_i$.

I do not know how to characterize this contrast, which I have not investigated.

Similarly, with *impress,* which obligatorily undergoes raising if it takes a complement, we find:

(50)   *Jack impressed Sally$_i$ as being fond of her$_i$.

These facts might then suggest a principle something along the lines of:

(51)   A verbal V$_i$ which undergoes psych movement and raising cannot have its underlying "subject" NP be a coreferent of one of the NP elements of its subjectless complement clause.

Actually, however, even (51) is not general enough. Facts like those in (47)–(50) are equally characteristic of the analogous passive constructions of verbs with complements which undergo raising. Compare:

(52)   a.   Harriet$_i$ believes Jack to have been unfaithful to her$_i$.
       b.   It is believed by Harriet$_i$ that Jack has been unfaithful to her$_i$.
       c.   *Jack is believed by Harriet$_i$ to have been unfaithful to her$_i$.

And:

(53)   a.   Harriet$_i$ proved Melvin to be inferior to her$_i$.
       b.   It was proved by Harriet$_i$ that Melvin was inferior to her$_i$.
       c.   *Melvin was proved by Harriet$_i$ to be inferior to her$_i$.

Finally:

(54)   a.   Greg$_i$ assumed that Linda was fond of him$_i$.
       b.   It was assumed by Greg$_i$ that Linda was fond of him$_i$.
       c.   *Linda was assumed by Greg$_i$ to be fond of him$_i$.

Triples like those in (52)–(54) show that main clause verbals which undergo both passive and raising behave exactly like those which undergo psych movement and raising with respect to the possibility of coreference between their underlying "subjects" and NP elements of the subjectless complement produced by raising.[14] Consequently, (51) must be replaced by something more general. To state this more general restriction, let us speak of an NP which would show up as the subject of a clause if some particular rule R[15]

[14] It goes without saying that these facts provide a strong argument for the existence of the rule psych movement, a rule whose reality has often been doubted, probably because of the fact that it is subject to a mass of lexical and semantic constraints of largely unexplored character.

[15] The rule in question must be one like passive, whose operation is upward bounded in the sense of Ross (1967b), that is whose operation does not cross higher clause boundaries. Hence rules like those which move *wh*-marked NP are not relevant here.

does not apply, but which shows up as a *non*subject in case R does apply to it as having been *downgraded*.[16] Thus both passive and psych movement have the effect of downgrading NP. The NP $Mary_i$ in (47)a, $Louise_i$ in (48)a,b, *me* in (49)a,b, $Sally_i$ in (50), $Harriet_i$ in (52)b,c, and $Greg_i$ in (54)b,c are all downgraded NP. Given this notion, one can give the more general reformulation of (51) in a way something like:

(55)   A downgraded NP, NP_k of a Verbal V_i, which takes a complement sentence and undergoes raising, cannot be the antecedent of a coreferential NP which is one of the main constituents of the subjectless infinitival or gerundial phrase produced by the application of raising to the complement of V_i.

(55) thus predicts that all sentences which fail this noncoreference condition will be ill formed.

The crucial feature of (55) is that it relates the notion of downgraded NP to that of subjectless infinitival/gerundial clauses produced by the application of raising to complement structures. The contrasts in triples like (54) show that all of the properties are relevant. (54)a has a verb with a complement, but the antecedent has not been downgraded and the complement has not become subjectless through application of raising. (54)b has a downgraded antecedent, but again the complement has not become subjectless through raising. In (54)c though, both conditions are met, and the restriction is manifested.

Consequently, if, as appears to be the case, a principle like (55) is valid for English, our explication of the IO-O coreference restrictions of *remind* clauses in terms of the properties of the verb *strike* is not just the reduction of the properties of *remind* to those of some individual item. Rather, the reduction of *remind* to an underlying propositionally complex structure containing *strike* reduces these properties of *remind* to a general regularity of English, (55), a regularity which, because of its reference to *raising*, cannot possibly apply to *remind* if it is not given an underlying analysis with a complex structure containing a complement. In this way, the IO-O coreference restrictions of *remind* clauses provide a striking and powerful argument for such a complex underlying structure. For such an analysis turns an apparently mysterious and *ad hoc* feature of *remind* clauses into a consequence of a general principle of English which relates pronominalization possibilities to downgrading and raising.

Overall, then, *the strike-like analysis* reduces each of the three corefer-

---

[16] Downgrading should be taken as a special case of a more general notion of a change in what G. Lakoff (1969b) has called *priority* relations between constituents. What I have previously treated as intraclause cross-over restrictions (Postal, 1971a) should, I think, actually be subsumed under the principle that coreferent NP within a clause cannot have their priority relations altered.

ence peculiarities of *remind* clauses to an independently motivated restriction in the grammar of English. I should like here to make a comment strengthening the conclusion just reached. I have spoken of three types of constraints in *remind* clauses:

(56) a. S-O constraints
      b. S-IO constraints
      c. IO-O constraints

I have so far categorized these only in terms of *severity,* suggesting that those of the type (56)c might be slightly less bad than the others. There is, however, another classification of such constraints. Consider violations of each, namely,

(57) a. *Joe_i reminds me of $himself_i$.
      b. *Joe_i reminded $himself_i$ of you.
      c. *Joe reminded $Betty_i$ of $herself_i$.

If one considers (57)a, it can be seen that not only is it ill formed, but that it involves a *semantic peculiarity.* I proposed to explain the restriction in (57)a in terms of the restrictions in sentences like:

(58) a. *Joe is like himself.
      b. *Joe is similar to himself.

But observe that these involve the same semantic peculiarity. We might describe this roughly as follows. To say that 'x is similar to y' is to *presuppose* that x and y designate distinct entities and to *assert* that these entities share certain properties. Hence, sentences like (58) violate the presupposition involved in the English items *like* and *similar,* since with unstressed reflexive forms, there is the presupposition that reflexive and antecedent designate the same entity. What is wrong with sentences like (58) is that they contain incompatible presupposition of the form 'x designates same entity as y' and 'x designates a different entity from y'. But just this property is manifested in sentences like (57)a, a property explicable in terms of *the strike-like analysis,* which provides (57)a with an underlying structure of the form:

(59) *It strikes me that Joe is similar to himself.

which has just the properties of (58).

Consider on the other hand (57)b. This is perceived as completely ill formed, probably even more so than (57)a. Yet when we examine the meaning of (57)b, we find no semantic peculiarity whatever. (57)b says that an individual named Joe was struck by the similarity between himself and *you*, a completely natural and well-formed semantic entity. But, significantly, under *the strike-like analysis* of (57)b, restrictions like those in (57)b are explained in terms of restrictions in sentences like:

(60)   a.   *Joe struck himself as being similar to you.
       b.   *Joe struck himself as being like you.

And these, while ill formed, are free of semantic violation, a fact brought out more clearly by their paraphrase relations to the well formed:

(61)   a.   It struck Joe$_i$ that he$_i$ was similar to you.
       b.   It struck Joe$_i$ that he$_i$ was like you.

The absence of semantic violation in sentences like (60) is a theorem of the general fact that so-called "cross-over" violations never yield semantic violations, but rather simply ill-formedness or blockage of anaphoric connections. For instance, ill-formed reflexive passives like:

(62)   *Harry was criticized by himself.

have perfectly clear and normal semantic interpretations. Therefore, the explanation of the restriction in (57)b in terms of *the strike-like analysis* predicts not only the degree of severity of the well-formedness violation, but also the fact that the violation in (57)b, unlike that in (57)a, has no correlated semantic effects.

For (57)c, the situation is analogous to (57)b, not to (57)a. There are no semantic violations. This is also predicted by the proposed analysis of *remind* clauses, since violations like those in (57)c are derived from those in examples like:

(63)   a.   *Joe struck Betty$_i$ as being similar to her$_i$.
       b.   *Joe struck Betty$_i$ as being like her$_i$.

and these are without semantic violations, as shown by their paraphrase relations to the well-formed:

(64)   a.   It struck Betty$_i$ that Joe was similar to her$_i$.
       b.   It struck Betty$_i$ that Joe was like her$_i$.

Consequently, *the strike-like analysis* of *remind* sentences not only accounts correctly for the degree of severity of restrictions in sentences like (57), but it also predicts correctly for all cases whether or not these will have semantic violations associated with them.

II.   Further Special Properties of *Remind* Clauses

A.   Comment

The facts concerning reflexivization constraints discussed in Section I provide a central core of evidence for *the strike-like analysis* of *remind* clauses. This body of facts does not, however, by any means exhaust the grounds for such a description. There are a large number of other facts of diverse sorts which point in exactly the same direction. These may be properly divided into two types, just as the reflexive constraints can, although they were not previously so categorized.

The essential claims of *the strike-like analysis* are two. One is that the structure of *remind* clauses involves an embedded propositional structure of the similarity predicate (*resemble, similar, like*) sort. The other is that the main verb in the underlying structure is of the type *strike*, that is, among other things, a verb which takes animate "subjects" and abstract, propositional "objects," and which undergoes both raising and psych movement. Consequently, one can divide up the evidence into two groups: that which supports the postulation of an underlying embedded similarity predicate structure and that which supports postulation of a main verb like *strike*. Looking back at the arguments concerning reflexivization, it can be seen that the S-O constraints support the postulation of an embedded similarity predicate. The S-IO, and O-IO constraints, on the other hand, support the postulation of a *strike* type main verb. Henceforth, I shall separate these two types of evidence, beginning with arguments for the *strike*-type main verb element of *the strike-like analysis*.

B.   Arguments for a *Strike*-type Main Verb in *Remind* Clauses

1.   Reciprocal arguments.   With *remind*, one observes the following pattern of acceptability:

(65)   a.   *John and Bill reminded each other of Louise.
      b.   John and Bill reminded me of each other.
      c.   *I reminded John and Bill of each other.
      d.   *John and Bill reminded each other of each other.

This pattern follows, as far as I can discern, from no *fully general* principles governing English reciprocals in surface clauses, even those containing one verb and three NP. Compare:

(66)   a.   John and Bill talked to each other about Louise.
      b.   John and Bill talked to me about each other.

c. *I talked to John and Bill about each other.
d. *John and Bill talked to each other about each other.

The paradigm in (65) does, however, correlate closely with that in:

(67) a. *John and Bill struck each other as being similar to Louise.
      b. John and Bill struck me as being similar to each other.
      c. *I struck John and Bill as being similar to each other.
      d. *John and Bill struck each other as being similar to each other.

Consequently, *the strike-like analysis* reduces the special reciprocal constraints of *remind* clauses to those of *strike* sentences like (67). Moreover,
further investigation suggests that the properties of (67) are not totally
ad hoc features of *strike,* but are a general characteristic of clauses whose
derivation involves both raising and psych movement. Compare, for instance, the paradigm of *seem* clauses in which raising has applied:

(68) a. *John and Bill seemed to each other to be fond of Louise.
      b. John and Bill seemed to me to be fond of each other.
      c. *Max seemed to John and Bill to be fond of each other.
      d. *John and Bill seemed to each other to be fond of each other.

In other words, it is apparently a general fact that in those surface clauses
which have resulted from joint application of psych movement and raising,
the downgraded NP can be neither a reciprocal, as in (68)a,d nor the antecedent of a reciprocal, as in (68)c. The natural explanation of these facts
is in terms of the requirement that such reciprocal phrases meet the same
kind of clause mate[17] condition required for standard reflexivization. That
is, the reciprocal and its antecedent must be in the same clause in structures
defined before raising applies. Hence:

(69) a. John and Bill know each other.
      b. *John and Bill think that Mary hates each other.
      c. *John and Bill talked to the boy who visited each other.

Given these facts, the explanation of the distribution of acceptability
in raising-derived clauses like those in (68) is the distribution in the preraising structures, namely, for *seem,* those in:

(70) a. *It seemed to John and Bill that each other were fond of Louise.
      b. It seemed to me that John and Bill were fond of each other.

---

[17] The term is from Postal (1971a). Elements are clause mates if there is no clause to which
one belongs but the other does not.

    c. *It seemed to John and Bill that Max was fond of each other.

    d. *It seemed to John and Bill that each other were fond of each other.

Thus the situation is as follows. The raising analysis of *seem* sentences like those in (68) and of *strike* sentences like those in (67) reduces their reciprocal constraints to underlying multi-clause structures like those in (70). The pattern of acceptability in *remind* clauses mirrors that in raised *seem* and *strike* sentences like (67) and (68), and not that in underived multi-NP clauses like those with *talk* in (66). This fact is explained by *the strike-like analysis* which derives *remind* clauses in a way which forces them to pass through a pattern like the sentences in (70), and then through one like that in (68). Because of this, the reciprocal constraints of *remind* clauses provide a powerful argument for *the strike-like analysis.*

    Actually, the argument is somewhat stronger than has so far appeared. It can be observed that the properties illustrated in (65) are highly dependent on quite superficial properties of sentences. In particular, note the difference, if, instead of a contiguous reciprocal expression, *each other* or *one another,* one has instead the form *each* on the antecedent:

(71) a. John and Bill each reminded the other of Louise.

       b. John and Bill each reminded me of the other.

       c. I reminded each one of the men of the other.[18]

       d. ?John and Bill each reminded the other of the other.

Under these conditions, all except possibly the last of the paradigmatic examples are well formed. But, crucially, exactly this is true of *seem* and *strike* derivations in which raising has applied:

(72) a. John and Bill each struck the other as being similar to Louise.

       b. John and Bill each struck me as being similar to the other.

       c. I struck each of the men as being similar to the other.

       d. ?John and Bill each struck the other as being similar to the other.

(73) a. John and Bill each seemed to the other to be fond of Louise.

       b. John and Bill each seemed to me to be fond of the other.

       c. Max seemed to each of the men to be fond of the other.

       d. ?John and Bill each seemed to the other to be fond of the other.

And these facts are of course due to the underlying principle that such sentences are not ruled out by constraints on underlying preraising structures containing complements and main verbs of the *seem, strike* type:

---

[18] The switch to plurals here and in several other examples below is due to constraints, irrelevant to our argument, on the possible surface structure co-occurrences of *each* and conjoined NP in nonsubject position.

(74) a.   It struck each one of the men that the other was similar to
           Louise.
      b.   It struck me that John and Bill were each similar to the other.
      c.   It struck each one of the men that I was similar to the other.
      d.   ?It struck each one of the men that the other was similar to the
           other.

Consequently, the facts in (71) also follow from the characteristics of main
verb-complement constructions as in (74), (characteristics which are carried
over in raising derivations as shown by (72) and (73)), if *the strike-like anal
ysis* is the correct derivation of *remind* clauses.

2.   Stative properties.   If one considers the verb *strike* in sentences like:

(75) a.   John strikes me as being intelligent.
      b.   John struck Barbara as having a quick mind.

it can readily be determined that it falls into that class which has come to
be called (G. Lakoff, 1966b) *stative* or *nonactive*. The properties typical of
this class are, *inter alia*:

(76) a.   No occurrence with *do so*
      b.   No imperatives
      c.   No occurrence with the modal *may* of permission
      d.   No occurrence with progressive
      e.   No occurrence as the embedded verb with main verbs such as
           tell (to), order, permit, force, persuade, and so forth
      f.   No occurrence with *what NP did was . . .*
      g.   No occurrence with subject-selected adverbs like *enthusiasti-
           cally, reluctantly*

To illustrate that this is true of *strike*, consider:

(77) a.   John thought about Bill but Tom wouldn't do so.
      b.   *John struck Bill as being dumb but Jack didn't do so.
(78) a.   Think about Bill.
      b.   *Strike Bill as being over six feet tall.
(79) a.   May I think about Bill?
      b.   *May Bill strike me as being clever?
           (on permission sense of *may*)
(80) a.   John is thinking about Bill.
      b.   *John is striking me as being too fat.
(81) a.   I ordered John to think about the digestion of rhinoceri.
      b.   *I ordered John to strike Bill as being overweight.

(82) a.   What John did next was think about rhinoceros digestion.
      b.   *What John did next was strike Bill as being overweight.
(83) a.   John thought about rhinoceros digestion enthusiastically.
      b.   *John enthusiastically struck Bill as being dumb.

It is a consequence of *the strike-like analysis* that all such properties of *strike* must be properties of *remind* sentences. And this is the case:

(84) a.   *John reminded Bill of Tom but Jack didn't do so.
      b.   *Remind Bill of Mary.
      c.   *May Bill remind you of Lucille?
           (on permission sense of *may*)
      d.   *John is reminding me of a gorilla.
      e.   *I ordered John to remind Betty of a tap dancer.
      f.   *What John did next was to remind Bill of a gorilla.
      g.   *John enthusiastically reminded Betty of Boris Karloff.

These facts support *the strike-like analysis,* since they show that under this analysis it is not necessary to specify the verb *remind* as being stative. This property is derivable from the underlying stativity of *strike.*

3.   Passive.   A property typical of *strike,* but not common to the whole class of verbs, nor even to the whole class of statives, is that it does not undergo passive, at least in some dialects, that of the present writer included:

(85) a.   *Harry was struck as being foolish by Jack.
      b.   *Harry was struck by a 1936 Chevrolet as being similar to a 1946 Packard.

But the same property is true of *remind* in these dialects:

(86) a.   *Harry was reminded of a 1936 Chevrolet by a 1946 Packard.
      b.   *Harry was reminded by a 1946 Packard of a 1936 Chevrolet.

Hence, given *the strike-like analysis,* the failure of *remind* to undergo passive is derivable without special statement from the failure of *strike* to undergo this rule. This, in turn, is itself not an accidental fact, but follows from the regularity that the applications of psych movement and passive are mutually exclusive. As we have seen, *strike* undergoes psych movement.

4.   Selectional features.   Another class of facts relevant to the derivation of *remind* sentences from underlying *strike* structures concerns nominal-verbal selectional properties. With the verb *strike* in surface clauses of the form:

(87)   Harriet struck me as being clever.

we find an initial subject NP, a postverbal NP, and a clausal fragment without its subject which is understood as a coreferent of the subject of *strike*. The selectional facts, then, are these:

(88)   a.   The subject in such cases is unrestricted with respect to *strike* itself, but is restricted with respect to the clausal fragment.
       b.   The postverbal NP in such cases must be animate, possibly "human" in some sense (exclusive of babies, for example).

These properties can be illustrated by such examples as:

(89)   a.   Harriet struck me as being nice.
       b.   That dump truck struck me as being nice.
       c.   That proposal struck me as being nice.
       d.   That month struck me as being a dreary one.
       e.   That location struck me as being a lonely one.
(90)   a.   ?Harriet struck the chicken soup as being too hungry.
       b.   ?That proposal struck most hydrogen bombs as being inconsistent.
       c.   ?Your first home run struck my second double as being shorter than Schwarz's fifth pop up.

Notice that I have made no claim as to the *nature* of such restrictions. In particular, I have taken no sides on the question as to whether they are syntactic, semantic, a mixture, facts about belief systems, facts about the world, and so forth. This is irrelevant, although I agree with G. Lakoff (1970d) that they involve semantic presuppositions. What is relevant here is only that *the strike-like analysis* predicts that the properties illustrated in (89) and (90) must carry over to *remind* sentences.

In particular, the derivation from *strike* sentence structures predicts that that NP which corresponds to the derived subject of *strike* must be largely[19] selectionally unrestricted with respect to *remind*, while being restricted to the remnants of the clause fragment. This NP is the surface subject of *remind*. Just so, the analysis predicts that the NP in *remind* sentences which corresponds to the postveral NP in *strike* sentences must be animate. This NP is the IO of *remind* sentences. Both predictions are borne out.

[19] Some facts indicating that *remind* is not *completely* free with respect to its subject are given and analyzed in Section IV.

(91) a.   Harriet reminded me of a monkey.
      b.   That dump truck reminded me of Harry's tractor.
      c.   That proposal reminded me of Harry's suggestion.
      d.   That month reminded me of last month.
      e.   That location reminded me of the place where Harry's mor-
           tuary used to be.

(91) illustrates that *remind* does not restrict the nature of its subjects. However, such subjects are restricted with respect to the remnant in *remind*
sentences of the clausal fragment of *strike sentences,* which is just the O NP.
Observe:

(92) a.   ?Harriet struck me as being similar to Willy Mays' 434th home
           run.
      b.   ?Harriet reminded me of Willy Mays' 434th home run.
(93) a.   ?Your right nostril struck me as being similar to Fermat's last
           theorem.
      b.   ?Your right nostril reminds me of Fermat's last theorem.
(94) a.   ?This onion soup strikes me as being similar to 1943.
      b.   ?This onion soup reminds me of 1943.

That the IO of *remind* sentences must, as predicted by *the strike-like analysis,* be animate is illustrated by such examples as:

(95) a.   ?Your nose reminded my foot of Harry's armpit.
      b.   ?That idea reminded that nonnull set of the Declaration of
           Independence.
      c.   ?Khrushchev's mother reminded the election of Nixon of Har-
           riet's sister.
      d.   ?Irving's notebooks will remind the arrest of Schwarz of the
           fact that everything either does or does not exist.

Consequently, each of the selectional predictions of *the strike-like analysis*
of *remind* structures is borne out by the selectional properties of surface
remind clauses.
    It should be further observed that if the surface *remind* is itself taken
as the entity whose selection must be stated, it becomes a unique element.
Under *the strike-like analysis,* the selections are broken down into two sub-
sets, those pertaining to a verb like *strike,* and those pertaining to a similarity predicate. Thus, the selections are bifurcated into selections common
to two large sets of verbs, those such as *strike, seem, appear, impress, taste,
perceive,* and so forth, on the one hand, and *similar, resemble, like, different,
identical* on the other. Thus *the strike-like analysis* not only predicts the

particular selections of *remind* but it does so through general statements about selections which can be given for classes of verbal elements. In this way, *the strike-like analysis* prevents *remind* from having to be regarded as a selectionally peculiar item.[20]

5.   Relative and question word extractability.   A significant argument showing that *remind* sentences have an underlying structure with a main verb *strike* involves constraints on moving NP out of certain environments under transformational rules. I shall refer to such processes as *extraction* and to their potential applicability as *extractability*.

The fact is that *remind* sentences manifest a peculiar restriction on *extractability* under whose rules involved in the reordering of *wh*-marked NP, rules I shall refer to as *Wh-Rel movement* and *Wh-Q movement*.

(96) a.   Harry reminded me of a gorilla.
      b.   Max thought that Harry reminded me of a gorilla.
      c.   Who did Max think reminded me of a gorilla?
      d.   the one who Max thought reminded me of a gorilla
      e.   What did Max think Harry reminded me of?
      f.   the thing that Max thought Harry reminded me of

In these examples both the S and O NP can be extracted by both *Wh-rel* movement and *Wh-Q* movement. For me, however, this is not possible with the IO:

(97) a.   *Who did Max think Harry reminded of a gorilla?
      b.   *the one who Max thought Harry reminded of a gorilla

It would be attractive if this constraint could be formulated generally in terms of all rules of a certain type, if, for instance, it could be stated as a restriction on the operation of any rule which extracts NP and which is not upward bounded in the sense of Ross (1967). However, I do not think this is possible, because it seems that *remind* sentences with extracted IO NP are all right if this NP is extracted by the rule Ross (1967) refers to as *topicalization*, and which I have called (see Postal, 1968) *Y-movement*:

(98) a.   Me Harry reminds of a gorilla.
      b.   Max Harry seemed to remind of Joe Dimaggio.
      c.   Pete I am sure Marsha reminded of Louise.

[20] In so doing, the analysis reveals in a clear way that *surface* verbals are not the elements which enter into the statement of selectional restrictions. Rather the relevant elements are the semantic verbals underlying the surface elements. This confirms the point made by McCawley (1968d) that selections are properly regarded as semantic. See Section V.

If it is agreed that the examples of (98) are well formed, in comparison to the starred examples of (97), it must be concluded that the ban on extracability is one relating to *wh*-forms and the rules which reorder them, rather than to unbounded reordering rules in general.

The importance of the restriction on IO extractability in *remind* clauses lies in the behavior of sentences with the verb *strike*. For, significantly, these manifest exactly the relevant extractability restriction:

(99) a.   Harry struck me as being similar to a gorilla.
      b.   Max though that Harry struck me as being similar to a gorilla.
      c.   Who did Max think struck me as being similar to a gorilla?
      d.   the one who Max thought struck me as being similar to a gorilla
      e.   What did Max think Harry struck me as being similar to?
      f.   the thing that Max thought Harry struck me as being similar to

But:

(100) a.   *Who did Max think Harry struck as being similar to a gorilla?
       b.   *the one who Max thought Harry struck as being similar to a gorilla

It follows that, under *the strike-like analysis,* the extractability constraint in *remind* sentences follows automatically from that which must be somehow built into *strike* sentences. Given in this way, however, the argument, while real enough, is not especially strong. It simply has the form that given *the strike-like analysis,* instead of two verbs, *strike* and *remind,* with an exceptional restriction, we have one. Hence, the apparent advantage of the analysis proposed for *remind* is the elimination of one exceptional property from one verb.

However, the facts in (96)–(99) provide a much stronger basis for *the strike-like analysis* than this. The argument has the following form. The restriction manifested by the verb *strike* and predictably carried over to *remind* under *the strike-like analysis* is actually not an *ad hoc,* exceptional feature of *strike*. Rather, it is apparently a largely predictable feature of a significant set of verbal elements, and, most crucially, predictable in terms of properties which include the presence of a complement sentence. Therefore, the alternatives with respect to properties like those in (96)–(99) are not two exceptional verbs versus one. Rather, they involve setting up as an exceptional property of a verb a feature which is really governed by regularities, and, moreover, regularities statable just in terms of the underlying structures provided by *the strike-like analysis*. In short, the alternatives are: treating the extractability constraint of *remind* sentences as a function of the regularity operating for *strike* sentences; or treating it as an exception, a mere accident.

I do not as yet fully understand the regularity which predicts the extractability constraint, but it seems to involve *at least four* factors. First, it is limited to verbs which undergo psych movement. Second, it is, *remind* aside, limited to verbs which take complement sentences. Third, it seems to be at least partially determined by the position of the underlying complement sentence, or its deformed remnant, in the surface clause. Finally, the position of prepositions before the extracted NP plays a distinct role in degree of acceptability.

Let us specify some properties of psych movement verbals. These occur with an NP which designates the individual who experiences whatever psychological state, process, activity, event, and so forth, the verbal describes. Call this NP the *experiencer* NP. This is a fundamental category of NP like agent, instrument, and so forth, psych-movement verbals have the property that the experiencer NP ends up not as the surface subject, but within the surface predicate. They occur in clauses which cannot be reflexive. And they occur in clauses whose nonsubjects can occur with the strange adverbial *personally* in the meaning distinct from that of 'in person'. Compare the psych movement verbal *boring* with the nonpsych movement verbal. *understand*.

(101) a.   I personally understand Max.
       b.   *I understand Max personally.
       c.   I understand myself.
(102) a.   That is boring to me personally.
       b.   *Harry personally is boring to me.
       c.   *Harry is boring to himself.

It appears then that something like the following constraint operates in my dialect of English:

(103) Extraction Constraint

      Given a verbal element V_i which takes a complement sentence S_i and which undergoes psych movement, the *derived* object of V_i, that is, its *underlying* experiencer NP, is unextractable by the rules of *Wh-Q* movement or *Wh-rel* movement if S_i or its transformational remnant end up postverbally.

      Moreover, the unextractability is

  (i)   *mild* if the experiencer NP is preceded by a preposition which accompanies it under extraction or is not preceded by a preposition

  (ii) *severe* if the experiencer NP is preceded by a preposition which does *not* accompany it under extraction

Let us begin with the most minor of the features of (103), the requirement that the complement end up postverbally. The reason for this restriction, which emerged in conversation with G. Lakoff, is the contrast between sentences of the following sorts:

(104) a.   (the fact) That Billy kissed Greta was disgusting to Melvin.
       b.   It was disgusting to Melvin that Billy kissed Greta.
       c.   To whom was the fact that Billy kissed Greta disgusting?
       d.   *To whom was it disgusting that Billy kissed Greta?
       e.   **Who was it disgusting to that Billy kissed Greta?

The key contrast is between (104)c and (104)d, the chief difference between them being that (104)d has undergone the rule extraposition, which throws the complement sentence to the end of the clause. The fact that (104)d is clearly more ill formed than (104)c is especially noteworthy, in view of the fact that independent factors would tend to make (104)c worse. That is, (104)c has a very long, "heavy" subject NP and a very short VP, properties which generally yield unacceptable sentences. (104)d has a maximally short subject and the "heavy" complement has been placed postverbally, normally a happy condition for an English sentence. Yet, in spite of this, (104)d is not nearly as acceptable as (104)c, a clear indication, I think, of the operation of that part of (103) which mentions postverbal position of the complement.

Other examples include those which show that, with a gerundive complement in subject position, there is no extraction constraint, even when the other conditions are met:

(105) a.   Harry's proposing to Sally annoyed Louise the most.
       b.   Who did Harry's proposing to Sally annoy the most?
       c.   The one who Harry's proposing to Sally annoyed the most
            was Max.

Such sentences seem to suffer only from the property of having too heavy a subject.

Having indicated now that the postverbal position of the complement is relevant, let us next indicate that the presence of a complement sentence is required to induce extractability constraints. Compare:

(106) a.   That was obvious to me.
       b.   That Max was a Hungarian was obvious to me.
       c.   It was obvious to me that Max was a Hungarian.
       d.   To whom was that obvious?
       e.   Who was that obvious to?

> f. *To whom was it obvious that Max was a Hungarian?
> g. **Who was it obvious to that Max was a Hungarian?

Consider, too, sentences with a pure verb, rather than an adjectival verbal:

(107) a. That disturbed me.
      b. That Max was a Hungarian disturbed me.
      c. It disturbed me that Max was a Hungarian.
      d. Who did that disturb?
      e. *Who did it disturb that Max was a Hungarian?
      f. *the one who it disturbed that Max was a Hungarian

The difference between (107)d and (107)e illustrates the role of an occurring complement sentence in inducing the constraint on experiencer NP extraction for verbals that have undergone psych movement, and hence have this NP in their predicates.

There are several hundred verbal elements like *disturb,* that is, forms like *annoy, disgust, puzzle, amuse, bore,* and so on. These have the interesting feature of occurring in several different kinds of verbal constructions, both adjectival and pure verbal. Typically, they have at least the following possibilities:

(108) a. A pure verbal construction in which the experiencer NP is surface object
         (i) Max disgusted me.
      b. An adjectival construction in which the experiencer NP is a surface object, the verbal has present participle-like form together with a following preposition *to:*
         (ii) Max was disgusting to me.
      c. An adjectival construction in which the experiencer NP is surface subject, and the verbal has a past participle-like form followed by prepositions like *with, at, by,* and so forth:
         (iii) I was disgusted with Max.

Now, of these three, the *a* and *b* types are characterized by the obligatory occurrence of psych movement, the *c* type by its absence. This is shown by, among other things, the possibility of reflexive sentences in the *c* construction, their impossibility in the others:

(109) a. *Max disgusted himself.
      b. *Max was disgusting to himself.
      c. I was disgusted with myself.

Consequently, such constructions provide a clear testing ground for the extraction constraint (103). According to (103), the derived objects in the *a* and *b* constructions should be unextractable for all such forms, in the presence of postverbal complement. And this appears to be exactly the case:

(110) a.   It disgusted Max that I refused to play.
          b. *Who did it disgust that you refused to play?
          c. *the one who it disgusted that you refused to play
(111) a.   It was disgusting to Max that I refused to play.
          b. **Who was it disgusting to that I refused to play?
          c. **the one who it was disgusting to that I refused to play
          d. *To whom was it disgusting that I refused to play?
          e. *the one to whom it was disgusting that I refused to play

Observe, on the contrary, that the experiencer NP in the *c* construction may be freely extracted in the presence of a complement, due to the inapplicability of psych movement:

(112) a.   Max said Barbara was disgusted by the fact that Pete quit.
          b.   Who did Max say was disgusted by the fact that Pete quit?
          c.   the one who Max said was disgusted by the fact that Pete quit

I will now give evidence that for the two types of elements in (108) which have undergone psych movement, the presence of a complement is necessary to induce the extraction constraint:

(113) a.   Max disgusted me the most.
          b.   Who did Max disgust the most?
          c.   It disgusted me the most that Max quit.
          d. *Who did it disgust the most that Max quit?
(114) a.   Max was most disgusting to me.
          b.   Who was Max most disgusting to?
          c.   To whom Max was most disgusting?
          d.   the one to whom Max was most disgusting
          e.   It was most disgusting to me that Max quit.
          f. **Who was it most disgusting to that Max quit?
          g. *To whom was it most disgusting that Max quit?
          h. *the one to whom it was most disgusting that Max quit

We have thus illustrated with verbals of the type *disgust, puzzle,* and so on, the relevance of both psych movement, and an occurrence of a complement sentence. This class of verbals by no means exhausts the set for which the extraction constraint in (103) holds. This is also predictably the case for the elements *seem, appear,* and *impress* in sentences like the following. The reader can easily determine for himself that these are psych movement verbals in terms of the position of the experiencer NP, the impossibility of reflexives, and the distribution of *personally*.

Consider first *impress*. This verb must undergo psych movement, and, if it takes a complement, it must also undergo raising. Consequently, an underlying structure such as:

(115)

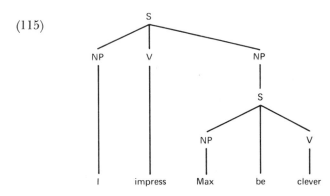

becomes:

(116)

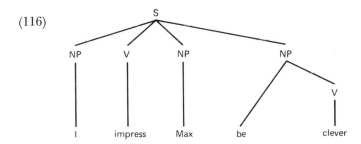

by raising, which precedes psych movement on a cycle, and then:

(117)

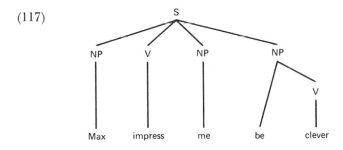

by psych movement, ending up finally as:

(118)   Max impresses me as (being) clever.

by certain late rules and constraints of an unclear sort. No complement is, however, required:

(119)   That impressed me.

The functioning of the extraction constraint is clearly illustrated by such examples as:

(120)   a.   Max impressed everyone as (being) honest.
        b.   That impressed everyone.
        c.   *Who did Max impress as (being) honest?
        d.   *the one who Max impressed as (being) honest
        e.   Who did that impress?

In particular, observe how the contrast between (120)c and (120)e illustrates the role of a complement sentence.

The verbs *seem* and *appear* are like *impress,* except for a number of minor features. First, they do not take the *as* element in their complement remnants. Secondly, for them, a complement in their underlying object is obligatory, not optional. Thirdly, in the presence of this complement, the application of raising is optional, not obligatory. A final difference is that *seem* and *appear* preserve the *to* preposition associated with experiencer NP, while *impress* requires it to delete. As with *impress,* however, psych movement is obligatory in all cases. One finds:

(121)   a.   It seemed to Max that Paulette was nervous.
        b.   Paulette seemed to Max to be nervous (seemed nervous to Max).

These have essentially the same underlying structure, roughly:

(122)

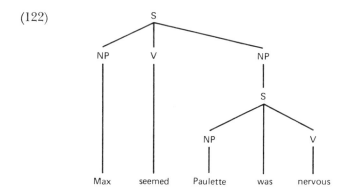

The difference is that (121)b has undergone optional raising, while (121)a has not. Consequently, when psych movement comes to apply, it makes a subject, not out of the raised complement subject in (121)b, but out of the whole complement in (121)a. This latter complement is then later thrown to clause-final position by extraposition. Observe, then, the constraints predicted by (103):

(123) a. **Who did it seem to that Paulette was nervous?
       b. *To whom did it seem that Paulette was nervous?
       c. **Who did Paulette seem nervous to (*seem to to be nervous)?
       d. *To whom did Paulette seem (to be) nervous?
       e. *the one to whom it seemed that Paulette was nervous
       f. *the one to whom Paulette seemed nervous

The constraints for *appear* are exactly the same, and I will illustrate them only briefly:

(124) a.   It appeared to Max that Paulette was nervous.
       b.   Paulette appeared nervous to Max.
       c. **Who did Paulette appear nervous to?
       d. *To whom did Paulette appear nervous?
       e. *To whom did it appear that Paulette was nervous?
       f. *the one to whom it appeared that Paulette was nervous

The properties of *seem* and *appear* just illustrated not only support the formulation of (103) as given, but indicate something further. The extraction constraint holds in these cases, regardless of whether or not raising has applied, that is, in both (123)b,c and in both (124)d,e, demonstrating that this rule is not a relevant factor in the constraint.

A class of verbal elements with behavior similar to *seem, appear, impress,* and *strike,* is the set of verbs of sensation, *smell, feel, sound, look, taste,* in those constructions where these have complements and undergo psych movement. In these cases, the complement clauses are of the type which begin with *like* or *as if*:

(125) a.   This book $\begin{Bmatrix} \text{feels} \\ \text{looks} \end{Bmatrix}$ to me as if it were made of iron.

       b. *To whom does this book $\begin{Bmatrix} \text{feel} \\ \text{look} \end{Bmatrix}$ as if it were made of iron?

       c. *the one to whom this book $\begin{Bmatrix} \text{feels} \\ \text{looks} \end{Bmatrix}$ as if it were made of iron

       d. *It was Harry to whom this book $\begin{Bmatrix} \text{felt} \\ \text{looked} \end{Bmatrix}$ as if it were made of iron.

(126) a.   That monkey $\begin{Bmatrix} \text{sounds} \\ \text{smells} \end{Bmatrix}$ to me as if it were dying.

b. *To whom does that monkey $\begin{Bmatrix} \text{sound} \\ \text{smell} \end{Bmatrix}$ as if it were dying?

c. *the one to whom that monkey $\begin{Bmatrix} \text{sounds} \\ \text{smells} \end{Bmatrix}$ as if it were dying

d. *It was Harry to whom that monkey $\begin{Bmatrix} \text{sounded} \\ \text{smelled} \end{Bmatrix}$ as if it were dying.

(127) a.   That soup tasted to me like it was made out of wombat meat.
  b. **Who did that soup taste to like it was made out of wombat meat?
  c. **the one whom that soup tasted to like it was made out of wombat meat
  d. *It was Harry who that soup tasted to like it was made out of wombat meat.

In all of these cases, the occurrence of psych movement in the derivation is indicated by:

(128) a.   The fact that the experiencer NP is the surface object;
  b.   The fact that *personally* can occur with the surface object;
  c.   The fact that the surface object cannot be (a noncontrastively stressed) reflexive.

It is significant to compare these sentences with others containing phonologically identical verbals, but where psych movement has not applied and there is no complement.

Consider for instance:

(129) a.   I smelled the statue.
  b.   What did you smell?
  c.   the thing that you smelled

Here the objects are freely extractable, as we would expect. It is particularly striking to take pairs like:

(130) a.   I smelled the gorilla.
  b.   I smelled funny to the gorilla.

(130)a has not undergone psych movement, and has no complement, while (130)b meets both of these conditions. And predictably:

(131) a.   Who did you smell?
  b. **What gorilla did you smell funny to?
  c. *To what gorilla did you smell funny?

As further evidence of the role of psych movement, it is significant to consider those verbals like *believe, regard, consider, find,* and so on which take complements which end up postverbally, and which undergo raising, giving them a derived object suitable for questioning and relative formation. Uniformly, we find that these derived objects are extractable.

(132) a. I believe (that Max is a vampire).
 b. I believe Max (to be a vampire).
 c. Who do you believe to be a vampire?
 d. the one who he believes to be a vampire
(133) a. I regard Max as a vampire.
 b. Who do you regard as a vampire?
 c. the one who he regards as a vampire

However, this follows from our analysis, since (103) requires the application of psych movement and verbs like *believe, regard, consider,* and so on have not undergone this, as indicated by the free reflexivization possibilities together with the position of their experiencer NP as surface subjects:

(134) a. I believe myself to be a vampire.
 b. Max regards himself as a genius.
 c. I find myself unable to go.
 d. I consider myself to be innocent.

Returning now to a more direct discussion of *remind,* the following facts are relevant:

(135) a. The IO NP of *remind* clauses is unextractable by the rules *Wh-Rel* movement and *Wh-Q* movement.
 b. There is a general constraint, formulable roughly and preliminarily as (103),[21] blocking the extractability of derived

---

[21] Clearly, (103) must be reformulated in a more general way, so that it will at least take account of similar behavior of many sentences which have undergone passive rather than psych movement. Thus observe:

(i) a. It was claimed by Max's mother that Arthur was a vampire.
 b. *By whom was it claimed that Arthur was a vampire?
 c. **Who was it claimed by that Arthur was a vampire?
 d. Who was that claimed by?
 e. By whom was that claimed?

Hence quite possibly, the proper formulation of the constraint sketched in (103) will refer to a notion like downgrading, or its more general basis in Priority relations, rather than to particular rules like psych movement per se.

One should also consider whether the constraint in (10), and that indicated by (i), are linked to the constraint observed by Ross (1967b) which prevents indirect objects from undergoing *wh*-movements after they have undergone the rule which places them directly postverbally:

(ii) a. I gave a shrunken head to someone.
 b. I gave someone a shrunken head.
 c. Who did you give a shrunken head to?
 d. To whom did you give a shrunken head?
 e. *Who did you give a shrunken head?

object NP which are the experiencer NP of verbals which undergo psych movement, and which take complements which end up postverbally.

c. The regularity in *b* holds for the hundreds of verbals in the class *annoy, bother, disgust,* in their pure verbal forms, and in their *ing-to* adjectival forms, for pure verbs like *seem, appear, impress, smell,* and other verbs of sensation, for pure adjectives like *obvious, important, vital.*

d. The regularity in *b* holds predictably for the verb *strike.*

e. Given a superficial analysis of *remind* as a deep verb occurring with no complement and three NP within its immediate clause, fact *a* and fact *b* are unrelated, merely accidental cofeatures of English.

However:

(136) Given *the strike-like analysis,* (135)b, by way of its special case, (135)d, automatically has (135)a as a consequence.

(136) is thus the deeper argument for *the strike-like analysis* derivable from the extractability constraints on *remind* clauses. It shows that this analysis permits reduction of the apparent exception in (135)a to the regularity in (135)b, which must somehow be part of English grammar, regardless of how *remind* sentences are analyzed. In fact, this regularity would exist in English even if *remind* were not part of the vocabulary. *The strike-like analysis* thus shows the extractability constraint on *remind* clauses to be a predictable consequence of the deeper generalization about English which is roughly formulated in (103). The precondition for this is a description of *remind* clauses which provides them with an underlying main verb + complement sentence structure, where the main verb is like the verb realized elsewhere as *strike,* a verb which undergoes psych movement.

C.   Arguments for an Embedded Similarity Predicate Clause

1. Remarks. In Part B of this section, several arguments were given showing that the underlying structures of *remind* sentences must contain a main verbal element with the properties of that verb *strike* which undergoes both raising and psych movement. In the present section, I take up arguments suggesting that this main verb takes as complement clauses with a similarity predicate, that is, one with the properties of members of the class *like, similar, resemble,* and such. At least one such argument has already been given, namely, the fact that the S-O coreference constraint of *remind* sentences corresponds to the restrictions in examples like:

(137) a. *Martha is like herself.
      b. *You no longer resemble yourself.
      c. *I used to be similar to myself.

2. Plural generic objects.   In sentences like:

(138) a.   Chevrolets resemble Volkswagens.
      b.   Monkeys are similar to acrobats.
      c.   Reptiles are like diplomats.

Similarity predicates occur with plural generic NP as their *objects*. However, this occurs under a special condition, namely, that such NP also occur in the subjects. When this condition is not met, sentences with similarity predicates[22] and plural generic NP are ill formed, in my dialect:

(139) a. *Harry is like gorillas.
      b. *Joan resembles tap dancers.
      c. *I am similar to researchers.

I do not even find such sentences acceptable when the subject is conjoined or a nongeneric plural:

(140) a. *You and I resemble linguists.
      b. *Jack and Jill were like idiots.
      c. *The men were similar to villains.

This generic restriction provides support for the embedded similarity predicate aspect of *the strike-like analysis,* since exactly the same restriction shows up between S and O of *remind* sentences:

(141) a.   Chevrolets remind me of Volkswagens.
      b.   Monkeys remind me of diplomats.
      c. *That Chevrolet reminds me of Volkswagens.
      d. *Jack reminds me of tap dancers.
      e. *Jack and Jill remind me of travellers.

It should be emphasized that the constraint on similarity predicates is not a general one having to do with verbal forms per se, but is a special property of this class:

(142) a.   John is fond of diplomats.
      b.   Jack and Jill are friendly to travellers.
      c.   Harry understands monkeys.

---

[22] This regularity is one of those holding for the wider class of predicates mentioned in footnote 6.

Therefore, the restriction in *remind* sentences requires special explanation, unless *the strike-like analysis* is taken as the derivational basis.

3.   *Average, typical.* Words like *average* and *typical*, when preceded by the definite article, function like quantifiers in sentences like:

(143)   a.   The average linguist is a university employee.
        b.   The typical Nazi liked to hit people on the head.

That is, the NP of which they are part are semantically interpreted as *variables* rather than as *constants*, just like NP such as *every dog, most employees,* and so on.

In general, it might be assumed that the subject and object of a similarity predicate are related to it symmetrically. It is not clear that this is the case, however, when quantified NP are involved. And it is definitely not the case when *average* or *typical* occurs in either subject or object. Thus:

(144)   a.   The typical linguist is similar to Max.
        b.   ?Max is similar to the typical linguist.
(145)   a.   The typical communist is like that man over there.
        b.   ?That man over there is like the typical communist.
(146)   a.   The average gorilla resembles your mother.
        b.   ?Your mother resembles the average gorilla.
(147)   a.   The average bureaucrat is like Nixon.
        b.   ?Nixon is like the average bureaucrat.

That is, in my dialect at least, when we have two NP with a similarity predicate, one of which is a normal constant-interpreted one with definite reference, the other a variable NP of the kind with *average* preceded by a definite article, there are natural sentences only when the variable NP is subject.[23] Notice that this restriction on *average, typical,* and so on is limited in scope to similarity predicates, and other members of the wider class including *different, equivalent,* and so on. It is not true for verbals in general. Thus the *b* sentences in (144)–(146) are fine if one replaces the similarity predicate by *know, fond of,* and so forth.

Significantly, the analogous restriction on *typical, average,* and so on, exists for me in *remind* clauses between S and O NP:

---

[23] The reason for this probably lies in the fact that in these symmetrical predicate cases there is an asymmetry between subject and object in that the object NP serves as the "standard." To say:

(i) John is like Bill.

is to presuppose that the listener knows what Bill is like and to assert that in some respect John matches Bill. Consequently, it is odd to have in the "standard" position an NP which does not designate a particular (set of) entities.

(148) a.   The typical linguist reminds me of Max.
      b.   ?Max reminds me of the typical linguist.
(149) a.   The typical communist reminds me of that man over there.
      b.   ?That man over there reminds me of the typical communist.
(150) a.   The average gorilla reminds me of your mother.
      b.   ?Your mother reminds me of the average gorilla.
(151) a.   The average bureaucrat reminds me of Nixon.
      b.   ?Nixon reminds me of the average bureaucrat.

Consequently, the strange variable NP restriction of similarity predicates is automatically carried over to *remind* clauses under *the strike-like analysis*. Without this analysis, the facts in *remind* clauses are again *ad hoc* restrictions related to nothing else in the grammar.[24]

It should be observed that the argument goes somewhat beyond *average, typical* and similar adjectives (such as *usual, normal*) to include, for me, certain ordinary quantifiers. Hence, the distribution of acceptability in (144)–(151) is, for example, unaffected by substituting *every* for *the* $\left\{ \begin{array}{c} average \\ typical \end{array} \right\}$ in all of these examples.[25]

4.   *In that* + *S*. Arguments for *the strike-like analysis* of *remind* clauses can be obtained by investigation of the rather special construction of the form *in that* + *S* (henceforth abbreviated Z). Z occurs with *remind* sentences:

(152) a.   Johnson reminded me of de Gaulle in that he had a long nose.
      b.   Pete reminded me of Fast Louis Parsons in that he could run the mile in 4.2 seconds.

However, obviously Z does not occur freely with most types of verbals:

[24] In the light of footnote 23, one could formulate an argument in somewhat different terms as follows. *The strike-like analysis* predicts that in *remind* clauses that NP which serves as the "standard" of comparison is the O, not the S.

[25] What is, I believe, the same restriction also carries over to the generic form *one*, not surprisingly, since such forms also involve in some way universal quantification. Hence observe:
   (i)   One is similar to other people.
   (ii) ?Other people are similar to one.
As a consequence of (ii), *the strike-like analysis* predicts that sentences like:
   (iii) ?Other people reminded Harry of one.
should be out, which is correct. It also seems that the well-formedness of (i) should predict that:
   (iv) ?One reminded Harry of other people.
is well formed, and this is not obvious. Observe, however, that (iv) seems no worse than the explicitly embedded structure:
   (v)   ?One struck Harry as being similar to other people.

(153) a. * Joe$_i$ punched Bill in that he$_i$ was sick for a week.
       b. *My doctor$_i$ fell down in that he$_i$ knows French very well.
       c. *Harry$_i$ knows algebra in that his$_i$ mouth is open.
       d. *Lucille$_i$ is singing in that she$_i$ is wiggling her vocal cords.[26]

That is, there must be a cross-classification of verbals with respect to whether or not they occur with Z. Observe, though, that Z does occur with similarity predicates:

(154) a. Harry$_i$ is similar to Jack in that he$_i$ has a big nose.
       b. That man$_i$ resembles my brother in that he$_i$ has red hair.
       c. Betty$_i$ is like Lucille in that she$_i$ has an enormous liver.

Thus there exists the following situation:

(155) a. Z does not occur with most verbals;
       b. Z occurs with similarity predicates (and also the related forms *different, equivalent,* and so on);
       c. Z occurs with *remind.*

The argument is clear. Under *the strike-like analysis,* the asymmetry of (155) is eliminated, since case *c* is reduced to case *b.* Without this analysis, there is the preposterous situation of a construction occurring with a set of elements, symmetrical predicates, which take two NP, not occurring with most other verbals, but then occurring with a special verb, *remind,* which takes three NP.

This argument is stronger than appears at first, for the following reason. Obviously, the syntactic fact that Z occurs with similarity predicates, *different, equivalent,* and so on is no accident, semantically. This is a semantically natural association, since Z serves to characterize the parameter(s) along which the similarity (difference) specified by the predicate is defined. In short, given *the strike-like analysis,* one can say simply that Z occurs with the class of symmetrical predicates, serving to specify the relevant parameter of relatedness. One thus *expects* Z to occur with such items, and under the analysis proposed here, this expectation carries over naturally to *remind.*

Another argument for *the strike-like analysis* can be derived from the facts of the Z construction. This second argument actually supports the claim that the main verb underlying *remind* is *strike,* and thus properly belongs in Part B.

I have considered only cases where Z occurs with an unembedded simi-

---

[26] If (153)d seems better than the other examples, it is, I believe, due to the fact that there is a distinct *in that + S* construction interpreted as meaning roughly 'because'. This is subject to the constraint that its main verbal be active. I am concerned in the text only with the "parameter" reading of *in that + S.*

larity predicate. Yet if these are to be the sources of Z with *remind* clauses, it is necessary that Z be embeddable. This is in fact possible in such cases as:

(156) a. Lucille impressed me as resembling her mother in that both of them have red hair.
     b. This meat looks to me like it is rotten in that it is covered with bugs.
     c. That child seems to me to resemble Pete in that it has dark skin.
     d. That dog appears to me to be similar to my wolf in that it eats rabbits.

However, quite strangely, Z with a similarity predicate can *not* be freely embedded with many sorts of main verbs:

(157) a. *Fred believes that Harry was similar to James in that he had no judgment.
     b. *I claim Lucille resembles her mother in that both of them have blonde hair.

I do not get Z readings for either of these. If they are well formed at all, it is only on a 'because' reading of *in that* + *S*, where the phrase is interpreted *as a constituent of the main clause*. Observe the contrast between (157), on the one hand, and:

(158) a. Fred believes that Harry was similar to James.
     b. I claim Lucille resembles her mother.

These show that the constraint is one concerning Z, and not similarity predicates as such.

How can one characterize the difference between those verbs like *impress, look, seem, appear* in (156), which permit embedded Z, and those like *believe* and *claim* in (157), which do not? The answer, if one recalls the analysis of verbs presented in Part B(5), is that the verbs in (156) undergo psych movement, while those in (157) do not. Hence the latter have their experiencer NP in subject position, while the former have them in the predicate. There would then appear to exist in English, in some form, the restriction:

(159) Z can occur with an embedded similarity predicate, just in case the first verb above the similarity predicate undergoes psych movement.

Now, given (159), we predict that it must be the case that *strike,* a psych movement verbal, can occur with an embedded Z. This is exactly right:

(160) a. John struck me as being similar to Pete in that he was ex-
           citable.
       b. John struck me as resembling his mother in that he was not
           too bright.
       c. John struck me as being like his father in that he was musi-
           cally inclined.[27]

Therefore, given (159) and *the strike-like analysis,* it is an automatic fact
that *remind* sentences can occur with the Z construction. Under *the strike-
like analysis,* this follows from two necessary facts: (i) Z occurs with similarity predicates; (ii) Z can occur with an embedded similarity predicate only
if the next verbal up undergoes psych movement. Hence, in a double sense,
it can be seen that the occurrence of Z with *remind* clauses is not exceptional
but follows from regularities statable on structures provided by *the strike-
like analysis* of *remind* clauses.

There is a further detail to the relation between Z and the next verb
above the symmetrical predicate it modifies. Sentences like (156) show that
Z can occur with psych movement verbals. This is necessary, but not sufficient, however, as seen from:

(161) a. *Lucille impressed Max as being similar to her mother in that
           she had red hair.
       b. *That child seemed to Bob to resemble Pete in that he had
           dark skin.
       c. *That dog appeared to you to be similar to my wolf in that
           it eats rabbits.

These show that in unembedded, declarative, nongeneric sentences, the
psych movement verbal must have a *first person* derived object, that is,
experiencer NP. However, this is not a fully general-form of the restriction.
For we notice that when the relevant constructions are explicitly embedded
below a verb of saying or thinking, the restrictions are rather different:

(162) a. John$_i$ says Lucille impressed him$_i$ as being similar to Mary
           in that she was very emotional.

---

[27] Notice that to preserve the regularity in (159), we must either claim that *be* is not a
real verb, or else indicate in some other way that it is "transparent" to this restriction.
This property of *be* is not particular to this case. Note that it is, for example, also transparent to such restrictions as that the first verb below a verb like *tell* must be a "self-
controllable" verb (see Kuno, 1970).

   (i)   I told John to visit Sally.
   (ii)   *I told John to resemble Mary.
   (iii) I told John not to be seen in public without his beard.
   (iv)   *I told John not to be found guilty.
   (v)   *I told John not to be betrayed by Sally.

       b. *John says Lucille impressed me as being similar to Mary in
           that she was very emotional.

(163)   a. $Doris_i$ claimed that Lucille seemed to her_i to resemble Gladys
           in that she was seven feet tall.

       b. *Doris claimed that Lucille seemed to me to resemble Gladys
           in that she was seven feet tall.

In these sentences, the restriction is clearly that the experiencer NP of the
psych movement verbal must be a coreferent of the agent NP of the next
higher verb of saying. This restriction can be generalized to cover unembedded cases like (161), where it seems that the requirement is that the
experiencer NP be first person, by adopting the analysis suggested by Ross
(1968) which provides each declarative sentence with an underlying performative verb of saying. Under this view, most first person NP are coreferents of the agents of deleted performative verbs. I will not go into this matter
further here, other than to say that the restrictions uncovered provide further support for the deleted performative verb analysis. Almost exactly
parallel restrictions are uncovered in part (6) below.

It appears then that there exists the following restriction:

(164) Z can occur with a symmetrical predicate which is embedded be-
      low a psych movement verbal just in case the experiencer NP of
      the psych movement verbal is a coreferent of the agent NP of the
      next higher verb of saying or thinking.

Given (164) and *the strike-like analysis,* one predicts that *remind* should
occur naturally with Z only when its IO NP is first person. But this is the
case:

(165)   a. Lucille reminded me of Betty in that she was beautiful.
       b. *Lucille reminded Max of Betty in that she was beautiful.

On the other hand, when *remind* is embedded below a verb of saying, one
predictably finds:

(166)   a. Max_i says Lucille reminded him_i of Betty in that she was
          beautiful.
       b. *Max_i says Lucille reminded me of Betty in that she was
          beautiful.

It follows that *remind* reveals a property otherwise manifested by main verbs
occurring with complement symmetrical predicates modified by Z constructions. Thus the facts provide clear evidence that underlying *remind* there
is, indeed, a main verb + complement sentence structure, as *the strike-like
analysis* claims.

5. In + the + way + that + S.   Arguments quite similar to those
derivable from *in that* + *S* are derivable from the related construction

$$in + the + way + \begin{Bmatrix} that \\ in\ which \end{Bmatrix} + S$$ (henceforth abbreviated X). Again, this

occurs with similarity predicates, and the wider set of related elements including *different, equivalent,* and so on, but not with most other verbals.
X does, however, occur with *remind* clauses:

(167) a. Max is similar to Pete in the way that he talks.
       b. Max reminds me of Pete in the way that he talks.
(168) a. Max resembles Barbara in the way he gives an argument.
       b. Max reminds me of Barbara in the way he gives an argument.

Thus the same kind of argument as the first given for the Z construction is
immediately derivable.

6. *Parallel deletions.*   Sentences of the form:

(169) a. Meeting Mary is like kissing a gorilla.
       b. Hitting a home run is similar to finding a hundred dollars.

reveal a peculiar restriction between the nominalized clauses in the two
nominals. For me, such sentences are only natural when the deleted subject
NP in both are coreferents. Moreover, the subject deletion in both clauses
is obligatory.
Hence:

(170) a. Shaving is like cutting one's throat.
       b. Shaving oneself is like torturing oneself.
       c. *Shaving himself was like torturing herself.
       d. *Shaving himself was like scratching myself.
       e. *Mary's criticizing herself was similar to Pete's praising him-
           self.
       f. *Criticizing Mary was similar to Pete's praising himself.
       g. *Mary's criticizing Lou was similar to praising yourself.

There are, then, the following restrictions on the subjects and objects
of similarity predicates in these cases.

(171) a. The underlying subjects of the nominalized clauses must be
           coreferents.
       b. These subjects must be deleted.[28]

---

[28] Both of the conditions (171) are valid only for noncontrastive NP. With strong contrastive stress, the deletion is unnecessary and coreference is not only not required but
unnatural:

(i)   Yoúr shaving Max is like mý torturing Pete.
(ii) ?Mý criticizing Billy is like mý attacking Tom.

However, (171) by no means exhausts the restrictions peculiar to sentences like (169). A further restriction is that the subject NP which are deleted in both clauses must be either the special general pronominal element *on* or else they must be coreferents of an NP in the clause of the immediately higher *verb of saying or thinking*.[29]

Consequently:

(172) a. Harry$_i$ says that shaving himself$_i$ is like torturing himself$_i$.
       b. *Harry$_i$ says that shaving herself is like torturing herself.
       c. (Harry$_i$ says) shaving oneself is like torturing oneself.

(173) a. Mary$_i$ thinks criticizing herself$_i$ is similar to torturing herself$_i$.
       b. *Mary$_i$ thinks criticizing myself is similar to torturing myself.
       c. (Mary$_i$ thinks) criticizing oneself is like torturing oneself.

(174) a. Pete$_i$ told Louis$_j$ that criticizing himself$_i$ would be like torturing himself$_i$.
       b. Pete$_i$ told Louis$_j$ that criticizing himself$_j$ would be like torturing himself$_j$.
       c. Pete told Louis that criticizing oneself would be like torturing oneself.

Now, on the face of it, this restriction does not hold for the unembedded constructions like those in (169). For these, the restriction is that the deleted subjects must be either of the type *one* or else must be first person elements in declarative sentences or second person elements in interrogatives:[30]

(175) a. Shaving myself is like torturing myself.
       b. *Shaving yourself is like torturing yourself.
       c. *Is shaving myself like torturing myself?
       d. Is shaving yourself like torturing yourself?

However, it is natural to regard facts like those in (175) not as indicative of some special restrictions distinct from those operative in (172)–(174), but

---

[29] A better statement would be one which referred to verbs that are "world creating" in the sense of G. Lakoff (1970a). That is, some verbs are such that their complements describe the world not fully in the terms of the speaker but at least partially in the terms of the individual designated by the experiencer NP of the verb itself.

[30] Even this statement is too general and requires further restriction at least for plurals, and to distinguish *yes-no* questions from others:

   (i)   *Is shaving myself like torturing myself?
   (ii)   Is shaving yourself like torturing yourself?
   (iii) Why is shaving myself like torturing myself?
   (iv)   *Why is shaving yourself like torturing yourself?

Also, modality is relevant:

   (v)   Is shaving myself going to be like torturing myself?

I have held these factors constant in the text, rendering them, I think, thereby irrelevant to the argument.

rather as instances of the same restrictions defined in terms of the performative verbs occurring in the underlying structures of (175).³¹ That is, it is
natural to reduce the facts of (175) to the principles underlying those of
(172)–(174) by way of an analysis like that suggested in Ross (1968), which
provides every declarative sentence with a performative verb which is a
verb of saying.³² Hence this induces restrictions just like the undeleted nonperformative verbs of saying and thinking in (172)–(174). Assuming this,
then, we can summarize the restrictions on constructions of the type (169)
as follows:

(176) a.   The underlying subjects of the nominalized clauses must be
            coreferents;
       b.   these subjects must be deleted;
       c.   (i) these subjects must be coreferents of an NP in the clause
            of the immediately higher verb of saying or thinking, or:
            (ii) they must be the general pronominal element *one*.³³, ³⁴

---

³¹ Observe that such an analysis of sentences like (175)a serves in part to bring the deletion
in such constructions under general principles operative for other cases of complement
subject deletion. That is, in general, such deletion takes place only when the subject has
a coreferent "controller" in a dominating construction. But the proposed performative
analysis of sentences like (175) provides them with just such a higher NP. The deletion
still remains partially unique, however, since in this case, but not in others, the "controller" NP is not in the next highest clause, but is two away. This is very peculiar.

³² As with the facts mentioned in part (5) about *in that* + *S* and agents of higher verbs
of saying, these facts can, of course, be developed into a very strong argument supporting
the postulation of performative verbs of saying which are deleted.

³³ Ross (personal communication) points out that these generalizations are not quite right
since there is also the possibility, without contrastive stress, of having *there* in both positions:

  (i)   There being no love between us is similar to there being no food in China.
  (ii) There being trouble in Africa is equivalent to there being trouble in Persia.
Moreover, in these cases *there* is undeletable:
  (iii) *Being no love between us is similar to (there) being no food in China.
I do not understand these facts.

³⁴ The peculiar element *one* must be represented as a *variable* NP, quantified over by
the same kind of universal quantification typical of generic NP, in contrast to *I* and *you*,
whose representations must involve constants. Intuitively, though, *I/you* and *one* are
closely, if obscurely, related. I think this relation can be described something like this.
One is a variable over just the range of entities that can be designated by *I* or *you*. That
is, roughly, *one* varies over sentient beings, beings capable of addressing or being addressed.
Hence, if we can say:

  (i)   On Mars, one builds one's house near a canal.
to refer to Martians, then we can say:
  (ii) Do you like having your house near a canal?
to a Martian. However, this does not exhaust the relation between the variable element
one and *I/you*. For in fact, *one* has the same inherent subjectivity that *I* does. Thus
observe the contrast between a science-fiction computer saying:

  (iii) People (sentient beings) should not destroy valuable property.
  (iv) One should not destroy valuable property.
In using (iv), the computer assumes itself to be a being of the type covered by *one*. Thus
in using (iv) the computer expresses a law which covers the computer itself. This is not

It should be emphasized that the properties of (176) are valid not only for the similarity predicates *similar, resemble, like,* and so forth, but also for their negative cousins, *different, differ, distinct, contrast,* and for the wider set of logically symmetrical predicates, *equivalent, identical, same, equal, equal (to).*

We observe next that these peculiar properties carry over to similarity predicate clauses which are embedded below *strike,* with this verbal acting as a verb of saying/thinking:

(177) a.   It strikes me that shaving myself is like torturing myself.
       b.   *It strikes me that shaving himself is like torturing himself.
       c.   It strikes me that shaving oneself is like torturing oneself.

(178) a.   It struck Harry$_i$ that shaving himself$_i$ was like torturing himself$_i$.
       b.   *It struck Harry that shaving myself was like torturing myself.
       c.   It struck Harry that shaving oneself is like torturing oneself.

(179) a.   It struck Lucille$_i$ that praising herself$_i$ was similar to criticizing herself$_i$.
       b.   *It struck Lucille$_i$ that my praising her$_i$ was similar to Pete's criticizing her$_i$.
       c.   *It struck Lucille$_i$ that praising herself$_i$ was similar to Pete's criticizing her$_i$.
       d.   *It struck Lucille$_i$ that my praising her$_i$ was similar to criticizing herself$_i$.

Given *the strike-like analysis* then, the grammar must predict that the restrictions summarized in (176) must all carry over to *remind* clauses. And this is the case:

(180) a.   Shaving myself reminds me of torturing myself.
       b.   *Shaving himself reminds me of torturing himself.
       c.   Shaving oneself reminds me of torturing oneself.

(181) a.   Shaving himself$_i$ reminded Harry of torturing himself$_i$.
       b.   *Shaving myself reminded Harry of torturing myself.
       c.   Shaving oneself reminded Harry of torturing oneself.

---

the case with (iii). Consequently, *one* is, in unmarked cases, used to express purported laws which necessarily cover their speaker. In this sense *one* is a quantified NP whose scope necessarily includes the individual designated by *I*. This provides, I think, the beginning of an understanding of why sentences like those in the text should allow either *I/you* on the one hand, or *one* on the other. There is a common structure here, differentiated by the constant-variable distinction. This analysis also makes it seem less arbitrary that the colloquial form of *one* in many dialects is *you*. Similarly, it provides some insight into that dialect of British English which, in some styles at least, uses *one* as a variant of *I*, that is, as a constant rather than variable NP.

(182) a.   Praising herself$_i$ reminded Lucille$_i$ of criticizing herself$_i$.
       b.   *My praising her$_i$ reminded Lucille$_i$ of Pete's criticizing her$_i$.
       c.   *Praising herself$_i$ reminded Lucille$_i$ of Pete's criticizing her$_i$.
       d.   *My praising her$_i$ reminded Lucille$_i$ of criticizing herself$_i$.

The key fact in the *remind* examples is that condition c(i) of (176), which requires coreference with an NP in a higher clause, predicts, given *the strike-like analysis* of *remind* clauses, that in *remind* sentences this identity will be to the IO of *remind* clauses, either when these stand in surface structure unembedded, or when embedded below some other verb. But this is right:

(183) a.   Shaving myself reminds me of torturing myself.
       b.   Shaving himself$_i$ reminded Harry of torturing himself$_i$.
       c.   *Shaving myself reminded Harry of torturing myself.
       d.   *Shaving himself reminded me of torturing himself.
(184) a.   Max thought that shaving myself reminded me of torturing myself.
       b.   *Max thought that shaving himself reminded me of torturing himself.
       c.   I thought that shaving himself reminded Max of torturing himself.
       d.   *I thought that shaving myself reminded Max of torturing myself.

One can imagine no more striking piece of evidence for the claims of *the strike-like analysis* than the fact that the IO of *remind* sentences behaves like an NP of an immediately dominating clause with respect to the application of principle (176) to the prediction of the facts in sentences like (183)–(184), facts which are, given *the strike-like analysis,* perfectly regular deductions from (176).

I have shown, then, in this section on parallel deletions that *remind* clauses obey in detail the law (176), a regularity whose domain must be given as two-term logically symmetrical predicates[35] embedded below some verb of saying/thinking. *Remind* clauses act *vis-à-vis* (176) just like a construction with a two-term symmetrical predicate, with the IO acting like an NP clause mate of the dominating verb of saying/thinking. But this is just the structure provided by *the strike-like analysis.*

To appreciate the strength of this argument in favor of *the strike-like analysis,* it must be observed that what has been shown is not only that the analysis predicts the properties of *remind vis-à-vis* the restrictions under

---

[35] That is, the regularity in (176) governs not just similarity predicates but the wider class mentioned in footnote 6.

consideration. In addition, it is obvious that *without* this analysis the grammar must specify both that: (i) *remind* is an exception to the regular rule (176)c (i); and (ii) there is a special rule for *remind* alone specifying that the NP which must be coreferent of the deleted subjects is the IO. Thus the alternative to *the strike-like analysis* in this case is a grammar in which there is:

(185) a. A regular rule (176)c (i);
       b. a statement to the effect that *remind* is an exception to (176)c (i);
       c. a special rule limited in scope to *remind* which says just what (176)c (i) says for the regular cases.

(185) shows that the alternative to *the strike-like analysis* is an account in which the perfectly regular properties of *remind* must be taken to involve two separate irregularities, an exception statement for (176)c (i) and a special rule to do the work of (176)c (i) in the single case. It is hard to conceive of a stronger argument for an analysis of the type under discussion.

7. **Constraints across conjunctions.** If we consider sentences of the form:

(186) a. Max_i thinks $Greta_j$ is similar to $Pete_k$ but $Lucille_l$ can't see that they are similar.
       b. Max_i thinks $Greta_j$ is similar to $Pete_k$ and I can see they are similar too.

where in each case the *they* is pronounced with weak, anaphoric stress, there is a restriction of interpretation of this *they* such that, in examples like (186), it is a coreferent of the NP subscripted *j, k* and no others. That is, *they* must be a coreferent of the n-ad of those NP which function as subject and object of the similarity predicate in the preceding clause. The same point is made when the second clause contains a nominalization:

(187) a. Max_i thinks $Greta_j$ is similar to $Pete_k$ but $Lucille_l$ can't see the similarity between them.
       b. Max_i thinks $Greta_j$ resembles $Pete_k$ and I can see the resemblance between them too.

Here it is weakly stressed *them* that must be a coreferent of the pair subscripted *j, k* and no others. The natural regularity here is that *they/them* in the second clauses must refer to the terms of the contrasting similarity predicate in the complement sentence of the preceding clause of thinking/saying. But exactly this regularity predicts the properties of sentences like:

(188) a.   Harry$_i$ reminds me of Larry$_j$ but Lucille$_k$ can't see that they
             are similar.
       b.   Harry$_i$ reminds me of Joe Dimaggio$_j$ but Lucille$_k$ can't see the
             resemblance between them.

in which *they/them* must be a coreferent of the pair of S and O NP of the
remind clause, if *the strike-like analysis* is accepted. That is, here again,
remind clauses behave like complex clauses with a saying/thinking main
verb and a complement containing a two term predicate of similarity, as
the strike-like analysis predicts.

There is, obviously, another argument based on the same facts. The one
just given was based on pronoun interpretation. But equally well one can
point out that those clauses which can occur as the first in sentences like
(186)(187) are just those with a thinking/saying main verb, and similarity
predicate complement. Hence, in general, complementless verbs are banned:

(189)   *Harry said something to Betty but Lucille can't see that they
         are similar.

as are verbs with complements of the nonsimilarity predicate type:

(190)   *Harry said that Max liked Bill but Lucille can't see the resem-
         blance between them.

Consequently, the occurrence of *remind* clauses in this position as illustrated
by (188) is quite anomalous if these have any structure other than that
provided by *the strike-like analysis*. Given the latter, on the other hand, the
occurrence is predicted directly.

III.   *The Strike-Like Analysis* and Predicate Raising

In a series of papers, McCawley (1968c, 1969b, 1970)[36] has proposed that
there exists in English a rule which he refers to as predicate raising. This
operation has the effect of taking the main verb of a complement sentence
and lifting it into the immediately higher main clause, attaching it to the
main verb of that clause, thus producing a kind of compound verb. This
rule is taken to operate prelexically, that is, before the lexicon has been
used to fill in the phonological form of constituents. Hence, an example of
the operation of predicate raising would be, according to McCawley, the
successive conversion of (191) into (192), (193), (194) by applying the rule
cyclically from bottom to top of (191).

---

[36] See also the discussion in de Rijk (1968) and Green (1969).

(191)

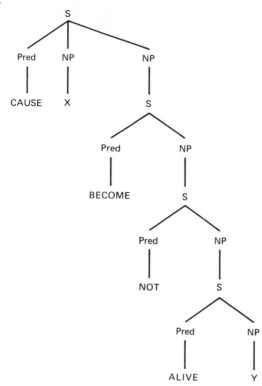

(192)

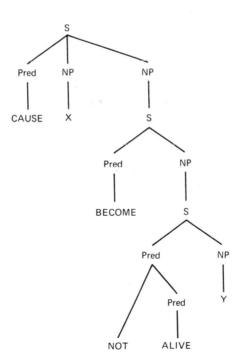

(193)

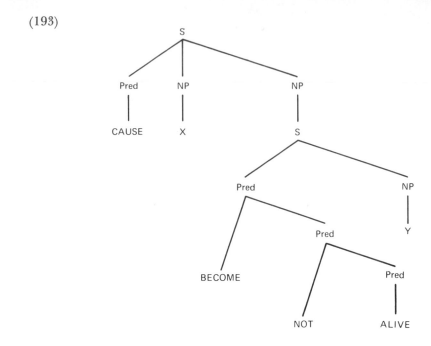

(194)

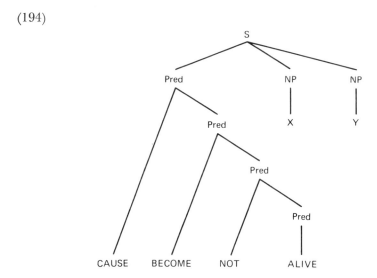

(194) is then the structure which, according to McCawley, underlies sentences of the form *x kill y*.

I have argued in Sections I and II that *remind* clauses have an underlying structure containing a main verb-complement sentence complex. Thus a sentence like:

(195)   Max reminded me of Pete.

would have, schematically, an underlying form like (196), where predicates are capitalized and where I adopt for the first time McCawley's (1970) notion that English has a VSO underlying order:

(196)

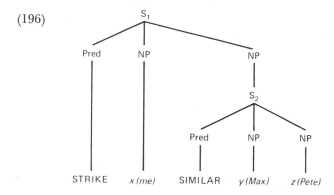

As I observed earlier in the discussion of Section I. B, some rule is necessary to convert structures that would otherwise end up as:

(197)   Max struck me as resembling Pete.

into those like (195). I referred to such an operation in passing as remind formation, but without serious discussion or justification. Observe, however, that what remind formation would have to do is simply take the predicate similar out of the complement clause of structures like (196) and attach it to strike to yield a compound verb, *strikesimilar* = *strikelike* = *strikeresemble*. But this operation is just what McCawley's predicate raising would do. In other words, there is no reason or need to propose a special rule of remind formation to make *the strike-like analysis* yield the right surface structures. The needed operation is simply a special case of McCawley's predicate raising.

Thus, one way of looking at the justification given in Sections I and II for *the strike-like analysis* is that this provides considerable support for the existence in English of a general operation which generates compound predicates out of main clause verbs and the main verbs of their complement clauses.

In these terms, sentences like (195) have a derivation from structures like (196) which involves the rules raising, predicate raising, psych movement, and subject formation, where the latter is the rule which converts the underlying VSO order to the SVO order typical of English surface clauses. The derivation would proceed schematically as follows:

(198) = (196) $\xRightarrow{\text{RAISING}}$

(199)

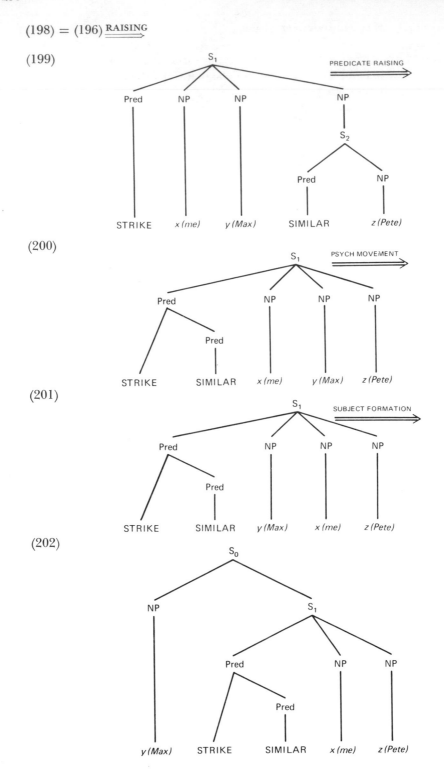

(200)

(201)

(202)

In the passage from (199) to (200), the node S_2 is destroyed by the operation of predicate raising, which leaves it without any branching structure. That is, S_2 is pruned, as posited by Ross (1969b). It is the operation of psych movement on (200) which guarantees that subject formation will make a subject out of *Max,* rather than *me,* since this rule operates on the NP immediately following the verb. At some point, of course, the dictionary or lexicon must be used to provide the derived compound verb in (202) its phonological form, *remind.* I leave open here just when this takes place.

It goes without saying that there are features of the derivation just discussed which are as yet unaccounted for; for instance, the origin of the preposition *of* of *remind* clauses. A more serious difficulty is the absence of any *single word* multi-morpheme verb such as *strikesimilar.* This is, so far, an unexplained gap. However, this seems to be a general difficulty with McCawley's rule of predicate raising. That is, although the structures produced by this rule are *compounds,* the clear cases of outputs seem to be monomorphemic. This fact requires analysis and explication.[37]

[37] This problem may be related to the question of how to describe the properties of a verb like *put* in sentences such as:

   (i)   Harry put the garbage in the can.
   (ii) I put the cat under the table.

Put clearly represents one of the causative verbs, but it is restricted to occurring with complements of locative type. This means that grammatical theory must be able to represent restrictions on the distribution of phonological lexical items in terms of the nature of the main verbs of their complement sentences. Given this fact, together with the postulated analysis of *remind* by way of predicate raising, one can begin to see a suspicious duplication. That is, given underlying, semantic structures of the form:

   (iii)

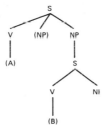

there are now *two* different mechanisms by which the shape of the main verb which represents (A) in surface structure can be determined. One is by way of constraints like those between *put* and a locative complement, the other by way of predicate raising analysis, as in the case of *remind.* That is, cause is pronounced *put* if its complement verb is locative. Perceive is pronounced *remind* if it undergoes psych movement, and predicate raising with a similarity predicate. Since there is no obvious way to reduce the description of *put* to an analysis in terms of predicate raising, one must consider reducing predicate raising descriptions to those of the type involved in *put.* This would mean rejection of a rule of predicate raising adjoining a complement verb to a main verb in favor of a rule deleting complement verbs given certain types of main verb. This proposal deserves consideration both as a way of eliminating the suspicious redundancy of two ways of stating main verb-complement verb restrictions and as a way of explaining why putative predicate raising outputs, which would be formally compounds, never show up as phono-

IV. Some Apparently Opposing Facts

In Sections I and II, I have given what I believe are many strong arguments supporting *the strike-like analysis* of *remind* clauses. In Section III,
I have sketched the transformational derivation of such clauses from underlying main verb + complement sentence structures given in the prelexical
form suggested by McCawley.

There are, however, some facts not yet considered which might easily
be taken to throw doubt on the validity of *the strike-like analysis*. I have
taken as supporting data all those facts which show that *remind* clauses
manifest properties of underlying *strike* + similarity predicate complement
sentence structures. Counterevidence would therefore arise if there were
properties of the latter sentences which did not carry over to *remind* clauses.
And there are apparently some such properties.

Similarity predicates can occur with nominalized prepositional phrases
of the form:

(203) a.   Max is similar to Pete in size.
       b.   Joe resembles you in weight.
       c.   Tom is like Bill in coloring and eyebrow texture.

These can, moreover, occur embedded below *strike*:

(204) a.   Max struck me as being similar to Pete in size.
       b.   Joe struck me as resembling you in weight.
       c.   Tom struck me as being like Bill in coloring and eyebrow
          texture.

Given *the strike-like analysis* then, one predicts that there should exist
remind clauses of the type:

(205) a.   *Max reminded me of Pete in size.
       b.   *Joe reminded me of you in weight.
       c.   *Tom reminded me of Bill in coloring and eyebrow texture.

---

logical compounds. Such a revised analysis would, as far as I can see, be as harmonious
with all of the facts discussed in this paper as the predicate raising analysis. However,
this proposal runs into considerable difficulties when complex cases involving more than
one embedding are considered, such as McCawley's derivation of *die* from the semantic
structure underlying *become not alive*. Under the deletion proposal, the lexical item *die*
would have to be inserted in the position of the predicate underlying *become,* just in case
the complement verbal has been deleted on both previous cycles. Since this process is
recursive, the constraints between lexical items, underlying structures and deletion become very complex and peculiar indeed.

But this deduction from the analysis is uniformly incorrect, and on the face of it, such a prediction failure is a serious blow to the analysis I have been trying to support.

I think, however, that on somewhat deeper investigation, this real problem will be seen as no serious obstacle to the validation of *the strike-like analysis.* For while I cannot *explain* the facts in (205), it is possible to provide a way of stating them without abandoning the analysis, and this description turns out to be necessary to account for certain further facts about *remind* clauses: Thus I will claim that while (205) reveals an *ad hoc* property of *remind* clauses, it is not a fully *ad hoc* property, since the restriction there revealed does other work.

It seems on the surface that similarity predicates, and, more generally, symmetrical, reflexive predicates like *equivalent, identical,* and so on can occur with almost any kind of NP whatever, regardless of what these refer to. This seems somewhat suspicious, because, intuitively, what are similar, identical, or not are only the properties of things. It is notable, therefore, that in general there are paraphrase sentences for similarity predicate sentences whose terms are not superficially property designators where the NP terms do refer to properties. Thus we can find pairs like:

(206) a. Max is similar to George in the way he treats girls.
      b. The way Max treats girls is similar to the way George treats girls.
(207) a. Max resembles Pete in coloring.
      b. Max's coloring resembles Pete's coloring.
(208) a. This proposal is equivalent to that proposal in empirical content.
      b. The empirical content of this proposal is equivalent to the empirical content of that proposal.

No method of relating such sentence pairs grammatically has, to my knowledge, ever been proposed, but clearly an adequate grammar must contain devices for accomplishing just this.[38]

---

[38] J. R. Ross (personal communication) observes that the rules involved in relating pairs like (206)–(208) in the text are essentially the same as those involved in pairs including *by* constructions like:
   (i) a. Harry's calling Mary annoyed me.
       b. Harry annoyed me by calling Mary.
   (ii) a. Harry's leaving early bothered me.
       b. Harry bothered me by leaving early.
Similarly, the same type of process seems involved in such pairs as:
   (iii) a. Mary's flashing smile brightened up the party.
       b. Mary brightened up the party with her flashing smile.
   (iv) a. Max's discovery excited everyone.
       b. Max excited everyone with his discovery.
Hence the rules involved seem to be a quite general and pervasive feature of English grammar.

Let us distinguish a-type from b-type sentences in examples like (206)–(208) as *entity sentences* and *property sentences,* respectively. It seems, then, that one must make at least the following distinction. For some kinds of properties, similarity predicate sentences may be of either the entity or property varieties. But for some properties, entity form is required. Thus, in the former class are properties represented by such words as *coloring, gestures, voice, speech, mannerisms, accent, expression.* In the latter are *size, height, weight, length,* and so forth. Hence:

(209) a. Max resembles Pete in weight.
       b. *Max's weight resembles Pete's weight.
(210) a. The Queen Mary is similar to the New Jersey in gross tonnage.
       b. *The Queen Mary's gross tonnage is similar to the New Jersey's gross tonnage.

But:

(211) a. The saint resembled Louis in mannerisms.
       b. The saint's mannerisms resembled Louis's mannerisms.

There is, evidently, a semantic generalization about which properties require entity sentence form, namely, just those which are abstract, and not directly perceptible, and which are quantitative rather than qualitative.

The distinction between examples like (209) and (210), on the one hand, and (211), on the other, carries over when similarity predicates are embedded below *strike*:

(212) a. It struck me that Max resembled Pete in weight.
       b. *It struck me that Max's weight resembled Pete's weight.
(213) a. It struck me that the Queen Mary was similar to the New Jersey in gross tonnage.
       b. *The Queen Mary's gross tonnage struck me as being similar to the New Jersey's gross tonnage.
(214) a. It struck me that the saint resembled Louis in mannerisms.
       b. The saint's mannerisms struck me as resembling Louis's mannerisms.

However, as already observed, the grammatical variants in (212)–(214) do not have *remind* analogues. If we replace the sentences in (212)–(214) by the "analogous" *remind* forms, all of them, except the analogue to (214)b, will be ill formed. This is an apparent disconfirmation of our analysis.

However, one can, without great difficulty, describe the facts as follows, while maintaining the analysis. As described in Section III, the difference between sentences like (212)–(214) and their potential *remind* analogues devolves on the optional application of the rule of predicate raising. The facts indicate, then, that no similarity predicate can undergo *both* predicate raising and that sequence of rules which converts property sentences into entity sentences. This is a kind of incompatibility between rule applications in a derivation which must be recognized as a general feature of grammar.[39] Suppose we refer to the sequence of rules in question jointly as property factoring. Then it is claimed that English contains the derivational constraint:

(215)   No similarity predicate may undergo both predicate raising and property factoring.[40]

(215) is to be regarded as a filter which marks any sentence arising through a derivation which violates (215) as ill formed. Hence, it will correctly mark sentences like (205) as ill formed.

Now it might be claimed that (215) is a special *ad hoc* addition to the grammar required only by *the strike-like analysis* of *remind* sentences. That is, it could be argued that (215) is an act of desperation forced by the incompatibility of our analysis with the ungrammaticality of sentences like (205). First of all, even if this were the case, it seems to me that the result is acceptable. That is, *the strike-like analysis* is so strongly supported by facts like those given in Sections I and II, that (215) would be a small price to pay for maintaining it in the face of facts like (205). There are, however, properties of *remind* clauses which show that (215) is not as *ad hoc* as it seems.

As observed earlier, in similarity predicate clauses, properties like that represented by *weight*, and so forth, must be represented by structures which

---

[39] For an obvious example of rule incompatibilities in a grammar, see the discussion in Postal (1971a), where it is shown how a condition of incompatibility between passive and the rule which positions indirect objects can serve to eliminate the duplication of indirect object positioning rules found necessary by Fillmore (1965a) on the basis of his observation that *to* indirect objects have two passives, but *for* indirect objects only one.

[40] Actually, this is too general. It really only governs those occurrences of property factoring which yield nominalizations, not those which yield full clauses. Hence while there is a contrast in (i):

   (i) a.   John's gestures are similar to Pete's gestures.
       b.   John is similar to Pete in gestures.
       c.   John's gestures remind me of Pete's gestures.
       d.   *John reminds me of Pete in gestures.
there is none in (ii):
   (ii) a.   The way John gesticulates is similar to the way Pete gesticulates.
        b.   John is similar to Pete in the way he gesticulates.
        c.   The way John gesticulates reminds me of the way Pete gesticulates.
        d.   John reminds me of Pete in the way he gesticulates.

The ultimate formulation of the constraint in (215) must thus take account of the difference between structures like *in gestures* and *in the way he gesticulates*.

result from property factoring, unlike those represented by words like *gestures,* and so forth, for which this is optional. Let us represent this as:

(216)   Property factoring is obligatory in similarity predicate clauses for abstract, measurable nominalizations.

Notice, then, that given *the strike-like analysis,* together with (215) and (216), we predict that no well-formed *remind* clause can contain S nominals of the type *John's weight, Pete's height,* and so forth, although nothing blocks the occurrences as *remind* clause S of nominals like *John's gestures, Pete's coloring,* and so forth. But these predictions are correct:

(217)   a.   *Pete's height reminds me of Joe's height.
        b.   *Pete's length reminded everyone of the box's length.
        c.   *Pete's weight reminded everyone of Max's mass.
(218)   a.   Pete's gestures reminded me of Harry's mannerisms.
        b.   Pete's coloring reminded me of Lucy's coloring.
        c.   Pete's accent reminded me of Herbie's accent.

The ill-formedness of (217) is predicted as follows. (216) requires that NP like those in the subject of (217) undergo property factoring when they occur in similarity predicate clauses. *The strike-like analysis* specifies that structures like (217) can only be derived from underlying representations in which the S NP of (217) are in similarity predicate clauses. However, given *the strike-like analysis,* surface forms like (217) can only be derived by application of predicate raising. Therefore, surface strings like (217) can only be derived by operation of both property factoring and predicate raising to the same similarity predicate. But (215) predicts that all such derivations will yield ill-formed examples.

Consequently, while initially (215) seems totally *ad hoc,* it turns out that this principle plays a real explanatory role in the grammar. That is, it shows how the peculiar properties of sentences like (217) are automatic consequences of the principle (216), required for similarity predicates. Further, it explains why similarity predicate clauses have both entity and property sentence variants, while *remind* clauses have only property sentence versions. That is, under the analysis suggested here, (215) explains in addition the contrast between:

(219)   a.   Harry's gestures struck me as being similar to Pete's gestures.
        b.   Harry struck me as being similar to Pete in gestures.

and:

(220)   a.   Harry's gestures reminded me of Pete's gestures.
        b.   *Harry reminded me of Pete in gestures.

The ill-formedness of (220)b and all similar examples is an otherwise totally mysterious fact about *remind* clauses, especially in view of the fact noted earlier that *remind* is in general almost selectionally free with respect to its S NP. Consequently, *the strike-like analysis* serves to show that the facts in (205), and (217)–(220) are all functions of the two underlying principles (215) and (216).

Still, one would be happier about (215) if it were not so limited. That is, while stated quite generally and in a way which, in particular, does not mention the lexical item *remind*, all data supporting (215) so far in fact derives exclusively from the properties of clauses containing this single lexical item. Hence suspicions about the validity of (215) are well founded, unless data independent of the lexical item *remind* can be found which bears positively on (215). That is, we need to find other lexical items whose behavior is partly predicted correctly by (215).

Fortunately, such items exist. One finds sentences such as:

(221) a.   This function's value is identical to that function's value.
       b.   This function is identical to that function in value.

Both entity and property sentence variants are well formed. There exist as well, however, sentences with the verb *identify*:

(222) a.   I identified the value of this function with the value of that function.
       b.   I identified this function's value with that function's value.

Now it is right, I think, to claim that *identify* in sentences like (222) arises from a main verb + complement sentence structure in which the verbal of the complement is the *identical* occurring in sentences like (221). The main verb is probably some variety of "judging" element.[41] Naturally, the derivation will precede by way of application of predicate raising. If this were the case, and if these derivations were subject to constraints analogous to (215), one would predict that sentences with *identify* could only have property form. But this is true:

(223) a.   I identified the value of this function with the value of that function.
       b.   *I identified this function with that function in value.

[41] Or, there may be an ambiguity with one reading such that the main verb has a meaning like the term *set*, used in discussions of computer programming, referring to the specification of a variable at a certain point as some particular constant. These remarks carry over to the following examples as well.

A parallel argument can be given for *equate* and $\begin{Bmatrix} equal \\ equivalent \end{Bmatrix}$:

(224) a. Harry's proposal's value is equivalent to your proposal's value.
       b. Harry's proposal is equivalent to your proposal in value.
(225) a. I equated Harry's proposal's value with your proposal's value.
       b. *I equated Harry's proposal to your proposal in value.

Just so for *differ, differentiate*:

(226) a. Harry's proposal's value differs from your proposal's value.
       b. Harry's proposal differs from your proposal in value.
(227) a. I differentiated Harry's proposal's value from your proposal's value.
       b. *I differentiated Harry's proposal from your proposal in value.

A parallel pair is *distinct* and *distinguish*:

(228) a. Harry's proposal's meaning is distinct from your proposal's meaning.
       b. Harry's proposal is distinct from your proposal in meaning.
(229) a. I distinguished Harry's proposal's meaning from your proposal's meaning.
       b. *I distinguished Harry's proposal from your proposal in meaning.

Another such pair is *connected* and *connect*:

(230) a. My idea's origin is connected to your idea's origin.
       b. My idea is connected to your idea in origin.
(231) a. I connected my idea's origin with your idea's origin.
       b. *I connected my idea to your idea in origin.

Finally, the same properties hold for *related* and *relate*:

(232) a. This invention's cost is related to that invention's cost.
       b. This invention is related to that invention in cost.
(233) a. I related this invention's cost to that invention's cost.
       b. *I related this invention to that invention in cost.

These facts show that (215) is both correct and general, that is, that it is not limited in coverage to *remind* clauses. In fact, it is obviously more general than I have stated. A correct formulation should refer not to similarity predicate per se but to the wider class of symmetrical predicates including similarity predicates, *identical, equivalent, different, related*. Thus the facts in (223)–(233) show that there is indeed a valid constraint in English blocking the joint application of predicate raising and property factoring to the same predicate in the course of a derivation. This being the case, far from being an *ad hoc* or desperation device, (215), or rather a correct, more general reformulation of it, is a constraint which must be part of the grammar of English, no matter how *remind* clauses are described. Consequently, the facts in (215) with which we began this section can in no sense be looked upon as throwing any doubt on the validity of *the strike-like analysis*. Rather, they should only be taken as indicating the existence of the previously unsuspected regularity indicated roughly in (215), as well as indicating the need for those principles I have tagged property factoring. These latter principles I have, of course, not been able to give any serious account of here.[42]

V.   Theoretical Implications

A.   Remarks

In Sections I, II, and IV a variety of arguments were presented, which, taken together, show unambiguously that surface *remind* clauses are derived by way of *the strike-like analysis*. In Section III, I sketched the transformational mappings involved. In the present section, I will consider the theoretical ramifications of this conclusion about the derivation of the surface verb *remind*.

One might sum up the result of previous sections as follows:

(234)   There is no deep verb *remind*.

That is:

(235)   The surface verb *remind* does not correspond to any single verbal element in those structures which are the input to transformational rules.

Consequently:

(236)   In general, those structures which provide the input to transformational rules are not defined even in part by a relation to surface structures which is "lexical item preserving."

---

[42] I note, however, that these principles have a good deal in common with the operation of what has been called *conjunction reduction*.

That is, one *cannot* assume that:

(237)   the lexical items occurring in the surface structure of a sentence provide a minimal skeleton out of which its "deep structure" is formed.

To understand the implications of these facts, it will be well to consider general aspects of the development of the generative-transformational theory of grammatical structure. In particular, I am concerned with what (234)–(237) show about the role of the lexicon in a grammar, as well as with certain more general issues of which this question is a part.

The development of generative-transformational grammar began in the early 1950s with the attempt of Chomsky to provide a generative formulation for some of the ideas of Zellig Harris. The early growth of transformational theory is, from the point of view of current concerns at least, quite strange, although this strangeness is understandable if one considers the state of linguistic theory in the early 1950s and the fact that the source of part of the development of generative grammar lay in Harris's work and conception of linguistic data. The strangeness lies in the fact that for some time no specific account of semantics was attempted. It was assumed that there was an independent syntax which was the basis of a possible semantic description, relegated to the future. This is clearly Chomsky's position throughout the first decade (1953–1963) of work in this genre (see, for example, Chapter 9 of Chomsky 1957).

In 1963, a significant change took place in generative-transformational thinking, with the development in the work of Katz and Fodor (1963) of a semantic theory which was linked to transformational grammar. While the notion that there is an autonomous syntax on which semantic description must be based was maintained, indeed elaborated, a conception of semantic structure itself emerged and its relation to grammatical form began to be specified. Largely under the stimulation of continued work by Katz,[43] there evolved a conception of transformational grammar in which a semantic component was accorded a central place. This conception, arrived at partially in Katz and Postal (1964) and more or less fully specified in Chomsky (1965), I will refer to as *classical transformational theory*.

In this view, there are three components in a grammar, one, the syntactic, being generatively basic in the sense that the other two components, semantic and phonological, operate on its output. The syntactic component was itself regarded as binary, containing a base component, which generated deep structures, and a transformational component, which mapped deep structures onto surface structures. The claim was that deep structures were the input to the semantic component, and surface structures the input to the phonological component. In this sense, then, transformational operations were regarded as semantically "irrelevant," in a restricted way.

[43] The relevant items include Katz (1964a, 1964b, 1966, 1967a, 1967b, 1968, in press).

The semantic component was, according to Katz, assumed to contain a set of projection rules which mapped deep structures onto semantic representations, or sets of *readings* for sentences and for the constituents which make them up. Under Katz's conception, projection rules require from deep structures the inherent meanings of lexical items which are included in their terminal elements, together with a specification of the various "deep" grammatical relations holding between the constituents of which these lexical items are terminal representatives. A first key point is that Katz-type projection rules are assumed to be defined minimally on lexical item-sized chunks of meaning, and to operate successively to derive "larger" meanings for macro-constituents up to the sentence level. A second feature is that, for Katz, individual readings consist of *sets* of semantic elements, so-called *semantic markers,* some of which are atomic, but some of which have a complex internal structure.[44] In this regard, then, Katz's semantic representations contrast with syntactic structures, of either the deep structure, surface structure, or intermediate structure sort, since these are without exception in transformational theories *trees* of elements, that is, labeled bracketings of, rather than sets of them. A third point is that Katzian projection rules are assumed to be quite distinct from grammatical transformations in structure, operation, and output. Where a transformation is a rule which takes a tree as input and gives a tree as output, a projection rule, in Katz's sense, takes a (subpart of a) deep structure tree with the meanings of lexical items specified in terms of semantic markers as input and gives as output a (possibly, null, possibly unary) set of readings, each consisting of a set of semantic markers. A final relevant point about classical transformational theory is that in it all of the rules of the transformational component are "post lexical," that is, all operate at a point after deep structures have already been fully specified by the insertion of lexical items like *dog, boy, pick up, fall, fat, intelligent,* and so forth.[45]

Overall, then, classical transformational theory recognizes the following significantly different levels of linguistic representation:

(238) a.   Semantic representation = sets of readings
       b.   Deep structure
       c.   Surface structure

[44] The fact that some markers have a complex internal structure, one which includes a bracketing, makes the claim that readings are simply sets of markers of dubious import. That is, it is not clear what arguments could be given for taking this view, rather than the view that a reading is a single complex, bracketed object, as in the view of generative semantics, which will be discussed below. This is a crucial matter, since taking the latter point of view makes readings, that is, semantic objects, much more like syntactic objects, which are labeled bracketings.

[45] One point where there is not full specification in classical terms concerns *suppletions* like *go/went,* where the proper suppletive forms are often determined by application of postdeep structure transformations. No explicit theory of how this is to be described was part of the classical theory.

       d.   Phonological representation[46]
       e.   Phonetic representation

Moreover, these levels are generated and related by at least the following distinct types of grammatical rules:

(239) a.   Base syntactic rules, whose function is to generate deep structures, or at least their nonlexical skeletons
        b.   Grammatical transformations, whose function is to map deep structures onto surface structures
        c.   Projection rules, whose function is to map deep structures onto sets of readings
        d.   Phonological rules, whose function is to map surface structures onto phonetic representations

Almost everyone working within the overall generative-transformational framework now seems convinced in one way or another that classical theory is incorrect, and incorrect in two ways. In the most minor sense, it is inadequate in that it has to be *supplemented* by further types of apparatus, for example, by output conditions of the sort discussed by Ross (1967b) and Perlmutter (1968). The latter provides what I think is overwhelming evidence for their inclusion in a grammar. More seriously, however, there is roughly equal conviction that at least some of the assumptions of the classical theory are wrong. Here, however, there is a great division of opinion with much disagreement as to just what is wrong, and as to how the theory should be reconstructed in a more adequate fashion.

To the present writer, the significant proposals are those of Bach (1968), Gruber (1967), G. Lakoff (1968b, 1969b), and McCawley (1967; 1968a,b,c,d,e; 1969b; 1970). They and others have arrived at a conception of grammatical structure in which the major revision lies in the relation between syntax and semantics, and how semantic representations are to be defined and generated. One can best describe this new approach which has, rather unhappily,[47] come to be called *generative semantics,* with the help of some terminology. In the classical framework, the notion deep structure is substantively defined by the output of the base rules, together with general conditions which require that deep structures be suitable for defining "deep" grammatical relations and for specifying selectional restrictions. Suppose, however, one defines deep structure in a way which is largely substantively

---

[46] One might, of course, assume that the phonological representation is simply a proper part of the surface structure.

[47] Unhappily, because (i) any theory of semantics must be generative in the sense that it must provide a formal means of generating the infinite class of semantic representations and (ii) what is crucial about generative semantics is its claims of the *homogeneity* of semantic and syntactic representations and the homogeneity of the mapping between them.

neutral, as follows: The deep structure of a sentence is that constituent tree which is input to the grammatical transformations. Suppose further one defines the notion semantic representation as that level of structure concerned with specifying the meaning of a sentence. The proposal of Bach, Gruber, Lakoff, McCawley and others in this approach is, then, just this:

(240) The deep structure of a sentence (in the neutral sense just given) *is* its semantic representation.[48]

This view has, *inter alia,* the following consequences and corollaries:

(241) a. The base component of the grammar must generate semantic representations directly.
       b. There are no projection rules.
       c. Semantic representations must be trees, rather than sets of markers.
       d. There must be transformations operating on "prelexical" structures.

The key feature of this proposal is that syntactic and semantic structures are taken to be homogeneous enough for the mapping between them to be accomplished by a single type of rule,[49] transformations. The homogeneity is, moreover, substantively assumed to mean that both types of structures are representable as labeled bracketings, that is, trees.

If there is a homogeneous mapping of semantic representations onto surface structures, it follows, as stated in (241)d, that some transformational rules will operate before lexical items, that is, before the phonological forms and the markings for arbitrary irregularities, have been inserted into representations. These "prelexical" transformations will be operating intuitively in part of that domain where projection rules were thought to operate in classical terms. That is, prelexical transformations, in the new framework,

---

[48] Actually, it is clearly the case, as assumed by G. Lakoff (1969b), that the input to the transformations is only a subpart of the semantic representation; in particular, a large body of structure providing in some sense the *presuppositions* of a sentence may not be in any natural sense input to transformations. However, some presuppositions are. For instance, *most* restrictive relative clauses are presuppositional in nature. (But those in predicate nominals are not.)

[49] If one identifies the single type of rule to be found in a homogeneous generative semantic theory with traditional transformations, then the theory will clearly be inadequate. Rather, it seems, as G. Lakoff (1969a) has insightfully observed, that the general type of rule consists of *derivational constraints,* where these are conditions on the possible trees in a derivation. Transformations, as he observes, can then be treated as *local* derivational constraints, where by local one refers to constraints on successive pairs of trees in a derivation. The degree to which the claim of homogeneity can be taken seriously in these terms will depend on the tightness with which the class of derivational constraints, both local and global, can be constrained.

will mediate between structures whose levels of abstractness correspond to semantic representations and deep structures in the classical theory.[50]

B. *Remind,* The Classical Theory, and Generative Semantics

In terms of the account in Part A, one can understand the relevance of the conclusions reached in earlier sections. (234)–(237) indicate that the correct analysis of *remind* clauses is simply incompatible with the classical theory of transformational grammar. In particular, it is incompatible with its assumption that there is a level of deep structure which is *distinct from* the level of semantic representation and which contains in it structures corresponding directly to the lexical items of the surface structure. We have seen that in those structures which are input to the transformations deriving surface *remind* clauses, there can be no single element corresponding to the lexical item *remind,* since such clauses are derived from complex main verb + complement sentence structures.

Consider the relation between this fact and the claim made by the classical theory that there exists an interpretive semantic component containing a special type of grammatical mapping, namely, projection rules. While the validity of *the strike-like analysis* of *remind* clauses does not, as such, show that this assumption is necessarily incorrect, it provides a crushing blow to its *plausibility.* The plausibility of such an assumption lay in the view that there was some *natural* level of structure containing syntactic atoms, that is, lexical morphemes, which could be assigned meanings. That is, the plausibility depended on there being a natural level of structure to provide just those elements which would serve as the units provided with meaning by dictionary entries. The projection rules then were to show how, given information about grammatical relations, these meaning "molecules" were combined into the macro-meanings of larger and larger constituents.

But the analysis of *remind* constructions shows that no such level exists for *remind clauses.* The lexical item *remind* cannot be inserted into representations at some major juncture in the mapping of semantic representations onto surface structures which is such as to define grammatical relations and contain all other lexical items. *Remind* cannot be inserted until after certain definite transformational rules have already operated, in particular raising and predicate raising. Hence, there is no basis for assuming an independently defined level of structure which is suitable to serve as the input to the putative projection rules. The claim of the classical theory that there is a basic juncture in the process of relating readings to surface structures is seen to have no support. As it stands, it is an arbitrary assumption.

---

[50] They will, of course, have a wider field of operation, since, as we have seen, prelexical transformations like raising were also taken in classical terms to be accomplishing part of the mapping between deep and surface structures.

There is no known evidence for it. It is notable that in the literature on interpretive semantics this assumption is not defended but is more or less taken as a necessary assumption. But it is certainly not true that it is a necessary assumption.

Moreover, given *the strike-like analysis,* it is quite unclear as to what principles could, in the face of the breakdown of the lexical item principle, determine the primitive semantic clusters which serve as the *meaning molecules* which form the input to projection rules. Anyone who continues to claim that there exist such projection rules must find just such a principle, a principle hitherto implicitly provided by the assumption that lexical items provide the boxes in which the semantic molecules are found. Supporters of interpretive semantics must state a principle alternative to the view that the meaning molecules upon which projection rules work are the lexically listed readings of lexical items like *dog, beard, good, fat, chew, chase, kill,* and *remind.* Needless to say, no such principle is in sight.

From the point of view of generative semantics, the absence of such a principle is expected. Since there are no projection rules in this view, there is no need for a semantic principle to determine appropriate semantic molecules from the semantic atoms. Readings will be constructed directly out of the set of primitive predicates and indices defining semantic NP on the basis of whatever turn out to be the appropriate organizational principles. The organization of these structures into lexical item-sized constituents of meaning is carried out by the mapping of semantic representations into phonetics, that is, by the (relatively) homogeneous grammar. But the only role played by the derived, molecule-sized chunks of meaning assigned to lexical items is in the determination of how particular readings can be represented phonetically. That is, the organization of semantic primitives into lexical molecules is of no relevance to semantic description per se.[51] Because of this, the destruction of the lexical item principle for defining the semantic molecules that are needed as input to projection rules in the classical scheme provides indirect, though relatively strong, support for the view of generative semantics. Notice, however, that the questions of inadequacy of the classical theory and of the truth of generative semantics, are independent. The former has been demonstrated sufficiently, both above and in several others places.[52] The latter naturally remains open.

The support provided for generative semantics by *the strike-like analysis* can and should be looked at in another way. Let us assume for English a specification of a large set of surface structures. That is, assume that we have some good idea of what the surface structures of many sentences are like. Then one can consider arguments justifying the existence of certain

[51] For discussion of the role of lexical insertion in a grammar of this type, see especially McCawley (1968c) and Morgan (1968).

[52] See Bach (1968), G. Lakoff (1968a, 1969b), McCawley (1968a, 1968d).

transformational rules. The literature of the last dozen years contains an array of such arguments. Each transformational rule which is justified in turn justifies the existence of a level of syntactic structure, that is, some class of trees, distinct from the surface structure and, in an obvious sense, "more abstract" than surface structure. Given a transformation T_i, with input structure R_i and output structure R_{i+1}, I shall speak of R_i as a *remote structure* (with respect to R_{i+1}). Hence, a set of justified transformations justifies a sequence of successively more abstract remote structures. For example, if two transformations of genitive NP preposing and pronoun stem deletion after genitives can be justified, surface structures like:

(242)   I washed Harry's.

will have successively more remote structures like:

(243)   I washed Harry's one.
(244)   I washed the one of Harry's.

If then it could further be argued that constructions like *of Harry's* in sentences like (244) are derived from reduced relative clauses (say with the verb *have*), (244) might have a more remote structure:

(245)   I washed the one which Harry had.

and so forth.

Transformations have usually been wholly or largely justified on assumptions independent of hypotheses about the semantic representations of sentences. Consequently, to a large extent, the remote structures which have been justified have a "directionality of abstractness" which is *defined independently* of assumptions about semantic representation. By the term in quotes in the last sentence, I mean the following. For a particular sentence (that is, surface structure) whose derivation contains a single application of each of a set of transformations T_1, T_2, T_3 there are three levels of remote structure R_1, R_2, R_3. Assuming that T_1–T_3 are extrinsically ordered, or at least that they necessarily apply always in the assigned order, R_1 provides in a clear sense the most abstract remote structure, from the point of view of surface structure. That is:

(246) $R_1 \xrightarrow{\text{by } T_1} R_2 \xrightarrow{\text{by } T_2} R_3 \xrightarrow{\text{by } T_3}$ Surface Structure

Now, by saying that the "directionality of abstractness" is defined independently of assumptions about semantic representation, I mean that it is not a logical truth in any sense that in general R_3, R_2, and R_1 will provide successively closer approximations to structures which are semantically relevant than the surface structure will. Consequently, if it is in fact true that for arbitrary sentences the various sequences R_3–R_1, and so on do come, in a clear sense, closer and closer to semantic representation, this is a fundamental empirical fact about human language, and a fact of the utmost importance. For it shows that the abstract syntactic structures uncovered by transformational analysis are not, as they might be, semantically arbitrary, but rather are in a direct way steps along the path of the mapping, known to exist, between semantic representations and surface structures.

I framed the above remarks conditionally. There is, however, no need to do this. For it can be shown that the transformations which have been discussed and accepted for English are overwhelmingly such that successively more remote structures are increasingly semantic-like. I will illustrate this with a few examples. Consider sentences like:

(247)   Stab yourself!

It is a celebrated argument in transformational work that such sentences must be derived from structures *from which a second person subject is deleted*. One argument for this is the peculiar restriction on the distribution of reflexive forms in which such imperatives, namely, that only second person reflexives are allowed:

(248)   a. *Stab himself!
        b. *Stab myself!
        c. *Stab themselves!

This distribution follows automatically, given the general conditions on reflexives, that is, conditions valid for sentences other than subjectless imperatives,[53] from the assumption of a remote structure of the schematic form:

(249)   You stab yourself!

[53] Completely parallel arguments can be given on the basis of other forms which involve "agreement" with subject NP. These include the form *own*, and expressions such as *blink NP's eyes*:

(i) a. Harry visited $\left\{ \begin{array}{l} \text{his} \\ \text{*my} \end{array} \right\}$ own father.

     b. You visited $\left\{ \begin{array}{l} \text{your} \\ \text{*my} \end{array} \right\}$ own father.

(ii) a. Harry blinked $\left\{ \begin{array}{l} \text{his} \\ \text{*my} \end{array} \right\}$ eyes.

     b. You blinked $\left\{ \begin{array}{l} \text{your} \\ \text{*my} \end{array} \right\}$ eyes.

But:

(iii) a. Visit your own father.
      b. *Visit my own father.
(iv) a. Blink your eyes.
      b. *Blink my eyes.

Notice that there is nothing in this argument which assumes anything about the meaning of sentences like (247). However, a consideration of the meaning of such sentences shows that structures like (249) provide a closer approximation to a semantically relevant structure than do those like the surface structure of (247) itself. That is, semantically, (247) involves a binary predicate[54] relating two terms, and these are represented by the two NP in the remote structure (249). Of course, (249) is still very far from a structure which could represent the meaning of (247), but then only one jump in remote structure has been considered, that mediated by the transformational rule which deletes the subjects of imperatives.

For a second example, consider the rule at work in sentences like (250)a:

(250)   a.   Harry wants to kiss Greta.
        b.   Harry wants Max to kiss Greta.

It is well known that (250)a must be derived by a rule which deletes the subject of the infinitival clause, a rule sometimes called *equi-NP deletion*. This rule operates subject to the condition that the subject be a presupposed coreferent of the subject of *want*. I have discussed such derivations extensively in Postal (1969b). Such a derivation provides a sentence like (250)a with a remote structure like:

(251)   Harry$_i$ wants Harry$_i$ to kiss Greta.

where identically subscripted lexical items serve as a gross and inadequate way of indicating nominal coreference.[55] The arguments for an analysis like (251) of sentences like (250)a are many. One is the parallelism with sentences like (250)b, which shows that *want* takes infinitival complements with full sentence form. Hence, to block complement subjects which are coreferents of the main clause subject would require an *ad hoc* statement. Similarly, the possibility of reflexive forms and *own* possessives in such subjectless complements reveals the existence of underlying subjects:

(252)   a.   Harry wants to justify himself.
        b.   Harry wants to visit his own father.

since these forms are in general subject to the constraint that a coreferent in the same clause must precede them. Other arguments include the fact

---

[54] This is actually only a gross approximation. There is no doubt that on a deeper level *stab* X must be further analyzed into something like "pierce the surface of X with a pointed instrument" or the like.

[55] A more natural method might be an adaptation of the diagrammatic approach of Geach (1962, 137), yielding something like the following for (251):

(i)   [i] want [i] to kiss Greta.
      └─Harry─┘

that the deletion analysis from remote structures like (251) explains such gaps as:

(253)   *I want me to go.

Thus the analysis is established without appeal to semantic facts. Again, however, we find that the remote structure provides a closer approximation to a semantic representation than does the surface structure. For clearly, the meaning of (250)a will involve a relation between an individual, *Harry*$_i$, and some hypothetical state of affairs described by the statement *Harry*$_i$ *kiss Greta,* just as (250)b involves a relation between this individual and a state of affairs described by the statement *Max kiss Greta.* But in such representations there are at least three terms, two of which happen to be coreferents in (251). The structure in (251) provides three NP to correspond to these terms, while (250)a does not.

Other obvious examples of the principle being illustrated would include the rules which deform relative clauses yielding structures like (254)a from those like (254)b:

(254)   a.   the boy who is sitting on the corner
        b.   the boy sitting on the corner

also the rules which yield preposed adjectives by deforming structures like (255)a into those like (255)b:

(255)   a.   the rocket which is unstable
        b.   the unstable rocket

and also the rules which yield "gapped" structures like (256)a from those like (256)b (see Ross, 1970):

(256)   a.   Morton singled to left and Tom to right.
        b.   Morton singled to left and Tom singled to right.

There is thus ample basis for the claim that it is an empirical fact that as one follows transformational derivations in reverse, one moves in a direction of semantic relevance, not in some arbitrary direction. This, I emphasize again, is an empirical fact, and one which does *not* follow as such from the definitions of transformation and transformational derivation.

Consider in this light *the strike-like analysis* of *remind* clauses. A vast array of evidence has been presented which shows that such clauses involve an underlying main verb + complement sentence structure, where the main verb is a perceptual verbal like *strike,* and the embedded verbal a similarity predicate. The evidence for this was of a nonsemantic nature. But, as noted almost at the outset, just such a structure is required to account for the semantic interpretation of *remind* clauses. Semantically, these do not involve a single ternary predicate, but rather a binary predicate relating an individual to a perceived state of affairs, where the state of affairs is itself representable as involving a binary predicate of similarity. Thus the structure appropriate for representing the meaning of *remind* clauses turns out to provide the appropriate syntactic basis for the derivation of these clauses. Consequently, *the strike-like analysis* itself is a very clear and striking case of the fact that the directionality of abstractness justifiable in transformational derivations is not arbitrary but rather oriented toward structures of increasing semantic relevance.

Now, although this state of affairs is unexplained by the definitions of transformation and transformational derivation per se, it is a consequence of the assumptions of generative semantics, since in this view the input to the transformations is (a subpart of) the semantic representation. Consequently, every step in reverse along the route of transformational derivation from surface structure is necessarily, in this view, a step toward the semantic representation.[56]

It might be claimed that the same prediction is made by the classical theory of transformational grammar, with its assumption that semantic representations are completely determined by the deep structure. It might seem that under this older view, every reverse step from surface toward deep structure must be a step toward increasing similarity with the semantic representation. In this way, it might be claimed that, with regard to this parameter at least, generative semantics and the classical theory are not distinguished in their empirical claims. There are two negative points to be made with respect to this claim, however.

First, given the existence of projection rules, rules of a type totally different from transformations, and the fact that the possible range and complexity of meanings of lexical items is enormous, there is no reason why deep structures should resemble semantic representations much more than surface structures do. In fact, in the classical theory, the only conditions which deep structures must meet but which surface structures are supposed to fail *vis-à-vis* semantics is that the former must contain all relevant lexical items, often deleted from the latter, and that grammatical relations must be definable. But, although hitherto ignored by many, including the present writer, these conditions have a necessarily restricted content, especially re-

---

[56] It might still be possible for a move from a less to a more remote structure to yield a less semantic-like structure, if derivations were allowed to "bulge" in certain ways, that is, if the class of possible rules permitted relatively arbitrary kinds of changes. The natural way to eliminate this possibility in generative semantic terms is with a very narrow and substantive set of universal constraints on derivations and the rules which generate them, for example, constraints preventing the insertion of arbitrary constituents, preventing most possible classes of restructurings, and so forth.

stricted from the point of view of requiring deep structures to be more semantic-like than surface structures. I will illustrate.

Consider a sentence like:

(257)   Harry likes meat from pigs.

Here the phrase *from pigs* must be viewed as a reduced restrictive relative clause. Consequently, (257) is just a variant of:

(258)   Harry likes meat which $\left\{ \begin{matrix} \text{is} \\ \text{comes} \end{matrix} \right\}$ from pigs.

Now, it would be claimed by the classical theorist that, in order to get the right meaning for the object NP in (257), the deep structure of this NP must be such as to indicate that *from pigs* bears some particular "deep" relation to the subject of the restrictive relative. And it would be claimed that this relation is the same as that in sentences like:

(259)   a.   This meat is from pigs.
         b.   Most meat is from pigs.

Consequently, it would be argued that a deep structure for (257) which provides its object NP with a structure something like:

(260)

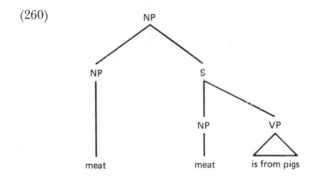

is required on grounds of grammatical relations.

My claim that such requirements have only the most limited content is illustrated by sentences like:

(261)   Harry likes pork.

The key fact about (261) is that it is an essential paraphrase of (257). However, in the classical theory, the object NP of (261) will have an entirely different deep structure from that in (260), a structure in which the lexical item *pork* itself occurs, together with some nonsyntactic, purely semantic, representation of the meaning, indicating that *pork,* in fact, designates meat from pigs.

What this shows, then, is that the semantic component of the classical theory was intended to be powerful enough to derive the meaning of sentences like (261) from deep structures which are hardly more abstract than their surface structures. Since the meaning of (257) is the same as that of (261) (or close enough to it for purposes of argument), it follows that a classical semantic component was intended to be powerful enough to derive the meaning of (257) from a deep structure as gross as the deep structure of (261). But such a deep structure is less closely related to the semantic representation of (257) than the surface structure of (257) is. In particular, where the surface structure of (257) provides an explicit analysis of the object NP into an element designating a type of substance, meat, and into another element designating the animal from which this substance originates, the deep structure of (261) provides, syntactically, no such analysis at all.[57] Consequently, it turns out the classical theory does not really require the deep structure of the object NP in (257) to determine its meaning, since it must be able to determine such meanings from surface NP with no structure, like the object in (261). It could do this in the case of the object NP of (257) by treating it in effect as an idiom, and assigning the same reading assigned to the lexical item *pork* to the whole NP *meat from pigs.* The classical theorist might, of course, object that while this could be done for the object NP of sentences like (257), it cannot be done for all constituents which have single lexical item paraphrases, still less for all constituents, because there are an infinite number of them. Thus, to a certain extent, the classical theory does require deep structure and does make use of the recursive structure assigned by the syntax. This is certainly true. The point is, however, that there is no nonarbitrary principle to determine when classical semantic theory assigns readings to nodes by way of projection rules and when it does so by simply assigning the node a reading in the lexicon (that is, treats the node as an idiom). The assumption was that this principle is provided by lexical items, that is, that these elements of deep structure (together with complex idioms) were assigned readings in the lexicon, all other structures by projection rules. But *the strike-like analysis* shows that this cannot be the case for *remind,* since the node corresponding to the lexical item *remind* is not present at a level corresponding to classical deep structure and cannot enter derivations until after certain transformational operations, thus at a postdeep structure point in classical theory.

In other words, we see that the classical theory necessarily must have the power to derive arbitrarily many, complex semantic representations such

---

[57] This information would be provided in classical terms by the semantic reading of the lexical item *pork,* which would be given as its dictionary entry.

as [MEAT WHICH COMES FROM PIGS] from deep structure representations which are related to them only in arbitrary ways, that is, in this
case deep structures like:

(262)   Noun
          |
         pork

Because of this fact, the claim that classical theory requires "deep" grammatical relations defined by the deep structures of the syntax (but not definable on surface structures) to generate semantic representations is a very
restricted truth, since, at least in the case of meaning subparts realized by a
lexical item, the theory must have the power to derive readings on the basis
of no "deep" grammatical relations at all.

Consequently, if the derivation of sentences in general is seen to yield
remote structures of successively greater similarity to semantic representations, this fact is not explicable in terms of the semantic requirements of
classical transformational theory, which, of necessity, is compatible with deep
structures that are only most indirectly related to semantic form. One can
even give a vague principle *partially* specifying the degree to which classical
theory fails to provide an explanation of this fact. Namely, it must fail to
do so at least to the extent that particular lexical items like *pork* can serve
as realizations of semantic representations which are realizable also as
syntactic structures of considerable complexity (*meat which is from pigs*).
For in these cases, the classical semantic theory must provide a technique
for representing structure "inside" of lexical items which is an essential
duplication of the structure provided by the syntax for the cases with surface structure complexity.[58] In the case of *pork,* a classical description must
analyze it into units referring to meat and to the animal pig, and must,
furthermore, specify that these units are related by a predicate "comes
from." From the semantic point of view, the structure relating such elements
as "meat" and "pig" must be given in two entirely different ways: once by
the syntax for cases which show up as surface structure phrases, once by
the readings of the lexical items for the cases which show up monomor-
phemically (or idiomatically).[59] Thus lexical items provide a clear area in

[58] For comments critical of this duplication, together with a general advocacy of a movement in transformational grammar away from the classical position and toward generative
semantics, see also J. Anderson (1968).

[59] The duplication of structure and relations for elements of meaning in classical theory
(that is, given semantically for lexical items and idioms, syntactically for productive surface phrases) was bad enough initially when there seemed to be a natural juncture between
projection rule and transformation, hence between semantics and syntax. But it is doubly
intolerable now that (i) there is no principle to draw this line; and (ii) there is the beginning of a conceptually more elegant theory which avoids the duplication entirely, namely,
generative semantics.

which classical deep structures must be unrelated to semantic form.[60] This is not the only area, however.

Given the existence of the special class of projection rules, rules which have not been characterized in a general way, which have not had their possible limitations seriously constrained (in the sense that transformational rules have, for example),[61] it is possible to derive semantic representations from deep structures of more or less arbitrary (semantically) structure. For example, nothing in the semantic assumptions of classical theory precludes setting up a deep structure for sentences like:

[60] The full *extent* of duplication is unclear, though obviously vast, since it is not known what constraints there are on the possibilities for individual lexical items to represent meanings. Nonetheless, it is probably the case, as observed by Weinreich (1966) that: ". . . every relation that may hold between components of a sentence also occurs among the components of a meaning of a dictionary entry." Further, it seems clear that there are no relations between the meaning components of lexical items which are not matched by overtly syntactic relations. That there are certain constraints, however, on the possibilities of representing structures with single lexical items is pointed out by Morgan (1968), who provides two constraints. Further restrictions are given in Postal (1969a), where it is shown that the same constraints govern lexical items and certain types of surface phrases. A particularly important general point made by Morgan (1968) is that the meanings of lexical items appear to obey the constraints on syntactic rules, a necessary consequence of the position of generative semantics. Thus Morgan observes that there are no lexical items with meanings whose parts could only be combined by rules which violated such syntactic constraints as those discussed in Ross (1967b). For example, there are no lexical items like *bralch* such that sentences like:

  (i) a.   Harry bralched Max.
      b.   Harry bralched a zebra.
mean respectively:
  (ii) a.   'Harry saw Max and a gorilla'.
       b.   'Harry saw a zebra and a gorilla'.

In generative semantic terms this is explicable, since such a derivation would involve a rule of noun incorporation, which is possible in many languages (compare in English the derivation of *kick* from "strike with foot," and so on), but a rule which violated Ross's coordinate structure constraint, which holds for syntactic constructions. The theory of projection rules offers, as far as I can see, no basis for such facts at all. Moreover, even if constraints are added to this theory such that no projection rule can derive the relevant meanings from structures like (i), these constraints will have to be essential duplications of the syntactic constraints, which must be present in the syntactic theory underlying the projection rule semantics. Only generative semantics seems to offer the possibility of generalization here, since only this theory claims that the internal semantic structure of lexical items *is* syntactic structure. Similar points are made in G. Lakoff (1968b) and Postal (1969a).

    As a general argument that the semantic structure of lexical items must *largely* duplicate the structure of phrases, one can note that in many styles of discourse, lexical items can be introduced as essential abbreviations for meanings whose previous description required complex form. This would force a projection rule theory to allow for arbitrarily complex Readings as both the output of projection rules and as the input (dictionary entries) to such rules.

[61] This is not to deny, of course, that transformations remain relatively unconstrained, that is, that the theory of such rules is much too weak. Nothing in the theory prevents all sorts of absurd rules. For example, one could give rules which would bring about situations in which subjects of verbs agreed with the tenses of other verbs embedded below them, where adjectives on subject nouns agreed with object nouns, and so forth.

(263)   John believes that Bill didn't come.

of the form:

(264)   John doesn't believe Bill came.

and having projection rules operate on the structure of (264) to determine, among other things, that the scope of the negative element is the subordinate clause, despite its deep structure appearance in the main clause. Thus in this case, the surface structure, which has the negative element in the subordinate clause which defines its scope semantically, would be closer to semantic representation in a clear sense than the deep structure. In fact, just such logical possibilities for "interpretive" rules applied to superficial, surface structure-resembling structures provide the heart of the recent proposals of Chomsky, Jackendoff, and others[62] advocating an even greater use of "interpretive" rules than is permitted in classical theory. However, the chief difference between these newer proposals and those of the classical theory is that the former advocates application of "interpretive" rules to structures other than deep structures.

I said above that there were two things to be said against the view that the classical theory predicts the fact that transformational analysis yields structures of increasing semantic relevance. The second is that *the strike-like analysis* shows that the transformationally justified directionality of remote structures in the direction of semantic representations continues beyond a point countenanced by classical theory. That is, as we have seen, *the strike-like analysis* must provide sentences with remote structures which are *prelexical* and hence on the other side of the classical juncture between projection rules and transformational rules. This fact is perfectly compatible with the assumptions of generative semantics.

One can diagram the conflicting claims of generative semantics and the classical theory in context with *the strike-like analysis* as follows:

(265)

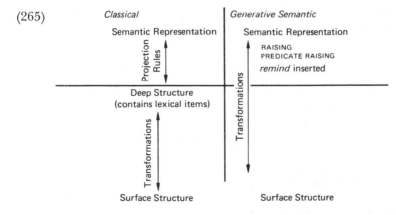

[62] See Chomsky (1969), Jackendoff (1968a, 1968b, 1969a, 1969b), and Dougherty (1968, 1969).

In the classical theory, all lexical items, hence in particular the item *remind*, must be inserted into the representations of deep structures, thus inserted before any transformations apply. In the theory of generative semantics, lexical items are inserted at some points in derivations, not necessarily all in a block. Transformations apply before lexical insertion as well as after it. (265) then reveals graphically how *the strike-like analysis* is incompatible with the classical theory, since in this analysis, transformations, in particular raising and predicate raising,[63] must apply before the lexical item *remind* can be inserted into linguistic representations.

The strike-like analysis shows then that in fact transformations, and not projection rules, are operating in that part of the range of mediation between semantic representation and surface structure which is prelexical. Consequently, the analysis reveals that part of the domain of mapping *claimed to be covered* by projection rules in the classical theory is *in fact covered* by transformational rules and conditions.[64] In other words, the rules operating *before* lexical insertion are of the same type as those operating *after* it. The full claim of generative semantics is that this particular case is typical, and that the range of projection rule application is null. This has, of course, not yet been shown.

However, the homogeneous theory of generative semantics is methodologically preferable on several grounds. It has a narrower theory of rule types (no projection rules, more generally no "interpretive" rules), and requires no unique, intermediate level of deep structure. Generative semantics assumes only the levels of semantic representation and surface structure, which no linguistic theory can do without. The classical theory posits in addition the level of deep structure and a distinct kind of grammatical rule. Thus the two views are not symmetrical, are not, as it were, equals from a methodological point of view. The classical view requires extra justification because of its necessary postulation of extra aspects of linguistic structure. The fact that the burden of justification lies with the supporter of these extra additions is important to stress in view of the fact that the historical priority of the classical theory within the framework of generative grammar tends to give it an air of validity that it does not have. That is, one tends to assume, wrongly, that its priority puts the newer theory in need of special justification.

But, notably, no justification for the extra apparatus of classical theory *vis-à-vis* generative semantics is known, and, as observed earlier, destruction of the insertion point of lexical items as a principled basis for the juncture between projection rule and transformation leaves the classical theory (and,

---

[63] That predicate raising is prelexical is self-evident from the discussion. That raising is depends on the point, which was made by Lakoff, and discussed in de Rijk (1968), that application of predicate raising is dependent on prior application of raising.

[64] The expression "and conditions" here is meant to cover the various derivational constraints we have considered, including that which makes predicate raising and property factoring incompatible. This matter is related theoretically to the discussion in footnote 49.

in fact, any theory claiming the existence of a level of deep structure distinct from semantic representation) with no known principle to determine this juncture. Thus at the moment a projection rule theory must necessarily be at least partly incoherent. Such a theory says that part of the mapping between semantic representations and surface structures is mediated by projection rules, but it cannot specify just how the juncture between projection rule and transformation is characterized. That is, there is no supportable notion of deep structure distinct from semantic representation.

Needless to say, on a deeper theoretical level, such a theory gives no explanation of why such a bifurcation of this mapping should exist. And this is the crux of the whole matter. The original plausibility of this so far unjustified assumption was the view that lexical items provided atomic elements with meanings from which the meanings of macroconstituents could be determined by rule. But this idea has collapsed. In the light of present knowledge, it can, I think, be seen to be nothing more than the traditional mistake of assuming that surface structures are relevant for semantic description, a view which classical theory, despite its emphasis on the role of deep structure in semantic interpretation, has not really moved very far away from.

I have argued *for* the generative semantic and *against* the classical view of transformational grammar by showing that in the derivation of *remind* clauses, there must be transformational rules operating at a point *prior* to, or on more "abstract," more semantic-like structures, than the deep structure permitted by classical theory. This will be, I think, a special case of the kind of argumentation which should be sought for to disconfirm the classical theory in these respects. That is, if the classical theory is wrong and something more along the lines of generative semantics is right, it will be possible in many cases to show that the mapping between semantic representations and structures approximating the abstractness of classical deep structures is mediated by grammatical transformations and not by some other special sort of rules like classical projection rules. Most striking cases of this sort have been found by Lakoff (1969b), who shows in a complex and revealing argument that items like *dissuade* cannot be inserted into linguistic representations until after some transformational operations have taken place. He gives a different argument for *prefer*. In Postal (1969a), I have given another argument to this effect, claiming that items like *pork* cannot be inserted until after certain compounding transformations have applied if generalizations covering both *pork* and words like *wombat-meat* are to be incorporable in the description.

Clarifying the general nature of at least one type of argumentation which is relevant to the choice between classical and generative semantic theories is important, both inherently, and because of some recent remarks by Chomsky, which seem to have obscured the issues here. In a paper in which are proposed modifications of the classical theory in a direction very different from that of generative semantics, Chomsky (to appear) suggests that much of the apparent difference between the generative semantic view and classical theory is merely notational. This statement is surprising in view of the empirical contrasts between the claims in (238)–(239) above on the one hand and (241) above on the other. It must be based on some terminological equivocation made possible by the introduction of a new term *standard theory*. This term, as far as I can see, distorts the properties of the classical theory, which Chomsky purports the term *standard theory* is general enough to characterize. I will not go into this matter in detail here. See Lakoff (1969b) for some discussion. Chomsky (1969) suggests that the difference between classical theory and generative semantics resides only in the "directionality" of the mappings. This follows, he claims, since both views generate quadruples of semantic representation, phonetic representation, deep structure, and surface structure for each sentence, with the two differing only in what is regarded as the "basic" structure, a question Chomsky takes rightly to be terminological or notational only.

However, (238)–(239) and (241) above differ in *substantive* ways, for example, in whether there is a level of deep structure "preceding" all transformational applications and containing all lexical items. Consequently, the warning that theories must be shown to be distinct both substantively and notationally is, though true, irrelevant to the choice between (238)–(239) and (241), a choice which is evidently factual, as we have seen. For example, (238)–(239) are incompatible with *the strike-like analysis,* while (241) is perfectly compatible with this feature of English. One must take into account such basic empirical differences between the two views as whether semantic representations are sets or trees, whether there exists in the mapping between semantic representations and surface structures a nonnull set of projection rules distinct from transformations, whether all lexical insertion can be pre-transformational, and so forth.

C.   Concluding Remarks on the Strike-Like Analysis.

In the light of the discussion in Part B, a few clarifying remarks about *the strike-like analysis* can be made. I have claimed that the underlying structure of *remind* clauses is of the form:

(266)

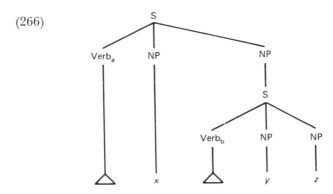

where Verb$_a$ is an element like *strike,* Verb$_b$ an element with the properties of a similarity predicate. In the context of the discussion of generative semantics, it is clear that there is no suggestion that these underlying verbals are *lexical items,* in particular none that they are the lexical *strike, resemble,* and so forth. The idea is that the underlying elements are *semantic* verbs, that is, predicates. Consequently, the claim is only that the underlying elements of *remind* clauses are those predicates which are lawfully connected to the various regularities documented for *strike* and similarity predicates. In particular, I would like to emphasize that it is not excluded that the actual lexical verb *strike* may have certain special properties not associated with the underlying predicate or predicate complex which shows up as the surface verb *remind.* Just so, the particular predicate of similarity which underlies *remind* may lack some *ad hoc* features of any or all of the verbals *similar, resemble, like.* In short, I have not intended to claim that *remind* is in any sense derived from underlying structures which contain the lexical verbs *strike,* or *resemble/similar/like.* Rather, I have argued that the derivation must be from elements whose properties are *included* in these lexical elements.

This fact raises the possibility of revealing some equivocation in earlier discussion. For instance, in footnote 12, it was observed that it is not clear that applicability of psych movement can be predicted from the meaning of a verb. If then the fact that *strike* undergoes psych movement were a mere idiosyncrasy of this lexical item, there would, in the terms just discussed, be no real explanation from *the strike-like analysis* of the behavior of *remind* with respect to psych movement.[65] Consequently, I am forced at this point to assume that the application of psych movement to a verb like *strike* is *not* idiosyncratic, but is rather a function of regularities describable in terms of the predicates which underlie *strike.* That is, I am forced, for example, to assume that there is a meaning difference between *strike* and *perceive,* analogously between *seem/appear* and *think,* etc. and, moreover, that the difference between these pairs is systematic and predicts applicability or nonapplicability of psych movement. I believe this is right and would now like to indicate briefly an outline of what I take this systematic semantic difference to consist in.

One can note that all the relevant verbals which undergo psych movement must, in nonhabitual, nonmodal, present tense, declarative[66] contexts

---

[65] An analogous remark would hold about other properties of *remind* predicted by *the strike-like analysis* from properties of *strike* if these were functions of something other than the semantic elements which underlie the lexical item *strike.*

[66] In interrogative contexts like:

    (i) Harry is asking Joan$_i$ whether Max strikes her$_i$ as crazy.

    (ii) *Harry is asking Joan whether Max strikes him as crazy.

the experiencer NP must apparently be a coreferent of the "indirect object" of the next highest verb of saying/thinking. Consequently, in superficially unembedded interrogatives, the experiencer NP must be second person:

    (iii) Does Max strike you as being crazy? [Footnote continues of the following page.]

have an experiencer NP which is a coreferent of the "subject" NP of the next highest verb of saying/thinking. In superficially unembedded declarative clauses, this means coreference to the "subject" of the deleted performative verb, discussed earlier in Section II. C (6). Such coreference requires the experiencer NP to be first person:

>   (267)   a.   *It seems to Pete that you are crazy.
>   b.   It seems to me that you are crazy.

Compare:

>   (268)   a.   Pete thinks you are crazy.
>   b.   I think you are crazy.

Similarly:

>   (269)   a.   *It strikes Pete that you are unfriendly.
>   b.   It strikes me that you are unfriendly.
>   (270)   a.   Pete perceives that you are unfriendly.
>   b.   I perceive that you are unfriendly.

When the relevant verbs are even superficially embedded, the requirement is that the experiencer NP be a pronoun coreferential to the relevant "subject." Hence:

>   (271)   a.   Harry$_i$ says I strike him$_i$ as being a vampire.
>   b.   *Harry$_i$ says Max strikes me as being a vampire.

Compare:

>   (272)   a.   Harry$_i$ says he$_i$ perceives that I am a vampire.
>   b.   Harry$_i$ says I perceive that Max is a vampire.

Similarly:

>   (273)   a.   Lucy$_i$ says I seem to her$_i$ to be an egomaniac.
>   b.   *Lucy$_i$ says Max seems to me to be an egomaniac.

(iv)   *Does Max strike $\begin{Bmatrix} \text{Lucy} \\ \text{me} \end{Bmatrix}$ as being crazy?

To get a uniform account of the coreference restriction for both declaratives and interrogatives, it will apparently be necessary to represent interrogatives with a structure schematically along the lines of:

(v)   x ask y that y tell z (S)

This will reduce the interrogative case to the "subject" condition. For simplicity, I ignore interrogatives in the text.

but:

    (274) a.   Lucy$_i$ says she$_i$ thinks I am an egomaniac.
             b.   Lucy$_i$ says I think Max is an egomaniac.

I conclude that this is a reflection of the fact that the psych movement verbals have some property not possessed by the parallel nonpsych movement verbals, a property which is such as to require first person/second person elements in the contexts indicated. What might this property be? Intuitively, it seems that in some way the psych movement elements are "more subjective" than the others. The question is, then, how this vague notion can be characterized semantically. I would propose a very rough analysis along the following lines. All verbals like *think, perceive, seem, strike,* and so on are descriptive of inner, subjective events, states, occurrences, and so forth. The psych movement verbals not only describe subjective matters, but manifest a presupposition that what they describe is subjective. That is, taking *seem* and *think* to contrast, it is true that both describe inner affairs which are, in fact, directly knowable only by the one who experiences them. However, *seem* not only describes such a domain, but it says it describes such a domain. A test of this contrast is provided by the possibilities of describing telepathy or mind reading devices of various sorts. Suppose that Pete is a telepath, reading the mind of Harry, and describing Harry's inner goings on to someone. It seems to me quite clear that he could do so by use of (275)a but not by use of (275)b or (275)c:

    (275) a.   Harry is thinking that you are an idiot.
             b.   ?It seems to Harry that you are an idiot.
             c.   ?You seem to Harry to be an idiot.

Just so, suppose Pete has a mind/feeling reading machine attuned to Harry. Again, it is clear that he could report the output of this machine by way of (276)a, but not by way of (276)b or (276)c:

    (276) a.   (The machine says) Harry perceives that you are a vampire.
             b.   ?(The machine says) it strikes Harry that you are a vampire.
             c.   ?(The machine says) you strike Harry as being a vampire.

Given the hypothesis that there are machines for telepathy, mind reading, and so forth, everyone's subjective experience is available to others. Consequently, it becomes possible to say directly what others are thinking, perceiving, and so forth. And one would do this by way of verbals like *think, perceive,* and so forth. This shows that these verbals do not, in their meanings, involve any presupposition that the realm they describe is inherently subjective. On the other hand, even given the hypothesis that sub-

jective experience is objectifiable by way of telepathy, and so forth, objectified experiences cannot be described by way of verbals like *seem, strike,* and
so forth. This shows, I conclude, that these verbals involve in their meanings the presupposition that the experiences they represent are inherently
subjective.[67]

Now, notice that this property of inherent subjectivity explains the restriction on such verbals that their experiencer NP must be a coreferent of
the "subject" of the next-higher verb of saying/thinking, because it is just
such verbs which are used to specify the reporting of inner experiences. But
under the subjectivity presupposition, only the individual who has the
experience is in a position to report it. Thus, (275)b,c and (276)b,c violate
this coreference requirement.

It is not immediately obvious how this account explains the permissi-
bility of sentences like:

(277)   It struck Harry that you were a vampire.

which are in the *past tense*. However, the natural interpretation of the conditions under which these are used is that the individual designated by
Harry has informed others of his subjective experience in the time interval
whose existence is guaranteed by the past tense. In short, sentences like (277)
seem equivalent to those of the form:

(278)   Harry$_i$ said that it struck him$_i$ that you were a vampire.

and may indeed be derived from the same source.

---

[67] Another way of saying this might be to specify that the psych movement verbals are
incorrigible because they are phenomenological. This is particularly clear with pairs like
look (psych movement) *see* (nonpsych movement).
Thus, if one says:

(i)   The wall looked green to me (it looked to me as if the wall were green).
(ii)   I saw that the wall was green.

one could be wrong only in the latter case. That is, if it is pointed out that the wall was
blue and only seemed green due to artificial light, one would agree that (ii) expressed a
false statement. But (i) would still express a truth. And indeed, if used honestly, it is
difficult to conceive of circumstances in which (i) could fail to express a truth. This difference also seems valid for such pairs as *seem, think,* although possibly not so clear for
them. Note the contrast between the following dialogues:

(iii)   a.   John seemed sick to me (it seemed to me that John was sick).
         b.   You're wrong.
(iv)   a.   I thought John was sick.
         b.   You're wrong.

If acceptable at all, (iii)b is interpreted, I think, as meaning that it is false to say John
was sick. (iv)b, however, is interpreted as meaning that it is false to say the speaker thought
John was sick. This follows from the fact that, being incorrigible, one cannot deny what
seem claims. Notice further that in reply to (iv)a one could say:

(v)   You didn't *think* John was sick, you *felt* he was sick.

But to (iii)a one cannot reply:

(vi)   ?It didn't *seem* to you John was sick, it *sounded* to you as if he were sick.

Again, the statement made by the psych movement verbal is incorrigible.

Similarly, one must account for the acceptability of the modal examples like:

(279)   I must strike $\left\{\begin{array}{l}\text{you}\\\text{everyone}\end{array}\right\}$ as being insane.

Here, however, it is noteworthy that there is no claim of direct knowledge of the inner experience of the individual designated by the experiencer NP of *strike*. Rather, such modal sentences really purport to be able to determine this indirectly by inference from some general law, regularity, or principle. That is, sentences like (279) are appropriate in contexts where the behavior of the subject is such as to guarantee, by assumption, such a reaction in an individual under general conditions.

While it is obvious that this semantic analysis of the contrast between pairs like *seem/think, strike/perceive,* and so forth, has barely begun and remains in a very gross state, I think it is sufficient to indicate that there are real, systematic semantic differences between such pairs. Consequently, I think it is justifiable to assume that the application of psych movement to verbals like *seem, strike* but not to the others is a systematic fact, which is predictable on the basis of the meaning of the predicates involved, and independent, by and large, of arbitrary lexical irregularities associated with the phonological form of the lexical items which represent these predicates.

Given this fact, the prediction of psych movement application to *remind* goes through, even under the generative semantic interpretation of *the strike-like analysis*. Notice, moreover, that this analysis predicts in addition that *remind* must have an inherently subjective interpretation, that is, that the experiencer NP must be a coreferent of the subject of the next highest verb of saying/thinking, and that *remind* is not appropriate for the description of hypothetically objectified subjective experience. And these claims are both true:

(280)   a.   Harry reminds me of a gorilla.
    b.   *Harry reminds Max of a gorilla.
(281)   a.   Max$_i$ says I remind him$_i$ of a gorilla.
    b.   *Max says Mary reminds me of a gorilla.
(282)   ?(The machine says) Max reminds Pete of a gorilla.

Consequently, not only has it been shown that *the strike-like analysis* is compatible with a generative semantic analysis of its underlying elements as semantic elements, but we have thereby uncovered another argument for this analysis. Namely, this analysis can explain why *remind* is interpreted as an inherently subjective verbal.

Finally, let me emphasize that there is no need to assume that the analysis given is as fine-grained as possible. Both the underlying main verbal element and the similarity predicate underlying *remind* clauses might themselves turn out to be susceptible of further analysis into more primitive semantic elements. That is, there is no need to assume that *strike* or *similar* necessarily corresponds to a single predicate. Indeed, the discussion of inherent subjectivity just finished already shows that this is not the case for *strike*. One can easily imagine an analysis of forms like *similar* which would provide them with a predicate common to items like *equivalent* and *identical*. Consequently, structures like (266) above, may turn out to be derived remote structures rather than a subpart of the semantic representation itself.

VERBS OF JUDGING: AN EXERCISE IN SEMANTIC DESCRIPTION

Charles J. Fillmore The Ohio State University

1. Preliminaries

In very many ways, assertions made by linguists about the meanings of utterances have been confused and misleading. In the earliest, *mentalist* conception of the meanings of linguistic forms, one spoke of an image or concept or idea that existed in the head of the speaker before the utterance and in the head of the hearer after the utterance. In *behaviorist* definitions of meaning, such as that proposed by Bloomfield, the meaning of a linguistic form was taken to be the situation which preceded the performance of an utterance and the behavior, on the part of the participants in the speech act, which followed it. In the purest of the *structuralist* notions of meaning, the meaning of a linguistic form was given as that feature of social situation which is shared by all utterances of the form, but not present in the utterances of at least some other linguistic forms.

The mentalist definition is of no use to anybody who wants to know whether he correctly understands some linguistic form, if only for the reason that there is no way of knowing whether the images he has in his mind when he produces or encounters the form are shared by his interlocutors. The behaviorist definition is a kind of disguised insult: if instead of telling you what a linguistic form means, I tell you something about when people have used it and what happened after they did, I'm not telling you what the form means, I'm asking you to figure out for yourself what it means. The pure structuralist definition is the most hopeless one of all: if we wish to understand the definition, we must presumably know something about the social situations in which language theorists have proclaimed it; but most of us have simply not heard it often enough or in enough contexts to come up with any particularly reliable conclusion. Completely formulaic "definitions" of meaning have never served our discipline well.

. There are theories of meaning, or rather techniques of describing meaning, which regard the meanings of linguistic forms as decomposable into smaller entities of one kind of another, usually called *features* or *components*. The ascription of such components to words and morphemes has often been completely ritualistic, and it is typically carried out in such a way that wherever there are problems, it is certain that the analyst is dealing with unclarities in our understanding of objects in the world or institutions in the associated culture, rather than with facts of the type that are correctly called linguistic.

To show what I mean by this, I ask you to consider one of the "acceptable" ways of determining the semantic properties of a noun like *wolf*. A procedure has been suggested by several authors that when a sentence is not semantically odd, the analyst can be sure that the selectional restrictions associated with the lexical items in that sentence are satisfied and he can perform various replacements in these sentences to detect both the selectional requirements of some of the words (especially the verbs) and the

inherent properties of others (especially the nouns). From such contempla-
tions we can discover that the word *wolf* has the feature *physical object*
because of its occurrence in the acceptable sentence (1); we note that it has
the feature *living* because of a sentence like (2); and we conclude that it
has the feature *animate* because we can say (3).

(1)   The wolf fell.
(2)   The wolf died.
(3)   The wolf felt it.

When both an affirmative sentence and its negative counterpart are odd,
the sentence being nevertheless fully grammatical, this is a sign of unsatis-
fied selectional restrictions; the analyst posits semantic properties of words
in ways that will account for the violation. Thus, from the fact that both
(4) and (5) are semantically anomalous, we are forced to conclude that,
while the verb-phrase requires a *human* subject, the noun *wolf* has the
feature *nonhuman*. We know from the oddity of sentence (6) that the noun
has the feature (say) *nonrigid*. And so on.

(4)   The wolf got a divorce.
(5)   The wolf didn't get a divorce.
(6)   I accidentally broke your wolf.

We would very soon discover, if we carried out this process much further, first of all, that there is no stopping place, and secondly, that wherever
it is unclear to us whether or not a sentence is odd in the intended sense,
this unclarity has a lot more to do with what we happen to believe about
the creatures known as wolves than with what we, as speakers of English,
know about the linguistic properties of the noun *wolf*.

The difficulties that I have mentioned exist, it seems to me, because
linguistic semanticists, like the philosophers and psychologists whose work
they were echoing, have found it relevant to ask, not *What do I need to
know in order to use this form appropriately and to understand other people
when they use it?* but rather, *What is the meaning of this form?* And having
asked that, linguists have sought to discover the external signs of meanings,
the reflexes of meanings in the speech situation, and the inner structure of
meanings. It is apparent that the wrong question has been asked.[1]

From the writings of the ordinary language philosophers, linguists can
learn to talk, not so much about the meanings of linguistic forms—where
"meanings" are regarded as abstract entities of some mysterious sort—but
about the rules of usage that we must assume a speaker of a language to

---

[1] This argument parallels the criticism of philosophical accounts of meaning found in
Austin (1961).

"know" in order to account for his ability to use linguistic forms appropriately. Although it is true that the use theorists in philosophy have not given linguists a tool which we can merely take over and turn instantly to our own use, I believe that we can profitably draw from some of the philosophers' discussion of language use when we propose or examine semantic theories within linguistics. In particular, we can turn our own inquiry toward the conditions under which a speaker of a language implicitly knows it to be appropriate to use given linguistic forms.

Among the ordinary language philosophers, there is some question of whether a use theory of meaning should begin with words or with sentences; we must hope that there is some way of resolving this conflict. Those philosophers who are particularly concerned with words[2] speak of there being rules for the use of words, and such rules include the principles for the composition of words into utterances; but these philosophers would deny that one can speak of the "use" of a sentence. The analogy is with chess: it makes sense to speak of what to do with a knight, or how to use a knight in a game of chess; but it does not always make sense to ask what one can do with a game of chess.[3]

On the other hand, there are philosophers who are mainly concerned with what one can do with sentences.[4] Utterances can be used in performing various acts (after J. L. Austin[5] we may call these *illocutionary acts*)—such things as informing somebody that a state of affairs exists, making a prediction, committing oneself to future actions, urging, promoting, suggesting, insulting, threatening, requesting, and so on. To such philosophers, the really basic notion of semantic theory is the *illocutionary act potential* of sentences—the range of things that one can do in saying specific sentences. In this view, the uses of words must be derivatively specified: to know how to use a word is to know how to use it in sentences with different illocutionary act potentials.[6]

Philosophers who have paid the most attention to the illocutionary forces of utterances have sometimes exemplified what they call the *happiness conditions* or *felicity conditions*[7] for the use of given sentences. The most common type of example is an imperative sentence like (7).

(7)   Please shut the door.

For this sentence, a reasonable set of happiness conditions is given on the following page.

[2] See Gilbert Ryle (1953).
[3] Ryle (1953), p. 35 of Chappell (1964).
[4] See especially Alston (1964).
[5] See Austin (1962a), especially pp. 98ff.
[6] See Alston (1964), p. 39.
[7] These locutions are due to J. L. Austin.

  i. The speaker and the addressee of this sentence are in some kind of relationship which allows the speaker to make requests of the addressee.

  ii. The addressee is in a position where he is capable of shutting the door.

  iii. There is some particular door which the speaker has in mind and which he has reason to assume the addressee can identify without any further descriptive aid on the speaker's part.

  iv. The door in question is, at the time of utterance, open.

  v. The speaker wants that door to become closed.

An important fact that is typically omitted from a philosopher's record of the set of happiness conditions of a sentence is that the various conditions are separately related to different specific facts about the grammatical structure of the sentence. For example, from the fact that the form of the sentence is imperative, we infer those conditions that relate to the speaker-addressee relationship; from the presence of the definite article, we infer the understanding that there is some mutually identifiable door to which the speaker is referring; the others are inferable from the ways in which we understand the verb *shut*.

More importantly, however, it needs to be pointed out that some of these conditions are really preconditions for the use of the sentence, rather than information about what the actual illocutionary force of utterances of the sentence is. Of the conditions I mentioned, for example, most of them are completely unaffected by negation. Thus, if I say (8),

(8)   Please *don't* shut the door.

the same conditions hold about the door being identifiable, about its being now open, and about the relations between speaker and hearer. The only one that changes is the one about the speaker wanting the door closed.

2.   The Discovery and Description of Presuppositions

I believe that the speech communication situation can be usefully analyzed into two levels or aspects, and these we might refer to as the presuppositional and the illocutionary. By the presuppositional aspects of a speech communication situation, I mean those conditions which must be satisfied in order for a particular illocutionary act to be effectively performed in saying particular sentences.[8] Of course, we need not be concerned with the

---

[8] On presuppositions see Frege (1892) and Strawson (1950).

totality of such conditions, but only with those that can be related to facts about the linguistic structure of sentences. In other words, while it is perfectly true that an utterance of sentence (7) cannot be effective if spoken to someone who does not know English or is out of hearing distance, these are necessary factors to every speech communication act, and do not have any special part in the understanding of that particular sentence.

In every conversation, we constantly make use of both the implicit, or presuppositional, and the explicit, or illocutionary, levels of communication. We know, for example, that our utterances can be judged as inappropriate or incorrect not only on the grounds that some state of affairs has been wrongly described, or that one has acted in bad faith in promising something or warning someone, but also on the grounds of presupposition-failure. We also know that by counting on the addressee's knowing the presuppositions of sentences, and by using sentences deliberately under conditions of presupposition-failure, we can sometimes communicate certain special messages or attitudes or achieve certain secondary communication goals—as would be the case if somebody were to ask me, *When did you stop beating your wife?*

Any complete account of the grammatical description of a language will need to bring in presuppositional facts at many points. In the counterfactual conditional description of a sentence, for example, one must mention that an utterance of the sentence presupposes the falsity of the proposition contained in the *if*-clause. In the most typical use of the definite determiner the speaker presupposes the existence of the object indirectly described by the associated noun phrase. An imperative sentence presupposes the kinds of speaker/addressee relationships mentioned earlier in connection with sentence (7). And so on.

I believe that linguistic theory is in need of a kind of analysis of the speech act that takes into account the presuppositional and the illocutionary aspects of speech communication, and I think that eventually linguists will be able to construct a system of rules by means of which, given the complete grammatical description of any sentence, one can "compute" the full set of the presuppositions which must be satisfied for any in-good-faith utterances of that sentence. The grammatical information that is needed for this computation is extremely complex, involving lexical information associated with individual words, global structural properties of sentences, the placement of contrastive stress, and just about anything imaginable. What I myself have been more directly interested in is that relatively small aspect of the problem which can be associated with the lexical description of particular verbs. One set of verbs in English that can serve to illustrate this aspect of lexically specific information is the one which includes the words speakers of English use in speaking about various types of interpersonal relationships involving judgments of worth and responsibility.

3. Verbs of Judging

I turn now to a consideration of some of the role concepts that one needs to have available for discussing the semantic structure of these verbs. I begin by identifying the terms needed for describing what I might like to call the *role structure*[9] of these verbs, that is, by identifying the various types or entities or aspects-of-situation that are needed for describing the conditions under which it is appropriate to use these verbs.

First of all, we will need to refer to some situation, action, deed, or state of affairs: for this I choose the term *situation*.

The situation we are speaking of may be one which favorably or unfavorably affects some individual: I refer to this being as the *affected*.

There may be some individual concerning whom it is relevant to ask whether he is responsible for the situation—he may have brought it about, or allowed it to come about. We may call him the *defendant*.[10]

Then there may be somebody who makes some kind of moral judgment about the situation or about the defendant's responsibility for the situation, or who makes a statement about such matters; we may call him the *judge*.[11]

The judge may simply make a judgment, and keep it to himself. On the other hand, he may make a statement—that is, he may say something about the situation or about the defendant. If he makes a statement, this statement is addressed to somebody: we may call that person the *addressee*. The term *addressee* in the descriptions offered below must be understood as referring to the addressee, not of the utterance which contains the verbs we are examining, but of the speech act which these verbs might refer to. Where needed, we shall refer to the speaker of the sentence in a speech-communication-situation as the *locutionary source,* and the addressee of that sentence as the *locutionary target.*

The words that we shall examine are *accuse, blame, criticize, credit, praise, scold, confess, apologize, forgive, justify,* and *excuse.* The ways in which the various role concepts I just mentioned can figure in semantic descriptions may be illustrated as follows: Suppose that somebody named

---

[9] The "role structure" proposed for this group of verbs is analogous to, but (I believe) distinct from the more general grammatical role structure of predicates of the type discussed in Fillmore (1968) and Halliday (1967–1968).

[10] I regret the courtroom connotations of the word *defendant,* but the other words that come to mind are more inadequate still. The word *culprit,* for example, presupposes that the individual so-identified was the one responsible; the word *suspect* presupposes that it is not known whether the individual is responsible. All three presuppose that the deed was blameworthy. What is needed is some word that is neutral with respect to all such presuppositions.

[11] Once again, the courtroom connotations are unwelcome. I mean merely one who makes or expresses a judgment about blameworthiness.

John told me that my Congressman was soft on Communism, and suppose that in referring to that event, I utter sentence (9).

(9)   John accused my Congressman of being soft on Communism.

I, the speaker of that sentence, am the locutionary source; and you, my intended addressees, are the locutionary target. John is the judge, my Congressman is the defendant; being soft on Communism is the situation; I am the addressee, since John's statement was addressed to me. Suppose now, by way of a second example, that John had written an obscene letter to Mary, and then told her that he was sorry; and suppose that in reporting this to you I utter sentences (10) and (11).

(10)   John apologized to Mary for writing the letter.
(11)   Mary forgave John for writing the letter.

In each of these cases John is the defendant and Mary the affected. In the sentence with *apologize,* Mary is also the addressee of John's utterance: an apology is directed to the affected.

In the lexical entries gathered in the Appendix, I have associated with each of these verbs—and with *blame* in three senses—various kinds of lexically specific information. In addition to the semantic properties that I attempted to exhibit in these entries, the verbs differ in various syntactic ways. For example, the phrase indicating the Situation is marked off by the preposition *of* in the case of *accuse,* by *with* in the case of *credit,* and by *for* elsewhere; observe sentences (12)a–c.

(12)   a.   John accused Harry of writing the letter.
        b.   John credited Harry with writing the letter.
        c.   John criticized Harry for writing the letter.

There are, moreover, fairly complicated conditions determining the responsibility of the situation as a noun or as a sentential object. Thus we can say (13) or (14) but not (15) or (16).

(13)   I accused John of causing the accident.
(14)   I scolded John for causing the accident.
(15)   *I accused John of the accident.
(16)   *I scolded John for the accident.

With *blame,* by way of contrast, we find either (17) or (18). On the other hand, we can say (19) but not (20).

(17)   I blamed John for causing the accident.
(18)   I blamed John for the accident.
(19)   I accused John of murder/treason.
(20)   *I blamed John for murder/treason.

A syntactic fact unique (in this set of words) to *blame* is that when the situation is represented with a noun, it can be realized as the direct object of the verb, with the defendant marked off with the preposition *on*. Thus we can say either (18) or (21).

(21)   I blamed the accident on John.

The words *criticize* and *scold* agree in that they can function in syntactically complete sentences even though the offending Situation is not explicitly mentioned. Thus we can say (22) or (23)

(22)   She criticized him.
(23)   She scolded him.

but we do not get, as syntactically complete utterances, (24) or (25).

(24)   *She blamed him.
(25)   *She accused him.

Sentences (24) and (25) may, however, be used elliptically when the nature of the offense is known from the context, but they cannot initiate a conversation. Put differently, (22) is a paraphrase of (26) while (24) is a paraphrase of (27).

(26)   She criticized him for something.
(27)   She blamed him for it.

The full roster of lexical information about these words, then, cannot be found in the entries exemplified in the Appendix. These contain only information relevant to semantic description.[12]

On examining these entries, the reader will notice that *accuse, criticize, scold, blame* in three senses, *credit* and *praise* are verbs that conceptually require an understanding of the three entities I have indicated as judge, defendant, and situation.[13] I am thinking of these verbs as they are understood in such sentences as (28)–(30).

---

[12] For an informal survey of the range of information required in a complete lexicon, see Fillmore (1969b).

[13] Notice that I am considering the word *criticize* only in the sense in which the concepts I have been talking about are relevant. There is also an esthetic sense of *criticize*, in which it is synonymous with 'evaluate on esthetic grounds'; but I do not consider here that sense of the verb.

(28)   John accused Harry of writing the letter.
(29)   John credited Harry with writing the letter.
(30)   John criticized/scolded/blamed/praised Harry for writing the letter.

The words *apologize* and *forgive* require in their role structure an understanding of the three entities affected, defendant, and situation.[14] I am thinking of these verbs as they would be understood in such sentences as (31) and (32).

(31)   Harry apologized to Mary for writing the letter.
(32)   Mary forgave Harry for writing the letter.

The words *justify* and *excuse* have much wider uses than I am able to discuss here, but we can limit our attention to their use in sentences like (33) and (34).

(33)   Harry justified his having written the letter.
(34)   Harry excused his writing the letter.

These involve the defendant and the situation.

Some of the verbs in our collection refer to linguistic acts. *Accuse, criticize* and *praise,* for example, are used to refer to situations in which the individual we have classified as the judge *says* something to someone.[15] The content of the linguistic production is represented in the entry as 'X' in quotation marks, a variable whose value is identified in the next line.

Certain others of the verbs—for example the second and third senses of *blame*—refer not to statements made public by the judge, but to inner experiences, to inner and possibly unspoken judgments made by the judge. For indicating these in the entries I have presented the judge and 'X' as the two complements of THINK, with the content of the judge's thoughts indicated on the next line.

The verbs *excuse* and *justify* are also linguistic-act verbs, and so is *apologize*; but *forgive* is not.[16]

Underneath the statements of what I have called the "meanings" of these verbs there can be found one or more formulas that capture what I

---

[14] It is only this sense of *apologize* that will concern us here.

[15] I use the word *say* in the entries, but it should be understood that the communicative act in question can be carried out in other ways besides speaking out loud.

[16] I have not, the reader will notice, succeeded in offering a very helpful description of the meaning of *forgive*.

take to be the necessary presuppositions of utterances having these items as their main verbs. The content of the presuppositions, the statements, and the judgments made by the subjects of these verbs, are all expressed as propositions or identity-conditions. They include the following: *The situation is blameworthy,* represented as the word *BAD* having, after it, the word *Situation* in square brackets; *the situation is praiseworthy,* represented as the word *GOOD* having, after it, the word *Situation* in square brackets; *the defendant is responsible for the situation,* represented as the word *RESPONSIBLE* followed by the words *Defendant* and *Situation* in square brackets; or *the situation is factual,* rather than merely conceived. This last I have represented as the term *ACTUAL* followed, in square brackets, by the word *Situation.*

We turn now to the description of the verbs *accuse* and *criticize.*

ACCUSE [Judge, Defendant, Situation (of)]   (Performative)
    Meaning: SAY [Judge, 'X', Addressee]
        X = RESPONSIBLE [Situation, Defendant]
    Presupposition: BAD [Situation]

CRITICIZE [Judge, Defendant, Situation (for)]
    Meaning: SAY [Judge, 'X', Addressee]
        X = BAD [Situation]
    Presupposition: RESPONSIBLE [Defendant, Situation]
    Presupposition: ACTUAL [Situation]

What is claimed by these descriptions is this: a speaker of English uses the word *accuse* when talking about a situation which is unquestionably bad and he wishes to report the claim that a certain person is responsible for that situation; he would use the word *cricitize* when talking about a situation in which there is no question about who is responsible for it and he wants to report the claim that the situation was blameworthy. Thus, if I say (35),

(35)   John accused Harry of writing the letter.

I presuppose that there was something blameworthy about writing the letter, and I'm telling you that John said Harry did it. If I say (36),

(36)   John criticized Harry for writing the letter.

I presuppose that Harry wrote the letter, and I'm telling you that John said that Harry's having written the letter was blameworthy. It is to be noticed that what is presupposed by the use of one of these verbs is part of the content of the linguistic act referred to by the other.[17]

These two verbs differ in two other interesting ways. Uses of the verb *criticize* presuppose the factuality of the situation; but not so for *accuse*. This distinction is not apparent in the examples given so far because of the use of the definite article in the phrase *writing the letter*. If we replace this by a situation-indicating expression that does not have its own existence presuppositions—such as one containing an indefinite noun-phrase—this other presuppositional difference between these two verbs becomes apparent. Consider the two sentences, (37) and (38).

(37)   I accused Harry of writing an obscene letter to my mother.
(38)   I criticized Harry for writing an obscene letter to my mother.

With *accuse,* there is no presupposition that such a letter was ever written; with *criticize* there is.

A second way in which *accuse* and *criticize* differ from each other is that *accuse* can be used "performatively," using that term in the sense it has been given by Austin.[18] An utterance of a sentence with this verb in its first person present tense form has a "force" that is different from that of simply conveying information. An utterance of sentence (39)

(39)   I accuse Harry of writing the letter.

can in itself be an accusing act; the verb *criticize* is not a performative verb, and what this means is that performances of sentence (40)

(40)   I criticize Harry for writing the letter.

cannot in themselves constitute criticisms.

The verb *scold* is like *criticize* in many respects, but it requires that the defendant be identical with the addressee in the linguistic act referred to by the verb. The addressee in the linguistic act referred to by uses of *criticize* can be anybody. Thus, I can criticize Harry to his face or behind his back, but I cannot *scold* him behind his back. The following is the lexical entry for *scold.*

---

[17] The basis for separating the presuppositions from the rest of the meaning is that the presuppositions obtain even when the sentence is negated or interrogated. Thus, if I say *John didn't criticize Harry for writing the letter,* I presuppose Harry's responsibility for the letter just as much as in the affirmative sentence; similarly, if I ask, *Did John accuse Harry of writing the letter?,* I can utter this question in good faith only if I believe that there is no question that the letter-writing act was objectionable.

[18] See Austin (1962a,b).

SCOLD [Judge, Defendant, Situation (for)]
    Meaning: SAY [Judge, 'X', Addressee]
      X = BAD [Situation]
    Presupposition: RESPONSIBLE [Defendant, Situation]
    Presupposition: THINK [Judge, 'ACTUAL [Situation]']
    Presupposition: Defendant = Addressee

There may be another presuppositional matter that separates *accuse* from *criticize* and *scold*. If the offending situation is extremely serious, the words *criticize* and *scold* seem inappropriate. Thus, a sentence like (41) sounds more natural than either (42) or (43).

(41)   I accused Harry of raping my daughter.
(42)   I criticized Harry for raping my daughter.
(43)   I scolded Harry for raping my daughter.

This observation probably has nothing to do with specifically linguistic facts about these verbs, however. It's just that we find it difficult to imagine a situation in which somebody is *explaining* to somebody else that an act of rape was immoral or in bad taste.

Blame in one of its uses is a linguistic-act verb; that is, there is one sense of the verb *blame* by which I would mean, in saying *He blamed me*, that he had said something to somebody. This is the sense I call *blame*$_1$.

BLAME$_1$ [Judge, Defendant, Situation (for)]
    Meaning: SAY [Judge, 'X', Addressee]
      X = RESPONSIBLE [Defendant, Situation]
    Presupposition: BAD [Situation]
    Presupposition: NOT (RESPONSIBLE [Defendant, Situation])
    Presupposition: Defendant ≠ Addressee
    Presupposition: Judge ≠ Defendant

It is this use of the verb that one would find in the following situation. Harry wrote the letter himself, and then he gave people to believe that I had written it; I say (44).

(44)   Harry blamed the letter on me.

In this sense of *blame*, the locutionary source reports the judge's statement that the defendant is responsible for the situation, but with the presupposition that the defendant was *not* the responsible one. With *blame*$_1$, it follows of necessity, the defendant is *not* the addressee of the judge's statement, and the judge is not the defendant. That is, it is not in the linguistic-act sense of *blame* that one can blame oneself. Otherwise, *blame₁* has much in common with *accuse*.[19]

The other two verbs *blame* are not linguistic-act verbs, but refer to opinions or thoughts or internal judgments on the part of the judge. Otherwise *blame₂* and *blame₃* are like *criticize* and *accuse* respectively.

BLAME₂ [Judge, Defendant, Situation]
    Meaning: THINK [Judge, 'X']
        X = BAD [Situation]
    Presupposition: RESPONSIBLE [Defendant, Situation]
    Presupposition: ACTUAL [Situation]

BLAME₃ [Judge, Defendant, Situation]
    Meaning: THINK [Judge, 'X']
        X = RESPONSIBLE [Defendant, Situation]
    Presupposition: BAD [Situation]
    Presupposition: ACTUAL [Situation]

This ambiguity of *blame,* that is, the division of *blame* into *blame₂* and *blame₃*[20] can be illustrated this way. Suppose there's no question in anybody's mind that I wrote a particular letter, and what I'm telling you is that John for some reason regarded my action as blameworthy. I can say, in reporting his state of affairs, sentence (45).

(45)   John *blámed* me for writing the letter.

This is *blame₂.* Or suppose that there is no doubt of the blameworthiness of this particular letter, and what I'm telling you is that John felt that I had done it. I can say sentence (46).

(46)   John blamed *mé* for writing the letter.

That is *blame₃.*[21]

We turn now to the verbs *excuse* and *justify.*[22]

---

[19] To some speakers, *blame₁* is a kind of achievement verb, implying that the Judge succeeded in affecting his addressee's beliefs. I think that I would not say **He blamed it on me, but fortunately nobody believed him.* I would have to say, *He tried to blame it on me, but fortunately nobody believed him.*

[20] The distinction being discussed here was pointed out in footnote 2 in Austin (1956).

[21] It is *blame₃* that we find in the request, *Don't blame mé!,* and *blame₂* that we find in the reassuring words, *I don't blàme you.*

[22] The distinction between these two verbs was described in very similar terms in Austin (1956), p. 42 of Chappell (1964).

EXCUSE [Defendant, Situation]
    Meaning: SAY [Defendant, 'X', Addressee]
        X = NOT (RESPONSIBLE [Defendant, Situation])
    Presupposition: BAD [Situation]
    Presupposition: ACTUAL [Situation]

JUSTIFY [Defendant, Situation]
    Meaning: SAY [Defendant, 'X', Addressee]
        X = NOT (BAD [Situation])
    Presupposition: RESPONSIBLE [Defendant, Situation]
    Presupposition: ACTUAL [Situation]

One *justifies* an action when there is no question of who is responsible, but where one wishes to say that the action was not really bad. One *excuses* an action when there is no question of the badness of the action, but where one wishes to disclaim responsibility. Thus, I can *justify* bombing a peasant village by pointing out that this deed was part of some larger endeavor that is essentially good. I can *excuse* my having bombed a peasant village by pointing out that I thought the button I pushed was the cigarette lighter.

This description does not tell the whole story. One very clear aspect of the use of these verbs is the presupposition that, in both cases, there is some reason for believing what the judge is denying. That is, it is only appropriate to speak of justifying an action if on the face of it it looks as if the action was bad; it is only appropriate to excuse one's behavior if there's some superficial evidence to believe that one *was* fully responsible for it.

In all of the descriptions that we have examined so far, there was something about badness and something about responsibility, and whenever one of these showed up in the description of the meaning, the other showed up in the statement of the presuppositions. With the words *apologize* and *forgive,* however, both of these show up in the presuppositions. If I say sentence (47),

(47)   Harry apologized to Mary for writing the letter.

I am presupposing both that Harry wrote the letter and that there was something bad about his doing that; and I make exactly the same presuppositions if I say sentence (48).

(48)   Mary forgave Harry for writing the letter.

APOLOGIZE [Defendant, Affected (to), Situation (for)]   (Performative)
    Meaning: SAY [Defendant, 'X', Addressee]
        X = REQUEST [Defendant, 'FORGIVE [Victim, Defendant, Situation]']
    Presupposition: BAD [Situation]

Presupposition: RESPONSIBLE [Defendant, Situation]
Presupposition: ACTUAL [Situation]

FORGIVE [Affected, Defendant, Situation (for)]   (Performative)
    Meaning: DECIDE [Affected, 'X']
        X = ? (Affected will not hold Situation against Defendant)
    Presupposition: BAD [Situation]
    Presupposition: RESPONSIBLE [Defendant, Situation]
    Presupposition: ACTUAL [Situation]

These words refer to changes, or requests for changes, in the negative relationship that has come about between affected and defendant as a result of the latter's having committed some offense.[23]

The verbs *credit* and *praise* have semantic descriptions very analogous to those of *blame₃* and *criticize* respectively, except that the evaluative predicate *GOOD* replaces *BAD* in the presuppositions of the one and in the "meaning" of the other.

CREDIT [Judge, Defendant, Situation (with)]
    Meaning: THINK [Judge, 'X']
        X = RESPONSIBLE [Defendant, Situation]
    Presupposition: GOOD [Situation]

PRAISE [Judge, Defendant, Situation (for)]
    Meaning: SAY [Judge, Addressee, 'X']
        X = GOOD [Situation]
    Presupposition: RESPONSIBLE [Defendant, Situation]

What is apparent from our examination of the semantic properties of this selected group of words is that we have identified a portion, at least, of a semantic "field," in the sense of the German field theorists.[24] It will of course be interesting to see, first of all, what structure is discoverable in the vocabulary field we have been examining (for example, whether it is clear that a language never needs words analogous to *excuse, justify, forgive* and *apologize* but with *BAD* replaced by *GOOD*, whether there are in the system of features suggested for these English verbs any "accidental gaps");

[23] I have called both of these verbs performatives, but I have described only *apologize* as a linguistic act verb. To say that they are performatives is to recognize that an utterance of the sentence *I apologize for writing the letter* constitutes in itself, if it is acknowledged, the performance of an act which will change the relationship between the two people; and so, I believe, is an utterance of the sentence, *I forgive you for writing the letter.* In nonperformative uses, however, only *apologize* is a verb of saying. This we can recognize if we see that it's acceptable to say *He apologized, but he didn't mean it,* but it's not acceptable to say, *He forgave me, but he didn't mean it.* One would have to say, *He said he forgave me, but he didn't mean it.*

[24] See for work representative of this school, Trier (1931) and Weisgerber (1953–1954).

secondly, whether there are other verbs so far unknown to me that fill out or extend the system I have proposed (there are a great many variants of *scold* that come to mind (*chide, castigate,* and so forth), *commend* has essentially the same analysis as *praise,* and there is a set of verbs including *admit, confess, concede,* and so forth, which lend themselves to description in the terms that have been discussed here); and thirdly, to what extent the concepts that have proved of service for this group of English verbs can provide descriptions of the nearest equivalents of these verbs in other languages. All of these questions I must unfortunately leave to the future.

Appendix

ACCUSE [Judge, Defendant, Situation (of)]   (Performative)
    Meaning: SAY [Judge, 'X', Addressee]
        X = RESPONSIBLE [Situation, Defendant]
    Presupposition: BAD [Situation]

CRITICIZE [Judge, Defendant, Situation (for)]
    Meaning: SAY [Judge, 'X', Addressee]
        X = BAD [Situation]
    Presupposition: RESPONSIBLE [Defendant, Situation]
    Presupposition: ACTUAL [Situation]

SCOLD [Judge, Defendant, Situation (for)]
    Meaning: SAY [Judge, 'X', Addressee]
        X = BAD [Situation]
    Presupposition: RESPONSIBLE [Defendant, Situation]
    Presupposition: THINK [Judge, 'ACTUAL [Situation]']
    Presupposition: Defendant = Addressee

BLAME$_1$ [Judge, Defendant, Situation (for)]
    Meaning: SAY [Judge, 'X', Addressee]
        X = RESPONSIBLE [Defendant, Situation]
    Presupposition: BAD [Situation]
    Presupposition: NOT (RESPONSIBLE [Defendant, Situation])
    Presupposition: Defendant $\neq$ Addressee
    Presupposition: Judge $\neq$ Defendant

BLAME$_2$ [Judge, Defendant, Situation]
    Meaning: THINK [Judge, 'X']
        X = BAD [Situation]
    Presupposition: RESPONSIBLE [Defendant, Situation]
    Presupposition: ACTUAL [Situation]

BLADE₃ [Judge, Defendant, Situation]
    Meaning: THINK [Judge, 'X']
        X = RESPONSIBLE [Defendant, Situation]
    Presupposition: BAD [Situation]
    Presupposition: ACTUAL [Situation]

EXCUSE [Defendant, Situation]
    Meaning: SAY [Defendant, 'X', Addressee]
        X = NOT (RESPONSIBLE [Defendant, Situation])
    Presupposition: BAD [Situation]
    Presupposition: ACTUAL [Situation]

JUSTIFY [Defendant, Situation]
    Meaning: SAY [Defendant, 'X', Addressee]
        X = NOT (BAD [Situation])
    Presupposition: RESPONSIBLE [Defendant, Situation]
    Presupposition: ACTUAL [Situation]

APOLOGIZE [Defendant, Affected (to), Situation (for)]   (Performative)
    Meaning: SAY [Defendant, 'X', Addressee]
        X = REQUEST [Defendant, 'FORGIVE [Victim, Defendant,
           Situation]']
    Presupposition: BAD [Situation]
    Presupposition: RESPONSIBLE [Defendant, Situation]
    Presupposition: ACTUAL [Situation]

FORGIVE [Affected, Defendant, Situation (for)]   (Performative)
    Meaning: DECIDE [Affected, 'X']
        X = ? (Affected will not hold Situation against Defendant)
    Presupposition: BAD [Situation]
    Presupposition: RESPONSIBLE [Defendant, Situation]
    Presupposition: ACTUAL [Situation]

CREDIT [Judge, Defendant, Situation (with)]
    Meaning: THINK [Judge, 'X']
        X = RESPONSIBLE [Defendant, Situation]
    Presupposition: GOOD [Situation]

PRAISE [Judge, Defendant, Situation (for)]
    Meaning: SAY [Judge, Addressee, 'X']
        X = GOOD [Situation]
    Presupposition: RESPONSIBLE [Defendant, Situation]

REFERENCES

Akmajian, Adrian. 1970. "On deriving cleft sentences from pseudo-cleft sentences." *Linguistic Inquiry* 1:149–168.

Alston, William P. 1964. *Philosophy of Language.* Englewood Cliffs, N.J.

Anderson, John. 1968. "On the status of lexical formatives." *Foundations of Language* 4:308–318.

Anderson, Steve. 1969. "On how to get even." Unpublished paper.

Annear, Sandra S. *See* Thompson, Sandra A.

Austin, John L. 1950. "Truth." Reprinted in Pitcher (1964, pp. 18–31).

———. 1956. "A plea for excuses." Reprinted in Chappell (1964, pp. 41–63).

———. 1961. "The meaning of a word." Reprinted in Caton (1963, pp. 1–21).

———. 1962a. *How To Do Things with Words.* Cambridge, Mass.

———. 1962b. "Performatif-constatif." Reprinted in Caton (1963, pp. 22–54).

Bach, Emmon. 1968. "Nouns and noun-phrases." In Bach and Harms (1968, pp. 90–122).

———, and Robert Harms, eds. 1968. *Universals in Linguistic Theory,* New York.

Baker, C. Leroy. 1970. "Double negatives." *Linguistic Inquiry* 1:169–186.

Bever, Thomas G., and William Weksel, eds. In press. *The Structure and Psychology of Language.* New York.

Bierwisch, Manfred, and Heidolph, Karl-Heinz, eds. In press. *Recent Advances in Linguistics.* The Hague.

Binnick, Robert I., Alice Davison, Georgia Green, and Jerry Morgan, eds. 1969. *Papers from the Fifth Regional Meeting of the Chicago Linguistics Society.* Chicago.

Black, Max. 1958. "Presuppositions and implication." Reprinted in Black (1962, pp. 48–63) .

———. 1962. *Models and Metaphors.* Ithaca, N.Y.

Butler, R. J., ed. 1962. *Analytical Philosophy,* Vol. I. New York.

Carden, Guy. 1967. *English Quantifiers.* Unpublished M.A. thesis. Harvard University.

Cartwright, R. 1962. "Propositions." In Butler (1962, pp. 81–103).

———. 1968. "Propositions again." *Noûs* 2:229–246.

Caton, Charles E., ed. 1963. *Philosophy and Ordinary Language.* Urbana.

Chapin, Paul. 1967. *On the Syntax of Word Derivation in English.* Unpublished Ph.D. dissertation, M.I.T.

Chappell, V. C., ed. 1964. *Ordinary Language.* Englewood Cliffs, N.J.

Chomsky, Noam. 1957. *Syntactic Structures.* The Hague.

———. 1962. "The logical basis of linguistic theory." In *Reprints of the Ninth International Congress of Linguists.* Cambridge, Mass.

———. 1964. "Current issues in linguistic theory." In Fodor and Katz (1964, pp. 50–118) .

———. 1965. *Aspects of the Theory of Syntax.* Cambridge, Mass.

———. 1966. "Linguistic institute lectures." Unpublished.

———. 1968. "Remarks on nominalization." Also in Jacobs and Rosenbaum (1970).

———. 1969. "Deep structure, surface structure and semantic interpretation." Also in Jakobson (1970, pp. 52–91).

Darden, Bill J., Charles-James N. Bailey, and Alice Davison, eds. 1968. *Papers from the Fourth Regional Meeting of the Chicago Linguistic Society.* Cambridge, Mass.

de Rijk, R. P. G. 1968. "A note on prelexical predicate raising." Unpublished paper.

Dougherty, Ray. 1968. *A Transformational Grammar of Coordinate Conjoined Structures.* Unpublished Ph.D. dissertation, M.I.T.

————. 1969. "An interpretive theory of pronominal reference." *Foundations of Language* 5:488–519.

Drubig, Bernhard. 1968. "Some remarks on relative clauses in English." *Journal of English as a Second Language* 3.2:23–40.

Feigl, Herbert, and Wilfrid Sellars, eds. 1949. *Readings in Philosophical Analysis.* New York.

Fillmore, Charles J. 1963. "The position of embedding transformations in a grammar." *Word* 19:208–231.

————. 1965a. *Indirect Object Constructions in English and the Ordering of Transformations.* The Hague.

————. 1965b. "Entailment rules in a semantic theory." *Project on Linguistic Analysis Report 10.* Columbus, Ohio.

————. 1966. "Deictic categories in the semantics of 'come'." *Foundations of Language* 2:219–227.

————. 1967. "On the syntax of preverbs." *Glossa* 1:91–125.

————. 1968. "The case for case." in Bach and Harms (1968, pp. 1–90).

————. 1969a. "Review of Bendix, *Componential analysis of general vocabulary.*" *General Linguistics* 9:41–65.

————. 1969b. "Types of lexical information." In Kiefer (1969, pp. 109–137).

Fischer, Susan. 1967. "A late paper on time." Unpublished paper.

Fodor, Jerry, and Jerrold J. Katz, eds. 1964. *The Structure of Language.* Englewood Cliffs, N.J.

Fraser, Bruce. 1969. "An analysis of concessive conditionals." In Binnick *et al.* (1969, pp. 66–75).

————. 1970. "Idioms within a transformational grammar." *Foundations of Language* 6:22–42.

Frege, Gottlob. 1892. "Über Sinn und Bedeutung." Translated in Feigl and Sellars (1949, pp. 85–102) and Geach and Black (1960, pp. 17–38).

————. 1918–1919. "The thought: a logical inquiry." Reprinted in Strawson (1967, pp. 17–38).

Garner, Richard. 1968a. "Utterances and acts in the philosophy of J. L. Austin." *Noûs* 2:209–227.

————. 1968b. "Austin on entailment." *The Philosophical Quarterly* 17.216–224.

————. 1969. "Caton on epistemic qualifiers." *Studies in Philosophical Linguistics* 1:55–77.

Garvin, Paul, ed. In press. *Cognition and Artificial Intelligence.*

Geach, Peter T. 1950. "Russell's theory of descriptions." *Analysis* 10:84–88.

————. 1962. *Reference and Generality.* Ithaca, N.Y.

————, and Max Black, eds. 1960. *Translations from the Philosophical Writing of Gottlob Frege,* Oxford.

Gleitman, Lila. 1965. "Coordinating conjunctions in English." *Language* 51:260–293. Reprinted in Reibel and Schane (1969, pp. 80–112).

Green, Georgia. 1968. "On *too* and *either,* and not just on *too* and *either,* either." In Darden *et al.* (1968, pp. 22–39).

————. 1969. *Some theoretical implications of the lexical expression of emphatic conjunctions.* Unpublished M.A. thesis, University of Chicago.

Grice, H. P. 1961. "The causal theory of perception." *Proceedings of the Aristotelian Society* Supp. Vol. 35:121–152.

————. 1968. "The logic of conversation." Unpublished paper.

Gruber, Jeffrey. 1967. *Functions of the Lexicon in Formal Descriptive Grammars.* Santa Monica, Calif.

Haas, Mary R. 1944. "Men's and women's speech in Koasati." Reprinted in Hymes (1964, pp. 228–233).

Hall, Barbara. *See* Partee, Barbara H.

Halliday, M. A. K. 1967–1968. "Notes on transitivity and theme in English." *Journal of Linguistics* 3:37–81, 197–277; 4:153–308.

Hancock, R. 1960. "Presuppositions." *The Philosophical Quarterly* 10:73–78.

Hoffman, Thomas R. 1966. "Past tense replacement and the English modal auxiliary system." In *Harvard Computation Laboratory Report NSF-17*. Cambridge, Mass.

Horn, Larry. 1969. "A presuppositional analysis of 'only' and 'even'." In Binnick *et al.* (1969, pp. 98–107).

Hymes, Dell H., ed. 1964. *Language in Culture and Society*. New York.

Jackendoff, Ray S. 1968a. "An interpretive theory of pronouns and reflexives." Unpublished paper.

———. 1968b. "Speculations on presentences and determiners." Unpublished paper.

———. 1969a. "An interpretive theory of negation." *Foundations of Language* 5:218–241.

———. 1969b. *Some Rules for English Semantic Interpretation*. Unpublished Ph.D. dissertation, M.I.T.

Jacobs, Roderick, and Peter Rosenbaum, eds. 1970. *Readings in English Transformational Grammar*. Waltham, Mass.

Jakobovits, Leon, and Danny Steinberg, eds. In press. *Semantics: an Interdisciplinary Reader*. Cambridge, England.

Jakobson, Roman, ed. 1970. *Studies in Oriental and General Linguistics*, Tokyo.

Joos, Martin, ed. 1957. *Readings in Linguistics*. Washington, D.C.

Katz, Jerrold J. 1964a. "Analyticity and contradiction in natural language." In Fodor and Katz (1964, pp. 519–543).

———. 1964b. "Semantic theory and the meaning of 'good'. *Journal of Philosophy* 61:739–766.

———. 1966. *The philosophy of Language*. New York.

———. 1967a. "Recent issues in semantic theory." *Foundations of Language* 3:124–194.

———. 1967b. "Some remarks on Quine on analyticity." *Journal of Philosophy* 64:36–52.

———. 1968. "Unpalatable recipes for buttering parsnips." *Journal of Philosophy* 65:29–45.

———. In press. *Semantic Theory*. New York.

———, and Jerry Fodor. 1963. The structure of a semantic theory." *Language* 39:170–210. Reprinted in Fodor and Katz (1964, pp. 479–518).

———, and Paul M. Postal. 1964. *An Integrated Theory of Linguistic Descriptions*. Cambridge, Mass.

Keenan, Edward L. 1969. *A Logical Base for English*. Unpublished Ph.D. dissertation, University of Pennsylvania.

Kiefer, Ferenc, ed. 1969. *Studies in Syntax and Semantics*, Dordrecht.

Kiparsky, Paul. 1968. "Tense and mood in Indo-European syntax." *Foundations of Language* 4:30–57.

———, and Carol Kiparsky. 1968. "Fact." To appear in Bierwisch and Heidolph, in press.

Klima, Edward S. "Negation in English." In Fodor and Katz (1964, pp. 246–323).

Kuno, Susumo. 1970. "Some properties of nonreferential noun phrases." To appear in Jakobson, in press.

Kuroda, Sige-Yuki. 1965. *Generative Grammatical Studies in the Japanese Language*. Unpublished Ph.D. dissertation, M.I.T.

Lakoff, George. 1966a. "Deep and surface grammar." Unpublished paper.

———. 1966b. "Stative adjectives and verbs in English." In *Harvard Computational Laboratory Report NSF-17*.

———. 1968a. "Instrumental adverbs and the concept of deep structure." *Foundations of Language* 4:4–29.

———. 1968b. "Repartee, or a reply to 'Negation, conjunction and quantifiers.' " Also in *Foundations of Language* 6:389–422, 1970.

———. 1969a. "On derivational constraints." In Binnick *et al.* (1969, pp. 117–139).

———. 1969b. "On generative semantics." To appear in Jakobovits and Steinberg (in press)

———. 1970a. "Counterparts, or the problem of reference in transformational grammar." *Harvard Computational Laboratory Report NSF-24*, 23–36.

———. 1970b. *Linguistics and Natural Logic (Studies in Generative Semantics* 1). Ann Arbor.

———. 1970c. "Presuppositions and relative grammaticality." *Harvard Computational Laboratory Report NSF-24*, 51–68.

———. 1970d. *Irregularity in Syntax.* New York.

———. 1971. "The role of deduction in grammar." This volume.

———, and Stanley Peters. 1966. "Phrasal conjunction and symmetric predicates." Reprinted in Reibel and Schane (1969, pp. 113–142).

Lakoff, Robin. 1968. *Abstract Syntax and Latin Complementation.* Cambridge, Mass.

———. 1969a. "Some reasons why there can't be any *some-any* rule." *Language* 45:608–615.

———. 1969b. "A syntactic argument for negative transporation." In Binnick *et al.* (1969, pp. 140–147).

———. 1971. "If's, and's, and but's about conjunction." This volume.

Langacker, Ronald. 1969. "Pronominalization and the chain of command." In Reibel and Schane (1969, pp. 160–186).

Langendoen, D. Terence. 1969. *The Study of Syntax.* New York.

Leech, Geoffrey. 1969. *Towards a Semantic Description of English,* London.

Linsky, Leonard. 1967. *Referring.* New York.

McCawley, James D. 1967. "Meaning and the description of language." *Kotoba No Uchū* 2, nos. 9–11.

———. 1968a. "The annotated respective." Unpublished paper.

———. 1968b. "Concerning the base component of a transformational grammar." *Foundations of Language* 4:243–269.

———. 1968c. "Lexical insertion in a transformational grammar without deep structure." In Darden *et al.* (1968, pp. 71–80).

———. 1968d. "The role of semantics in grammar." In Bach and Harms (1968, pp. 125–169).

———. 1968e. "Where do noun phrases come from?" Also in Jacobs and Rosenbaum (1970).

———. 1969a. "A programme for logic." To appear in *Synthese.*

———. 1969b. "Semantic representation." To appear in Garvin, in press.

———. 1969c. "Why you can't not say no sentences like these." Unpublished paper.

———. 1970. "English as a *VSO* language. *Language* 46:286–299.

———. 1971. "Tense and time reference in English." This volume.

Montague, Richard. 1969. "Presupposing." *The Philosophical Quarterly* 19:98–110.

Morgan, Jerry. 1968. "Remarks on the notion 'possible lexical item'." Unpublished paper.

————. 1969. "On the treatment of presuppositions in transformational grammar." In Binnick *et al.* (1969, pp. 169–177).

Nerlich, George. 1965. "Presupposition and entailment." *American Philosophical Quarterly* 2:33–42.

Palmer, Frank R. 1965. *A Linguistic Study of the English Verb.* London.

Partee, Barbara H. 1965. *Subject and Object in Modern English.* Unpublished Ph.D. dissertation, M.I.T.

————. 1968. "On some fundamental conflicts in the establishment of deep-structure subjects." Unpublished paper.

————. 1970. "Negation, conjunction and quantifiers: syntax vs. semantics." *Foundations of Language* 6:153–165.

Perlmutter, David. 1968. *Deep and Surface Structure Constraints in English.* Unpublished Ph.D. dissertation, M.I.T.

———— and John R. Ross. 1970. "Relative clauses with split antecedents." *Linguistic Inquiry* 1:350.

Peters, Stanley, and Robert W. Ritchie. 1969. "A note on the universal base hypothesis." *Journal of Linguistics* 5:150–152.

Pitcher, George, ed. 1964. *Truth.* Englewood Cliffs, N.J.

Postal, Paul M. 1967. "Restrictive relative clauses and other matters." Unpublished paper.

————. 1969a. "Anaphoric islands." To appear in *Linguistic Inquiry.*

————. 1969b. "On coreferential complement subject deletion." To appear in Jakobovits and Steinberg (in press). Also in *Linguistic Inquiry* 1:439–500, 1970.

————. 1971a. *Cross-over Phenomena.* New York.

————. 1971b. "On the surface verb 'remind'." This volume.

Reibel, David and Sanford Schane, eds. 1969. *Modern Studies in English.* Englewood Cliffs, N.J.

Rescher, Nicholas. 1967. "On the logic of presupposition." *Philosophy and Phenomenological Research* 21:521–527.

Rosenbaum, Peter. 1967. *The Grammar of English Predicate Complement Constructions.* Cambridge, Mass.

————, and Roderick Jacobs. 1968. *English Transformational Grammar.* Waltham, Mass.

Ross, John R. 1967a. "Auxiliaries as main verbs." To appear in Bever and Weksel (in press).

————. 1967b. *Constraints on Variables in Syntax.* Unpublished Ph.D. dissertation, M.I.T.

————. 1968. "On declarative sentences." Also in Jacobs and Rosenbaum (1970).

————. 1969a. "Adjectives as noun phrases." In Reibel and Schane (1969, pp. 352–360).

————. 1969b. "A proposed rule of tree-pruning." In Reibel and Schane (1969, pp. 288–299).

————. 1970. "Gapping and the order of constituents." In *Actes du Xe Congrès Internationale des Linguistes,* vol. 2. Bucharest.

Ryle, Gilbert. 1953. "Ordinary language." Reprinted in Chappell (1964, pp. 24–40).

Searle, John. 1959. "On determinables and resemblance." *Proceedings of the Aristotelian Society,* supp. vol. 33:14–58.

————. 1969. *Speech Acts.* Cambridge, England.

Sebeok, Thomas, ed. 1966. *Current Trends in Linguistics,* Vol. III. The Hague.

Sellars, Wilfrid. 1954. "Presupposing." *The Philosophical Review* 63:197–215.

————. 1968. *Science and Metaphysics.* New York.

Stockwell, Robert *et al.* (1969). *Integration of Transformational Theories on English Syntax*. Los Angeles.

Strawson, P. 1950a. "On referring." *Mind* 59:320–344. Reprinted in Caton (1963, pp. 162–193).

———. 1950b. "Truth." Reprinted in Pitcher (1964, pp. 32–53).

———. 1952. *Introduction to Logical Theory*. London.

———. 1954. "A reply to Mr. Sellars." *The Philosophical Review* 63:216–231.

———, ed. 1967. *Philosophical Logic*. London.

Thompson, Sandra A. 1968. "Relative clauses and conjunctions." The Ohio State University *Working Papers in Linguistics* 1:80–99.

Trier, Jost. 1931. *Der Deutsche Wortschatz im Sinnbezirk des Verstandes: die Geschichte eines Sprachlichen Feldes*. Heidelberg.

Weinreich, Uriel. 1966. "Explorations in semantic theory" in Sebeok (1966, pp. 395–477).

Weisgerber, Leo. 1953–1954. *Von Weltbild der Deutschen Sprache*. Düsseldorf.

Wierzbicka, Anna. 1967. "Against conjunction reduction." Unpublished paper.

INDEX OF AUTHORS AND TITLES